CL DEVON LIBRARY & IN
Please return this book on or be
Renew on tel. 0845 155 1001

GW01112360

Chulmleigh Library
Tel 580292 8/08 New Telephone Number
01769 582136

- 9 SEP 2005
20. APR 06
20. OCT 06

MCGOWAN, John
Decorating
747

D11230689 X 0 100

DECORATING
do-it-yourself step-by-step

Over 100 step-by-step techniques for painting, special paint finishes, papering walls and ceilings, tiling and laying floors

Consultant Editor: John McGowan

southwater

This edition is published by Southwater

Southwater is an imprint of Anness Publishing Ltd
Hermes House, 88–89 Blackfriars Road, London SE1 8HA
tel. 020 7401 2077; fax 020 7633 9499; www.southwaterbooks.com; info@anness.com

© Anness Publishing Ltd 2005

UK agent: The Manning Partnership Ltd,
6 The Old Dairy, Melcombe Road, Bath BA2 3LR;
tel. 01225 478444; fax 01225 478440;
sales@manning-partnership.co.uk

UK distributor: Grantham Book Services Ltd,
Isaac Newton Way, Alma Park Industrial Estate,
Grantham, Lincs NG31 9SD; tel. 01476 541080;
fax 01476 541061; orders@gbs.tbs-ltd.co.uk

North American agent/distributor:
National Book Network, 4501 Forbes Boulevard,
Suite 200, Lanham, MD 20706; tel. 301 459 3366;
fax 301 429 5746; www.nbnbooks.com

Australian agent/distributor:
Pan Macmillan Australia,
Level 18, St Martins Tower,
31 Market St,
Sydney, NSW 2000;
tel. 1300 135 113; fax 1300 135 103;
customer.service@macmillan.com.au

New Zealand agent/distributor:
David Bateman Ltd,
30 Tarndale Grove,
Off Bush Road,
Albany, Auckland;
tel. (09) 415 7664; fax (09) 415 8892

All rights reserved. No part of this publication may be reproduced, stored in a retrieval system, or transmitted in any way or by any means, electronic, mechanical, photocopying, recording or otherwise, without the prior written permission of the copyright holder.
A CIP catalogue record for this book is available from the British Library.

Publisher: Joanna Lorenz
Editorial Director: Judith Simons
Project Editor: Felicity Forster
Text: Diane Carr, Sacha Cohen, Mike Collins,
Jonathan Edwards, David Holloway
and Mike Lawrence
Illustrators: Peter Bull and Andrew Green

Photographers: Peter Anderson, Colin Bowling,
Jonathan Buckley, Sarah Cuttle, Rodney Forte,
John Freeman, Andrea Jones, Debbie Patterson,
Lucinda Symons and Jo Whitworth
Editor: Ian Penberthy
Designer: Bill Mason
Production Controller: Claire Rae

Previously published as part of a larger volume, Do-It-Yourself Essentials

1 3 5 7 9 10 8 6 4 2

The author and publishers have made every effort to ensure that all instructions contained within this book are accurate and safe, and cannot accept liability for any resulting injury, damage or loss to persons or property, however it may arise. If in any doubt as to the correct procedure to follow for any home improvements task, seek professional advice.

CONTENTS

Introduction 6

Painting skills 10
Painting materials • Painting preparation • Painting techniques

Paint finishes 52
Basic paint finishes • Patterned paint effects • Faux paint finishes

Papering walls & ceilings 92
Wallcovering materials • Wallcovering preparation • Wallcovering techniques

Home tiling 148
Tiling materials • Tiling preparation • Tiling techniques • Decorative tiling layouts

Laying floors 202
Flooring materials • Flooring preparation • Flooring techniques • Flooring variations

Safety & tools 258
Safety & preparation • Measuring, shaping & cutting tools • Assembling tools • Finishing tools

Index 318

INTRODUCTION

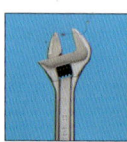

In recent years, the advent of the do-it-yourself superstore, the development of tools and materials aimed specifically at the amateur, and the proliferation of TV makeover shows have meant that when a job needs doing in or around the home, we no longer reach automatically for the telephone to call in a professional. First, we ask if we can do it ourselves, and more often than not, the answer is "yes". Today there are many home maintenance and improvement tasks that can be done by anyone with a practical frame of mind. The major advantage, of course, is a saving in money, but that's not always the prime reason for tackling a job. There is an immense amount of satisfaction to be gained from learning a new skill and, most of all, being able to stamp your own personality on your home.

ABOVE: Having the right tools will make any job go smoothly. As you learn new do-it-yourself skills, you can obtain the relevant special tools; look after them and they'll last a lifetime.

ABOVE: Many do-it-yourself tasks require working at a height, and it is essential to create a safe working platform. An access tower such as this, which can be hired, is invaluable.

SAFETY AND TOOLS

The most important requirements for any do-it-yourself job, even the simplest, are an understanding of the potential dangers involved and to take steps to protect not only yourself, but also others around you. Many tasks involve the use of sharp tools, electrical equipment or working from ladders, but there are other less obvious risks, such as injuries caused by lifting or dropping heavy objects, not to mention the mess caused by spilt paint. Always keep safety uppermost in your mind whatever you do.

ABOVE: Paint is a versatile decorating material and need not always be applied in wide swathes of a single colour. Among the many decorative paint techniques is stencilling.

Ensuring you have the right tools for the job will be a big help in carrying out the task safely. Never scrimp when buying tools; get the best you can afford and look after them. They'll pay you back with a lifetime's service.

PAINTING SKILLS

The most common of all do-it-yourself tasks is painting, and there is a wide range of paints and painting equipment available to suit the many different surfaces that can benefit from this decorative – and protective – treatment. Although modern materials and tools have made painting a simple procedure, it is still necessary to learn a variety of techniques to ensure the best finish. By far the most crucial aspect is the correct and thorough preparation of the surface.

PAINT FINISHES

One of the advantages of paint as a decorating material is that it can be used to create a wide variety of patterned effects on any surface, often with the simplest of techniques. Not only can you use ordinary paints in this way, but you can also buy special types that create unique finishes.

RIGHT: Decant paint into a paint pot rather than using it straight from the can. It will be easier to hold, and the paint in the can will not be exposed to air and form a skin.

ABOVE: Papering walls and ceilings requires the minimum of special tools and is an effective way of producing a good-looking decorative finish. It's not as difficult as many think either.

PAPERING WALLS AND CEILINGS

Applying patterned paper to walls and ceilings has been a popular decorative technique for centuries, and a common do-it-yourself task for decades. That said, many are put off by the thought of tripping over a bucket of paste, dealing with long strips of sticky paper and hanging the paper so that it is free of wrinkles and bubbles and the pattern lines up. Consequently, papering has fallen out of favour a little in recent years. In truth, the job is not that difficult, provided you take care, and the results can be positively stunning.

There are so many patterned papers to choose from, ranging from the subtle to the flamboyant, with various degrees of wear resistance that they are suitable for every room in the house. They are definitely worth considering if you want to create a particular sense of luxury.

HOME TILING

Ceramic tiles are a practical means of providing hard wearing, waterproof and easily cleaned surfaces on walls, floors and worktops, making them invaluable in kitchens and bathrooms. They can be decorative, too, offering many colours and patterns. Although tiling is a skilled job, there is no reason why

ABOVE: A freematch wallpaper or one with a continuous pattern, such as stripes, will not need an allowance for pattern matching.

ABOVE: A straight-match pattern has the same part of the pattern running down each side of the paper, making the cutting of drops simple.

ABOVE: An offset pattern has motifs staggered between drops, which must be taken into account when cutting and measuring the paper.

ABOVE: Ceramic tiles are ideal for creating waterproof splashbacks behind sinks and basins. The range of sizes, shapes, colours and patterns to choose from is huge.

ABOVE: Tiles need not always be used for practical purposes; they can make decorative features in their own right. Here, they have been used in place of a skirting (baseboard).

the amateur should not produce professional results, especially now that a variety of tiling tools have been designed with the do-it-yourselfer in mind.

LAYING FLOORS

Of all the surfaces in the home, the floors offer the greatest variety of potential finishes and coverings. You can choose from wooden boards, blocks, panels and strips; sheet vinyl and linoleum; vinyl, linoleum and cork tiles; carpet and carpet tiles; and even rubber. Some of these materials are easier to lay than others, but none is beyond the ability of anyone with a practical nature, and a few have actually been developed with the do-it-yourselfer in mind. As with so many do-it-yourself tasks, sound preparation is the key to success.

Another important consideration when selecting a floor covering is wear resistance – knowing what to use and where to use it is essential.

RIGHT: Wooden flooring comes in many forms and can make a really striking decorative feature. Here woodstrip flooring creates a sense of luxury.

PAINTING SKILLS

- Painting materials
- Painting preparation
- Painting techniques

INTRODUCTION

Painting walls, woodwork and other surfaces is, so all the surveys reveal, by far the most popular do-it-yourself job of them all. It can be an extremely satisfying activity, not only because you can completely transform the atmosphere of a room in a relatively short space of time, but also because painting itself is a relaxing and fun activity.

Modern paints and improvements in the design and manufacture of decorating tools have certainly made the task less arduous than it was in the days of traditional oil-bound paints and distemper (tempera), and have also made it easier for the amateur decorator to obtain professional-looking results.

One major shift in paint technology is the trend away from using solvent-based (oil) varnishes and paints for wood, toward water-based (latex) products that do not give off harmful vapours as they dry. Water-based finishes are not as durable as solvent-based ones, but are no longer as far behind them in performance terms as they once were, and they have other advantages, such as faster drying times, virtually no smell and easier cleaning of brushes, rollers and pads. Therefore, it is likely that their use in the home will become much more widespread than previously.

ABOVE: Traditional household paints are either water-based (latex) or solvent-based (oil) and are generally available in three finishes: matt (flat), satin (mid sheen) and gloss.

ABOVE: Careful preparation is one of the keys to successful painting. Buy a dust sheet (drop cloth) and use a sturdy set of steps to reach the tops of walls and ceilings.

No amount of clever technology can eliminate the need for proper preparation of the surfaces to be decorated, even though this part of the job is far less enjoyable and often more time-consuming than the actual painting. In many cases, it involves little more than washing down the surface, but sometimes more thorough preparation will be called for.

OPPOSITE: Emulsion (latex) paint is available in a huge range of ready-mixed colours. Most basic wall painting is done with water-based emulsion paint since it is easy to apply with a variety of brushes, rollers, sponges and rags. Several layers can be painted over each other.

RIGHT: Different paints are suitable for different surfaces and effects, so it is very important that you choose the right paint for the right surface.

The following pages describe the various types of paint, binders, diluents, varnishes and wood stains on the market; which to use where; how to prepare surfaces for redecoration; and how to apply the new finish – especially to the more awkward interior surfaces, such as casement and sash windows and flush and panelled doors.

PAINTING MATERIALS

There are some basic essentials that you will need for decorating. You can add to this equipment gradually as you work on different effects. For general painting, edging and painting woodwork, use household paintbrushes. The most useful sizes are 50mm (2in) and 25mm (1in). Finer artist's brushes are invaluable for dealing with difficult small spaces and touching up odd areas. Soft sable-haired artist's brushes with rounded edges are best for this purpose. When painting walls and ceilings, you can use larger brushes, but a roller will be quicker and less tiring to use. Good preparation is the secret of all successful painting jobs, so filling and sanding materials are also essential.

PAINTS

Paint works by forming a film on the surface to which it is applied. This film has to do three things: it must hide the surface underneath; it must protect it; and it must stay put. All paint has three main ingredients: pigment, binder and carrier. The pigment gives the film its colour and hiding power. The binder binds the pigment particles together into a continuous film as the paint dries, and also bonds the film to the surface beneath. In traditional paint, this was a natural material, such as linseed oil in oil paints and glue size in distemper (tempera); but modern paints use synthetic resins such as alkyd, acrylic, vinyl and polyurethane. The third ingredient, the carrier, makes the paint flow smoothly as it is applied and evaporates as the paint dries.

The ratio of pigment to binder in a paint affects the finish it has when it dries: the higher the pigment content, the duller the finish. By adjusting this ratio, paint manufacturers can produce paints that dry to a matt (flat) finish; to a silky sheen, eggshell; or to a high gloss. The choice depends on personal preference, tempered by the condition of the surface: high-gloss finishes highlight any imperfections, while matt finishes tend to disguise them.

PAINT TYPES

The paint types used in the home have different carriers. Water-based paint has the pigment and binder suspended in water as tiny droplets. It is an emulsion, like milk, and is usually called emulsion (latex) paint.
As the water evaporates, the droplets coalesce to form the paint film. Solvent-based (oil) alkyd paints have pigment and binder dissolved in a petroleum-based solvent, and take longer to dry than water-based paints. These are known as oil or oil-base paints, although the term "alkyd" is used for some primers of this kind. They give off a characteristic "painty" smell as they dry, which many people find unpleasant and to which some are actually allergic. Because of growing awareness of the health risks of inhaling some solvents, the use of these paints is declining in popularity and is already under legal restriction in some countries.

Paint also contains a range of other additives to improve its performance. The most notable is one that makes the paint thixotropic, or non-drip, allowing more paint to be loaded on to the brush and a thicker paint film to be applied; one coat is often sufficient.

LEFT: Emulsion (latex) paints are available in a tempting array of colours.

PAINT QUALITIES

	BASE	DILUENT	USES	NOTES
Matt emulsion (latex)	water	water, wallpaper paste, acrylic glaze, acrylic varnish; clean with water	basic walls; large choice of colours, flat finish	fast drying, needs varnishing on furniture, marks easily
Silk emulsion (latex)	water	as above	as above; faint sheen	fast drying, more hard-wearing than matt, needs varnishing on furniture
Soft sheen	water	as above	kitchens and bathrooms; mid sheen	fast drying, moisture-resistant, needs varnishing on furniture
Dead flat oil	oil	linseed oil, white spirit (paint thinner), oil glaze, oil varnishes	woodwork; flat/velvet finish	marks easily, not durable
Eggshell	oil	as above	woodwork, furniture; faint sheen	more resistant than above, but still marks
Satin (mid sheen)	oil	as above	woodwork, furniture; mid sheen	durable, washable finish
Gloss	oil	as above	woodwork, exterior furniture; high sheen	tough, hard-wearing finish, washable
Primer	oil	not to be diluted; clean with spirits (alcohol)	bare wood	necessary for porous or wood surfaces
Undercoat	oil	not to be diluted; clean with spirits (alcohol)	between the primer and top coat	saves on top coats, choose the right colour
Masonry	water	not to be diluted; clean with water	exterior masonry	limited colours, apply with a suitable roller
Floor	oil	not to be diluted; clean with spirits (alcohol)	floors, light or industrial use	tough, durable, apply with a roller

HOUSEHOLD PAINTS

These are available in a wide range of finishes, from completely matt (flat) through varying sheens to high glosses. There is a wealth of colour choice, and in many do-it-yourself stores you can have an exact colour matched and specially mixed for you. Read the instructions on the can to check that it is suitable for your surface. When thinning paint, make sure that you are using the correct diluent.

PAINT SYSTEMS

A single coat of paint is too thin to form a durable paint film. To provide adequate cover and performance, there must be a paint system consisting of several coats. These will depend on the type of paint system that has been chosen, and on the surface being painted.

The first coat is a sealer, which is used where necessary to seal in things such as the natural resin in wood, or to prevent the paint from soaking into a porous surface.

The second is a primer, which provides a good key for the paint film to stick to. On metal surfaces, this also stops the metal corroding or oxidizing. A primer can also act as a sealer.

The third is the undercoat, which builds up the film to form a flexible, non-absorbent base of uniform colour close to that of the fourth and final layer, the top coat. The latter gives the actual finish and colour.

On walls, for which water-based (latex) paint is generally used, the system consists simply of two or three coats of the same paint, unless there is a need for a sealer or primer to cure a fault in the surface, such as dustiness, high alkalinity or excessive porosity. The first coat is a "mist" coat of thinned paint. A primer is also used if walls are being painted with solvent-based (oil) paints.

On woodwork, the first step is to apply a liquid called knotting (shellac) to any knots to prevent resin from bleeding through the paint film. Then comes a wood primer, which may be water-based or solvent-based, followed by an undercoat, then the top coat. To speed up the painting process, paint manufacturers have perfected combined primer/undercoats, and have also introduced so-called self-undercoating gloss paint, which only needs a primer.

On metal, a primer is generally needed. A zinc phosphate primer is used for iron and steel indoors, but outdoors, it is common to apply a rust-inhibiting primer to these materials as soon as they have been stripped back to bare metal and any existing traces of rust removed completely. There are special primers for aluminium. This is then followed by an undercoat and top coat, as for wood. Copper, brass and lead can be painted directly without the need for a primer, as long as they are brought to a bright finish first and are thoroughly degreased with white spirit (paint thinner).

BELOW AND RIGHT: Acrylic primer and knotting (shellac).

BINDERS AND DILUENTS

Pigment needs a binder so that it will adhere to the surface on to which it is painted. As well as the binder in the paint itself, there are other binders that you can add to modify its consistency and texture. Diluents and solvents are added to thin the paint and to delay the drying time. Glazes also delay drying, and modern products such as acrylic glazes can be used instead of traditional scumble glazes for a more workable consistency.

There are many mediums for glazes such as wallpaper paste, linseed oil, PVA (white glue) and dryers that will change the nature of the paint. Solvents such as white spirit (paint thinner) can also be used to clean paintbrushes. Always use a diluent or solvent that is suitable for the type of paint you are using.

Regardless of how you employ them, remember that solvents other than water give off toxic fumes and are highly flammable. Treat them with respect and make sure your work area is well ventilated. Never smoke nearby.

Take care when disposing of empty containers and any rags soaked in paint. The latter can ignite spontaneously if exposed to even gentle heat. Do not pour solvent used for cleaning brushes into a drain; take it to a proper disposal site.

BINDERS AND DILUENTS

	BASE	DILUENT	USES	NOTES
PVA (white glue)	water	water	binder for emulsion (latex) washes	makes the mixture more durable
Linseed oil	oil		medium for powder	lengthy drying
Dryers			add to oil paint to speed drying	
Wallpaper paste	water		dilutes emulsions (latex)	retards the drying a little
Acrylic glaze	water	water	as above	retards drying
Scumble glaze	oil	water	medium to suspend colour pigments	difficult to tint to the right quantity
Methylated spirits (methyl alcohol)	oil	white spirit (paint thinner)	softens dried emulsion (latex)	
White spirit (paint thinner)	oil		paint thinner, brush cleaner	buy in bulk

VARNISHES AND WOOD STAINS

Varnish is basically paint without the pigment. Most contain polyurethane resins and are solvent-based (like oil paint), although water-based acrylic varnishes are becoming more popular for health and environmental reasons, just as solvent-based paints are losing ground to water-based types.

Varnishes are available with a matt (flat), satin (mid sheen)/silk or a high-gloss finish, either clear or with the addition of small amounts of colour. These coloured varnishes are intended to enhance the appearance of the wood, or to give it some extra colour without obliterating the wood grain, as paint would do.

Varnish is its own primer and undercoat, although it is best to thin the first coat with about ten per cent

ABOVE: Varnishes seal and protect the surface, and add colour to wood.

VARNISHES

	BASE	DILUENT	USES	NOTES
Polyurethane/oil-based	oil	white spirit (paint thinner)	strong varnishes in a range of finishes	tough, durable, slow drying
Polyurethane (aerosol)	oil		matt (flat) finish	
Acrylic	water	water	range of finishes	not as durable
Acrylic (aerosol)	water		matt (flat) finish	
Tinted varnish	oil acrylic	white spirit (paint thinner) water	for bare wood, or antiquing paint; range of colours	slow drying fast drying
Button polish	water	methylated spirit (methyl alcohol)	sealing bare wood	fast drying

white spirit (paint thinner) for solvent-based types, or water for acrylic types, and to apply it with a lint-free cloth rather than a brush so that it can be rubbed well into the wood grain. When this first coat has dried, it is keyed, or roughened, by rubbing very lightly with fine abrasive paper, dusted off, and a second, full-strength coat brushed on. For surfaces likely to receive a lot of wear, it is advisable to key the second coat as before, then apply an additional coat.

WOOD STAINS

Wood stains, unlike paint and varnish, are designed to soak into the wood. Subsequently, they may be sealed with clear varnish to improve the finish and make the surface more durable. They are available in water-based and solvent-based types, in a wide range of colours and wood shades; different colours of the same type can be blended to obtain intermediate shades, and the stain can be thinned with water or white spirit (paint thinner) as appropriate to give a paler effect.

Stains are often applied with a brush or a paint pad, but often it is quicker and easier to obtain even coverage by putting them on with a clean lint-free cloth. Quick work is needed to blend wet edges together and avoid overlaps, which will leave darker patches as the stain dries.

ABOVE: Pigments and stains can be stirred into water-based (latex) paint mediums to create unique colours and textures.

A water-based stain will raise fibres on the surface of the wood, which will spoil the evenness of the colour. The solution is to sand the surface smooth first, then moisten it with a wet cloth. This will raise the surface fibres. When the wood is dry, these fibres are sanded off with extra-fine abrasive paper, ready to receive the application of stain.

PAINTING PREPARATION

Perhaps the most important factor in achieving a successful result when decorating is to make sure that the surfaces are clean and smooth. Careful preparation can seem rather tedious, but it is worth the time spent. Wash walls with a solution of sugar soap (all-purpose cleaner), then rinse them well with clean water. Scrape off any flaking paint and fix any dents and cracks in the plaster with filler (spackle). When the filler has hardened, sand it smooth with fine-grade abrasive paper. Similarly, fix any defects in the woodwork. If knots are showing through the existing paintwork, sand them back to bare wood and apply knotting (shellac). When dry, paint on primer and undercoat to bring the area up to the level of the surrounding paintwork.

PREPARING THE ROOM

Paint is a popular decorative finish for walls and ceilings because it is quick and easy to apply, offers a huge range of colours and is relatively inexpensive compared with rival products, such as wallcoverings. It can be used over plain plaster, or applied over embossed relief wallcoverings and textured finishes.

Before starting to paint, clear the room and prepare the surfaces. Start by taking down curtains and blinds (drapes and shades). Remove furniture to another room if possible, or group it in the middle of the room and cover it with plastic sheeting. Take down lampshades and pendant light fittings (after turning off the power supply). Unscrew wall-mounted fittings and remove the hardware from doors and windows if they are being repainted at the same time.

Protect surfaces not being repainted, such as wall switches and socket outlets (receptacles), with masking tape. Finally, cover the floor with dust sheets (drop cloths), which will absorb paint splashes; vacuum-clean surfaces such as window sills, picture rails and skirtings (baseboards) where dust can settle, and turn off forced-air heating to ensure that dust is not re-circulated into the room.

ACCESS EQUIPMENT

Normally, most of the surfaces to be painted can be reached from a standing or a kneeling position, but for ceilings, the tops of walls and the upper reaches of stairwells, some access equipment is needed. A stepladder, ideally with a top platform big enough to support a paint kettle (paint pot) or roller tray, will be adequate for walls and ceilings.

For stairwells, use steps or ladder sections plus secured scaffold

PAINTING WALLS AND CEILINGS

Paint walls and ceilings in a series of overlapping bands. Start painting the ceiling next to the window wall so that reflected light on the wet paint shows whether coverage is even. On walls, right-handed people should work from right to left, and left-handed people from left to right.

boards, or access towers, to set up a platform. Always make sure that you can get to all the surfaces without overreaching.

PAINT COVERAGE

Paint coverage depends on several factors, including the roughness and porosity of the surface to which it is being applied and the thickness of the coating. For example, the first coat of paint will soak into new plaster, so the coverage will be less than is achieved with subsequent coats. Similarly, a textured surface will hold more paint than a smooth one, again reducing the paint coverage.

Manufacturers usually give an indication of coverage on the container; remember that it is an average figure.

LIGHT SWITCHES

When painting a wall that contains a light switch, protect the faceplate from splashes with masking tape. Paint around the fitting with a small brush before completing the wall with a larger brush or roller. Remove the tape before the paint has dried completely, otherwise the edges may lift as you pull the tape away.

ESTIMATING QUANTITIES

PAINT TYPE	SQ M PER LITRE	SQ FT PER GALLON
Liquid gloss (oil) paint	16	650
Non-drip gloss (oil) paint	13	530
Eggshell	12	490
Matt (flat) water-based (latex) paint	15	610
Satin (mid sheen)/silk water-based (latex) paint	14	570
Non-drip water-based (latex) paint	12	490
Undercoat	11	450
Wood primer	12	490
Metal primer	10	410
Varnish	15–20	610–820

The figures given here are intended as a rough guide only. Always check the manufacturer's coverage figure printed on the container, and use that together with the area to be painted to work out how much paint is required.

PREPARING PAINTED WOODWORK

Modern paints have excellent adhesion and covering power, but to deliver the best performance they must be given a good start by preparing the surface thoroughly.

Wash surfaces that have previously been painted with a solution of strong household detergent or sugar soap (all-purpose cleaner). Rinse them very thoroughly with clean water, and allow them to dry completely before repainting them.

Remove areas of flaking paint with a scraper or filling knife (putty knife), then either touch in the bare area with more paint or fill it flush with the surrounding paint film by using fine filler (spackle). Sand this smooth when it has hardened.

1 Use fine-grade abrasive paper wrapped around a sanding block to remove "nibs" from the paint surface and to key the paint film ready for repainting.

2 Wash the surface down with detergent or sugar soap (all-purpose cleaner) to remove dirt, grease, finger marks and the dust from sanding it. Rinse with clean water, ensuring that no detergent residue is left, as this will inhibit the new paint film.

3 Use a proprietary tack rag or a clean cloth moistened with white spirit (paint thinner) to remove dust from recessed mouldings and other awkward corners.

STRIPPING WITH HEAT

Every time a surface is repainted, this adds a little more thickness to the paint layer. It does not matter much on wall or ceiling surfaces, but on woodwork (and, to a lesser extent, on metalwork) this build-up of successive layers of paint can eventually lead to the clogging of detail on mouldings. More importantly, moving parts, such as doors and windows, start to bind and catch against their frames. If this happens, it is time to strip off the paint back to bare wood and build up a new paint system from scratch.

It may also be necessary to strip an old paint finish if it is in such poor condition – from physical damage for example – that repainting will no longer cover up the faults adequately.

1 Play the airstream from the heat gun over the surface to soften the paint film. Scrape it off as it bubbles up, and deposit the hot scrapings in an old metal container.

2 Use a shavehook (triangular scraper) instead of a flat scraper to remove the paint from mouldings. Take care not to scorch the wood if it is to be varnished afterwards.

3 Remove any remnants of paint from the wood surface with wire wool (steel wool) soaked in white spirit (paint thinner), remove any loose particles, then sand the surface lightly. Wipe with a clean cloth moistened with white spirit.

STRIPPING WITH CHEMICALS

As an alternative to stripping paint using a heat gun, you can use a chemical paint remover, which contains either dimethylene chloride or caustic soda. Heat works well on wood, but may scorch the surface and can crack the glass in windows; it is less successful on metal because the material conducts heat away as it is applied. Chemical strippers work well on all surfaces, but need handling with care; for safety, always follow the manufacturer's instructions.

You can choose between liquid and paste-type chemical strippers. The former are better on horizontal surfaces, while the latter are good for intricate mouldings since they take longer to dry. Whichever type you select, neutralize the chemical by washing it off in accordance with the manufacturer's instructions.

Both types of chemical stripper will cause injury if splashed on to bare skin or into the eyes, so be sure to cover up well when using them. Wear old clothes or overalls and vinyl gloves, together with safety spectacles or a similar form of eye shield. Make sure you work in a well-ventilated area and never smoke near the workplace until the stripper has been removed, as the fumes given off can be toxic when inhaled through a cigarette. If you should accidentally splash your skin, wash off the stripper immediately with plenty of cold water.

USING LIQUID REMOVER

1 Wear rubber gloves and old clothing. Decant the liquid into a plastic container or an old can, then brush it on to the surface. Leave it until the paint film bubbles up.

HOMEMADE PASTE REMOVER

Add caustic soda to water until no more will dissolve. Thicken to a paste with oatmeal and use as for proprietary paste remover. Be particularly careful when using this corrosive solution. If it splashes on the skin, rinse at once with plenty of cold water.

2 Use a flat scraper or shavehook (triangular scraper) as appropriate to remove the softened paint. Deposit the scrapings safely in a container.

3 Neutralize the stripper by washing the surface down with water or white spirit (paint thinner), as recommended by the manufacturer. Leave to dry.

USING PASTE REMOVER

1 Paste removers are especially good for removing paint from intricate mouldings because they dry very slowly. Apply the paste liberally to the surface.

2 Give the paste plenty of time to work, especially on thick paint layers. Then scrape it off and wash down the surface with plenty of water to neutralize the chemical.

REMOVING TEXTURED FINISHES

Textured finishes are tackled in different ways, depending on their type. Texture paints are basically thick water-based (latex) paints, normally used to create relatively low-relief effects, and can be removed with specially formulated paint removers. Some textured effects formed with a powder or ready-mixed compound are best removed with a steam wallpaper stripper, which softens the compound so that it can be scraped from the wall.

Never attempt to sand off a textured finish. There are two reasons. One is that it will create huge quantities of very fine dust; the other is that older versions of this product contained asbestos fibres as a filler, and any action that might release these into the atmosphere as inhalable dust must be avoided at all costs.

1 Strip texture paint by brushing on a generous coat of a proprietary texture paint remover. Stipple it well into the paint and leave it to penetrate.

2 When the paint has softened, scrape it off with a broad-bladed scraper. Wear gloves, and also safety goggles if working on a ceiling.

3 Once the bulk of the coating has been removed, use wire wool (steel wool) dipped in the paint remover to strip off any remaining flecks of paint.

4 Remove powder-based and ready-mixed types using a steam stripper, which will soften the finish. Never try to sand off this type of finish.

REMOVING TILES

When faced with a tiled surface, complete removal or a cover-up with plasterboard (gypsum board) are the two options. The former will leave a surface in need of considerable renovation, while the latter will cause a slight loss of space within the room, as well as some complications at door and window openings, where new frames, architraves (trims) and sills may be necessary. In addition, the skirtings (baseboards) will need removing from the walls and refitting to the plasterboard surface.

POLYSTYRENE (STYROFOAM) TILES

1 Lever the tiles away from the ceiling with a scraper. If they were fixed with a continuous coat of adhesive, consider covering the tiles with heavy lining paper as a temporary measure. For the best finish, fit a new plasterboard (gypsum board) ceiling, nailing through the tile layer into the ceiling joists.

CERAMIC TILES

ABOVE: On a completely tiled wall, use a hammer to crack a tile and create a starting point for the stripping. On partly tiled walls, start at the tile edge. Use a broad bolster (stonecutter's chisel) and a club (spalling) hammer to chip the old tiles off the wall. Replaster afterwards.

2 If the tiles were fixed in place with blobs of adhesive, use a heat gun to soften the old adhesive so it can be removed with a broad-bladed scraper.

STRIPPING WALLPAPER

Once the room is cleared, and dust sheets (drop cloths) are spread over the floor and any remaining furniture, the next step is to identify what type of wallcovering is to be removed. An ordinary printed paper will absorb water splashed on it immediately; other types will not. To tell washables from vinyls, pick and lift a corner, and try to strip the wallcovering dry. The printed plastic layer of a vinyl wallcovering will peel off dry, but the surface of a washable paper will not come off in the same way unless it is a duplex paper made in two layers. With paper-backed fabric wallcoverings, it is often possible to peel the fabric away from its paper backing; try it before turning to other, more complicated methods of removal.

Printed papers can usually be stripped relatively easily by soaking them with warm water containing a little washing-up liquid or a stripping compound. This will soften the adhesive, allowing the paper to be scraped off. Resoak stubborn areas and take care not to gouge the wall with the scraper.

Washable papers will not allow water to penetrate to the paste behind, so must be scored to break the surface film. Then they can be soaked, but removal will still be difficult; using a steam stripper will speed the process.

Wash all traces of adhesive from the wall and allow to dry before painting.

1 To strip printed wallpaper, wet the surface with a sponge or a garden spray gun. Wait for the water to penetrate, and repeat if necessary.

4 After removing the bulk of the old wallpaper, go back over the wall surface and remove any remaining "nibs" of paper with sponge/spray gun and scraper.

2 Using a stiff wallpaper scraper – not a filling knife (putty knife) – start scraping the old paper from the wall at a seam. Wet it again while working if necessary. Hold the scraper blade flat against the wall to stop it digging in.

3 Turn off the power before stripping around switches and other fittings, then loosen the faceplate screws to strip the wallpaper from behind them.

5 To strip a washable wallpaper, start by scoring the plastic coating with a serrated scraper or toothed roller, then soak and scrape as before.

6 For quicker results, use a steam stripper to remove washable papers. Press the steaming plate to the next area while stripping the area just steamed. Once the wallcovering has been removed, wash the wall to remove all traces of adhesive.

FILLING DEFECTS AND CRACKS

A perfectly smooth, flat surface is essential for a good paint finish, and regardless of whether you intend painting a wood or plaster surface, there are likely to be cracks and other minor blemishes that need filling before you can begin painting.

If you have chosen an opaque finish, cracks and small holes in wood can be filled with cellulose filler (spackle). However, if you intend applying a varnish or similar translucent finish, a tinted wood stopper (patcher) would be more appropriate, since it will disguise the damage. Cracks in plaster should be treated with cellulose filler.

Always apply filler so that it is a little proud of the surrounding surface. Then, when it has dried, sand it back to leave a perfectly smooth surface.

FILLING DEFECTS IN WOOD

1 Fill splits and dents in wood using filler (spackle) on painted surfaces, and tinted wood stopper (patcher) on new or stripped wood that will be varnished.

2 Use the corner of a filling knife (putty knife), or even a finger, to work the filler into recesses and other awkward-to-reach places. Smooth off excess filler before it dries.

3 When the filler or wood stopper has hardened completely, use abrasive paper (sandpaper) wrapped around a sanding block to sand the repair down flush with the surroundings.

FILLING CRACKS IN PLASTER

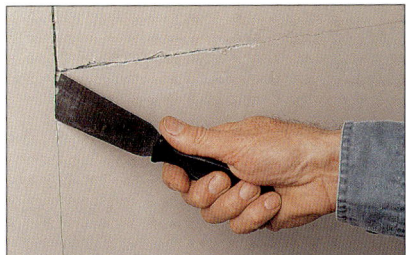

1 Use a filling knife (putty knife) to rake out loose material along the crack, and to undercut the edges so that the filler (spackle) grips well.

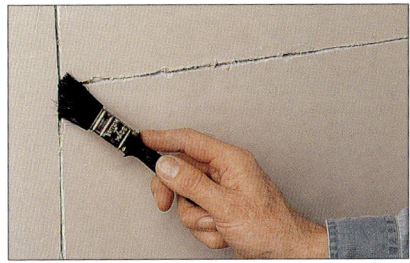

2 Brush out dust and debris from the crack, using an old paintbrush. Alternatively, use the crevice nozzle attachment of a vacuum cleaner.

3 Dampen the surrounding plaster with water from a garden spray gun to prevent it from drying out the filler too quickly and causing it to crack.

4 Mix up some filler on a plasterer's hawk (mortarboard) or a board offcut to a firm consistency. Alternatively, use ready-mixed filler or wallboard compound.

5 Use a filling knife to press the filler well into the crack, drawing the blade across it and then along it. Aim to leave the repair slightly proud.

6 When the filler has hardened, use fine-grade abrasive paper (sandpaper) wrapped around a sanding block to smooth the repair flush with the surrounding wall.

PAINTING TECHNIQUES

The most important requirement for successful results when painting is the proper use of the correct materials and tools. Make sure that you have the right type of brush, sponge, cloth, pad or roller for the specific technique you are planning. Read carefully through the steps to check that you have everything you need before you start.

In particular, make sure that you have enough paint to complete the job; running out could be disastrous. Remember that the quality of the finish will be determined by the effort you put into it. Don't rush or overload brushes in an attempt to speed the work, but bear in mind that you need to keep working from a "wet edge" to prevent seam lines from showing in the finish.

USING A PAINTBRUSH

The paintbrush is the most versatile and, therefore, the most widely used tool for applying paint. Choose the brush size to match the surface being painted. For example, for painting glazing bars (muntins) on windows or narrow mouldings on a door, use a slim brush – or perhaps a cutting-in (sash) brush if painting up to an adjacent unpainted surface, such as glass where a neat edge to the paint film is needed. For expansive, flat areas, select a larger brush for quick coverage. Remember that the largest wall brushes can be tiring to use, especially with solvent-based (oil) paints.

Get rid of any loose bristles in a new brush by flicking it vigorously across the palm of the hand before using it for the first time. Wash previously used brushes that have been stored unwrapped to remove any dust or other debris from the bristles, and leave them to dry out again before applying a solvent-based paint.

Always check that the metal ferrule is securely attached to the brush handle, and hammer in any projecting nails or staples. Check, too, that the ferrule is free from rust, which could discolour the paint. To remove rust, use either wire wool (steel wool) or abrasive paper (sandpaper).

PREPARING THE PAINT

1 Wipe the lid first to remove any dust. Then prise it off with a wide lever, such as the thicker edge of a table knife to avoid damage to the lip.

2 Decant some paint into a clean metal or plastic paint kettle (paint pot), or small bucket. This will be easier to handle than a full container, especially one without a handle.

3 Remove any paint skin from partly used containers. Then strain the paint into the paint kettle through a piece of old stocking or tights (pantyhose), or cheesecloth.

USING A BRUSH

1 To load the brush with paint, dip it into the paint to about a third of the bristle depth. An overloaded brush will cause drips, and paint will run down the brush handle.

2 Tie a length of string or wire across the mouth of the paint kettle (paint pot) between the handle supports, and use it to scrape excess paint from the bristles.

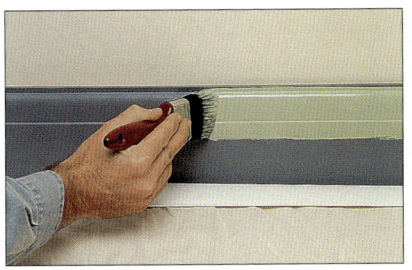

3 Apply the paint to the wood in long, sweeping strokes, brushing the paint out along the grain direction until the brush begins to run dry.

4 Load the brush with more paint and apply it to the next area. Blend the two together with short, light strokes, again along the grain direction.

5 Repeat this process while working across the area, blending the edges of adjacent areas together with light brush strokes to avoid leaving visible joins.

6 At edges and external corners, let the brush run off the edge to prevent a build-up of paint on the corner. Repeat the process for the opposite edge.

USING A PAINT ROLLER

Generally, paint rollers are used to apply water-based (latex) paints to large, flat areas, such as walls and ceilings. Choose a sleeve with a short pile for painting plaster, a medium pile for painting embossed or textured wall coverings and a long pile for deeply sculpted surfaces, such as those created with textured finishes (texture paints). Rollers can also apply solvent-based (oil) paint to flat surfaces, such as flush doors, but tend to leave a distinctive "orange peel" texture rather than the smooth finish left by a paintbrush.

There are some drawbacks with paint rollers: they cannot paint right up to internal corners or wall/ceiling angles, so these need to be painted first with a brush or pad. They can also splash if "driven" too fast, and the sleeves take a lot of time and effort to clean thoroughly, especially if they have been used for a long period and there is dried paint in the pile. Repeated cleaning eventually causes the sleeve to peel from its core.

It is possible to buy a roller washer for removing emulsion (latex) paint. It is designed to stand in a sink and be connected to a tap (faucet). When the tap is turned on, the running water causes the roller to spin and flush the paint from its pile. Oil-based paints should be removed by rolling the sleeve back and forth in white spirit (paint thinner).

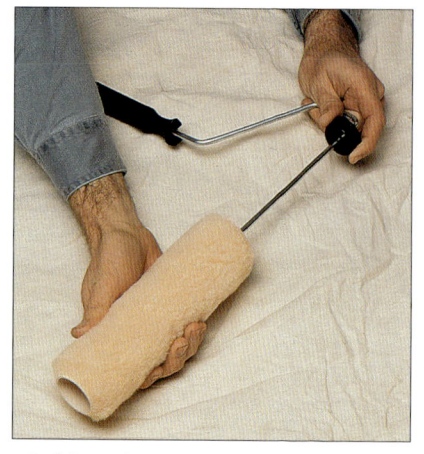

1 Select a sleeve with the required fibre type and pile length, and slide it on to the sprung metal cage until it meets the stop next to the handle. If painting a ceiling, fit an extension to the handle if possible.

4 Load the roller sleeve with paint by running it down the sloping section into the paint. Then roll it up and down the slope to remove the excess. Make sure the tray is placed out of harm's way so that it cannot be upset accidentally.

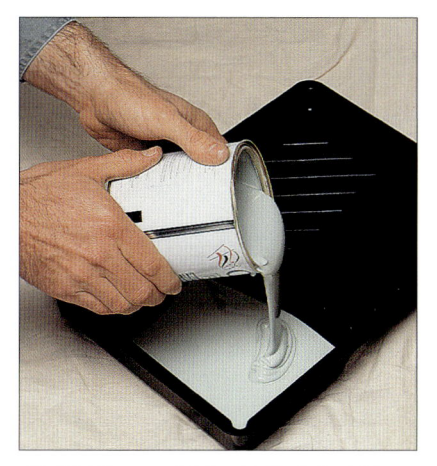

2 Decant some paint (previously strained if from an old can) into the roller tray until the paint level just laps up the sloping section.

3 Brush a band of paint about 50mm (2in) wide into internal corners and wall/ceiling angles, around doors and windows, and above skirtings (baseboards). Brush out the edge of the paint to feather it so that it does not form a seam.

5 Start applying the paint in a series of overlapping diagonal strokes to ensure complete coverage of the surface. Continue until the sleeve runs dry. Do not "drive" the roller too quickly, as it may cause the paint to splash.

6 Reload the sleeve and tackle the next section in the same way. Finish off by blending the areas together, working parallel to corners and edges.

USING A PAINT PAD

People either love or loathe paint pads. They tend to apply less paint per coat than either a brush or a roller, so an additional coat may be needed in some circumstances, but they make it easy to apply paint smoothly and evenly with no risk of brush marks.

For best results, pads should be used with the correct type of paint tray. This incorporates a loading roller that picks up the paint from the reservoir in the tray and applies it evenly to the pad as the latter is drawn across the roller. If you do not have the correct tray, a roller tray will suffice. Dip the pad carefully into the paint, then run it over the ridged section of the tray to ensure that the paint is evenly distributed on the pad sole and that the pad is not overloaded.

New pads should be brushed with a clothes brush to remove loose fibres. As with brushes, always select the correct size for the job, using the largest for painting walls and ceilings.

After use, dab the pad on newspaper to remove as much paint as possible. Then wash thoroughly in water, white spirit (paint thinner) or brush cleaner as appropriate. Work the fibres between your fingertips to clean them, finishing off by washing in hot, soapy water.

1 Pour some paint into the special applicator tray. Then load the pad by running it backward and forward over the ridged loading roller.

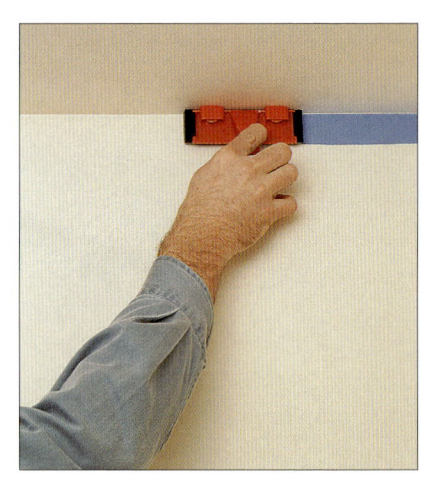

4 Special edging pads are designed for painting right up to internal angles. They have small wheels that guide the pad along the adjacent surface as you work. Make sure the wheels remain in contact with that surface.

PAINTING TECHNIQUES • 43

2 On walls, apply the paint in a series of overlapping parallel bands. Make sure the sole of the pad remains flat on the wall. Use a small pad or a special edging pad (see step 4) to paint right up to corners and angles.

3 Use smaller pads for painting narrow areas such as mouldings on doors or glazing bars (muntins) on windows, brushing out the paint along the direction of the grain. The pad will produce neat, straight lines.

5 Some larger pads can be fitted to an extension pole to make it easier to paint ceilings and high walls. Make sure the pad is attached securely.

USING AEROSOL PAINT

Aerosol paints and varnishes are ideal for hard-to-decorate surfaces such as wickerwork. Always follow the maker's instructions when using them.

USING TEXTURE PAINTS

Texture paints are water-based (latex) paints thickened with added fillers. Once the paint has been applied to the decorating surface, a range of three-dimensional effects can be created using various patterning and texturing techniques. These paints are ideal for covering surfaces in poor condition. Most have a natural white finish, but they can be overpainted with ordinary water-based paint for a coloured effect. Avoid using texture paints in kitchens – the textured surface will trap dirt and grease, which is difficult to clean.

1 Start applying the paint to the wall or ceiling surface in a series of overlapping random strokes, recharging the roller or brush at intervals. Do not push the roller too quickly, as it may flick the paint about.

4 Use a texturing comb to create overlapping swirls, working across the area. Practise the effect on paint applied to a piece of heavy cardboard first. When you are happy with your technique, begin on the wall.

5 Twist a sponge before pulling it away from the wall surface to create a series of small, overlapping swirls in the paint finish. Rinse the sponge regularly.

PAINTING TECHNIQUES • 45

2 When an area of about 1 sq m (11 sq ft) is covered, go over the whole area with a series of parallel roller/brush strokes to create an even surface texture. This can be left for a subtle effect or given a more obvious pattern, as shown here.

3 Give the textured finish the appearance of tree bark by drawing a flat-bladed scraper or similar edged tool over the surface to flatten off the high spots.

6 You can buy patterning roller sleeves in a range of different designs for use with texture paints. This one creates a regular diamond pattern.

7 This patterning sleeve gives a random streaked effect when rolled down the wall. Apply the texture paint with a brush first if using a patterning sleeve, but do not spread it too thinly, otherwise there will be insufficient to create a pattern.

PAINTING DOORS

The main problem with painting doors – or indeed any woodwork with a large surface area – involves keeping what professional decorators call a "wet edge". Obviously the door has to be painted bit by bit, and if the edge of one area begins to dry before it is joined to the next area, the join (seam) will show when the paint dries completely.

The secret of success is to work in a sequence, as shown in the accompanying drawings of flush and panelled doors, and to complete the job in one continuous operation, working as fast as reasonably possible.

Before starting to paint a door, wedge it open so there is room to walk through the doorway without touching wet paint, and also so that the hinged edge of the door can be reached easily. Remove handles, locks and other fittings; wedge a length of dowel in the latch hole to make a temporary handle for use until the paint has dried. Slide a dust sheet (dust cover) underneath the door to catch any drips. Finally, warn everyone else in the house that

PAINTING FLUSH DOORS

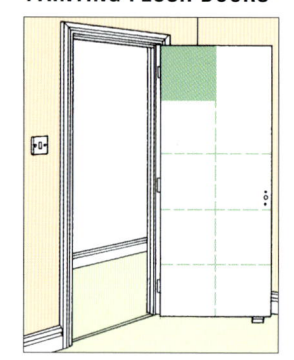

1 Remove the door furniture and wedge open the door. Then divide it into eight or ten imaginary squares, and start painting at the top of the door by filling in the first square. Brush the paint out toward the door edges so it does not build up on the external angles.

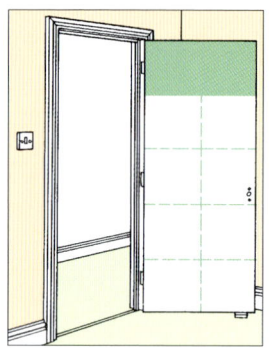

2 Move on to the next block at the top of the door, brushing paint out toward the top and side edges as before. Carefully blend the two areas together with horizontal brush strokes, then with light vertical laying-off strokes.

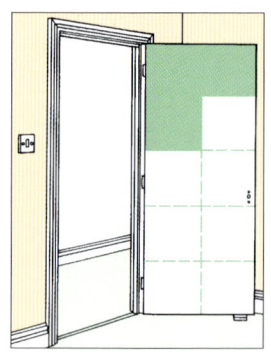

3 Continue to work down the door block by block, blending the wet edges of adjacent blocks as they are painted. Complete a flush door in one session to prevent the joins (seams) between blocks from showing up as hard lines. Replace the door furniture when the paint is dry.

the door is covered with wet paint, and keep children and pets out of the way in another room or out of doors.

If you intend painting the door frame and surrounding architrave (trim) as well as the door, do so after you have painted the door itself and the paint has dried. That way, you will only have one area of wet paint to avoid at a time when passing through the door opening.

PAINTING DOOR EDGES

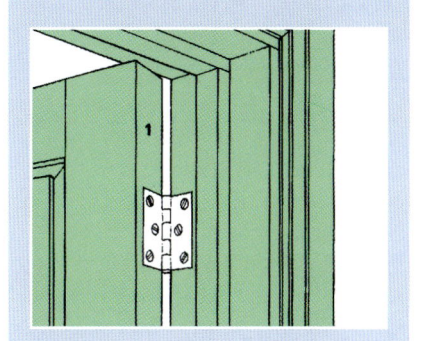

If each side of the door is to be a different colour, match the colour of the hinged edge (1) to that of the closing face of the door – the one facing the room – and the leading edge to the outer face.

PAINTING PANELLED DOORS

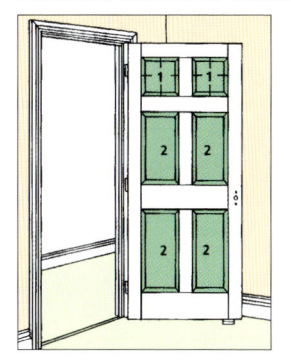

1 Tackle panelled doors by painting the mouldings (1) around the recessed panels first. Take care not to let paint build up in the corners or to stray on to the faces of the cross-rails at this stage. Then paint the recessed panels (2).

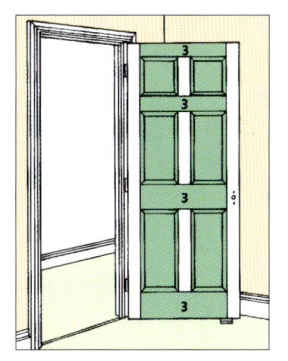

2 Next, paint the horizontal cross-rails (3), brushing lightly in toward the painted panel mouldings to leave a sharp paint edge. Feather the paint out thinly where it runs on to the vertical stiles at the ends of the rails.

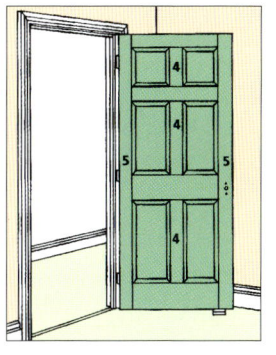

3 Finish the door by painting the vertical centre rail (4) and the outer stiles (5), again brushing toward the panel mouldings. Where the centre rail abuts the cross-rails, finish with light brush strokes parallel to the cross-rails. Work as quickly as possible.

PAINTING WINDOWS

Windows are more difficult to paint than doors because they contain so many different surfaces, especially small-paned types criss-crossed with slim glazing bars (muntins). There is also the additional problem of paint straying on to the glass. The ideal is a neat paint line that covers the bedding putty and extends on to the glass surface by about 3mm (⅛in) to seal the joint and prevent condensation from running down between putty and glass.

With hinged windows, the edges of the casement or top opening light (transom) should be painted to match the colour used on the inside of the window. With double-hung sliding sash windows, the top and bottom edges of each sash and the top, bottom and sides of the frame are all painted to match the inner face of the sashes.

Remove the window hardware before you start painting. On casement windows, tap a nail into the bottom edge of the casement and into the lower frame rebate (rabbet), and link them with stiff wire to stop the casement from swinging open or shut while you are working.

PAINTING A CASEMENT WINDOW

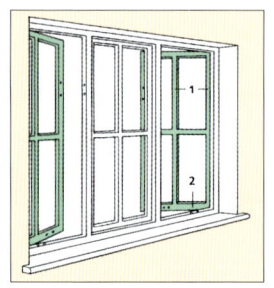

1 Remove the window furniture from the opening casement and wedge the window open while you work. Tackle the glazing bars (muntins) and edge mouldings first (1), then the face of the surrounding casement frame (2), and finally the hinged edge of the casement. Paint the remaining top, bottom and opening edges from outside.

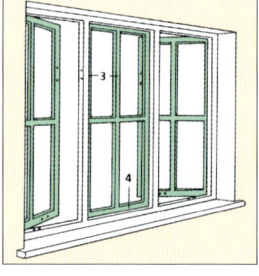

2 Move on to paint the glazing bars and edge mouldings (3) of the fixed casement. Use masking tape or a paint shield to ensure neat, straight edges here and on the opening casement; the paint should overlap the glass by about 3mm (⅛in) to ensure a good seal. Paint the face of the surrounding casement frame (4).

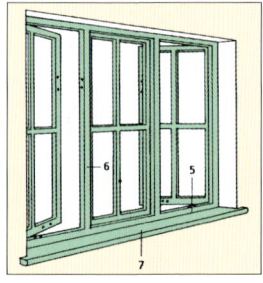

3 Paint the outer frame (5), then the centre frame member between the opening and fixed casements (6). Complete the job by painting the window sill (7) and the rebate (rabbet) into which the opening casement closes.

PAINTING A SASH WINDOW

For best results, sash windows should be removed from their frames before painting. Modern spring-mounted windows are easy to release from their frames. With older cord-operated types, remove the staff beads (window stops) first to free the sashes. Although quite a major task, take the opportunity to renew the sash cords (pulley ropes). This makes it possible to cut the cords to free the window. Some making good and finishing off will have to be done after the window is reassembled.

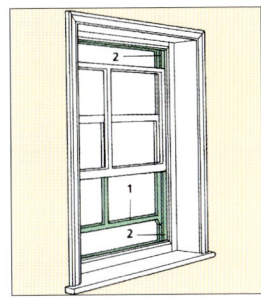

1 To paint sash windows without removing the sashes, start by raising the bottom sash and lowering the top one. Paint the lower half of the top sash (1), including its bottom edge, and the exposed parting beads (2) and the exposed sides of the frame.

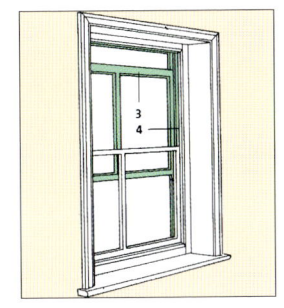

2 When the paint is touch-dry, reverse the sash positions and paint the upper half of the top sash (3), including its top edge, and the exposed and unpainted parting beads and frame sides (4).

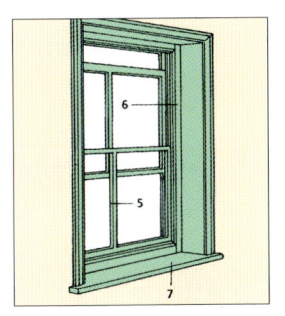

3 Finish off by painting the face and edges of the inner sash (5), the staff beads (window stops) and any other trim mouldings around the window (6). Finally, paint the window sill (7). Leave the sashes ajar until the paint has dried to prevent components from sticking.

PAINTING AROUND GLASS

◀ Stick masking tape to the glass with its edge 3mm (⅛in) from the wood. Paint the wood, then remove the tape.

▶ Alternatively, hold a paint shield against the edge of the glazing bar (muntin) or surrounding moulding. Wipe the shield to prevent smears.

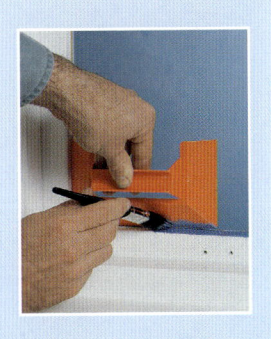

VARNISHING WOOD

Varnish is a useful means of providing a protective finish for wood while allowing the pattern of the grain to show through. The more coats of clear varnish applied, the darker the wood will appear, but coloured varnishes are also available that can give the wood the appearance of another species or simply make an attractive finish in their own right. Again, the more that is applied, the darker will be the appearance of the wood, so if possible test coloured varnish on scrap wood first to determine the number of coats you need to obtain the desired finish.

1 On bare wood, use a clean lint-free cloth to wipe the first coat of varnish on to the wood, working along the grain direction. This coat acts as a primer/sealer. Allow the varnish to dry completely.

2 Sand the first coat lightly when dry to remove any "nibs" caused by dust particles settling on the wet varnish, then wipe off the sanding dust.

3 Apply the second and subsequent coats of varnish with a brush, working along the grain and blending together adjacent areas with light brush strokes. Sand each coat, except the last, with very fine abrasive paper (sandpaper).

STAINING WOOD

Wood washing actually stains wood with a colour, so that the beauty of the grain shows through and is enhanced by the colour. The technique can only be used on totally bare, stripped wood once all traces of varnish, wax or previous paint finishes have been removed completely. If they are not, the result will be patchy. Depending on the product used, the surface may or may not need varnishing to seal it, so make sure you read the manufacturer's information on the container. Usually a matt (flat) finish looks appropriate for this technique.

Colours that often work well include yellow ochre, blue, Indian red, violet, cream and pale green.

WOOD WASHES

yellow ochre

blue

Indian red

violet

cream

pale green

1 Pour the pre-mixed wash into a paint kettle (paint pot). Then brush the stain evenly on the wood in the direction of the grain.

2 While the stain is still wet, wipe off the excess with a cloth. This will even the effect and expose slightly more of the grain. Then leave the stain to dry completely before varnishing the wood if required.

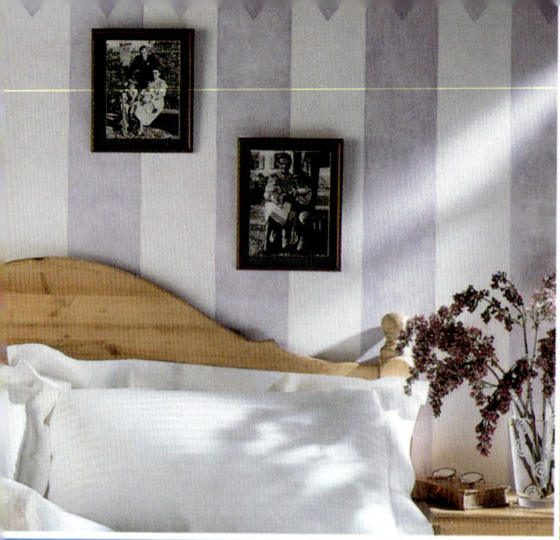
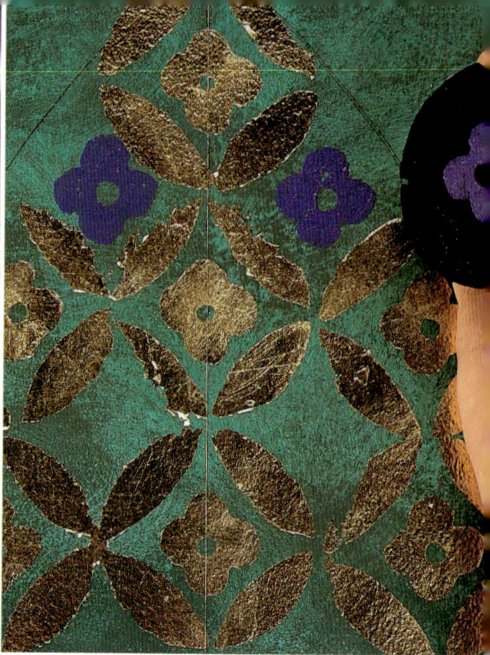
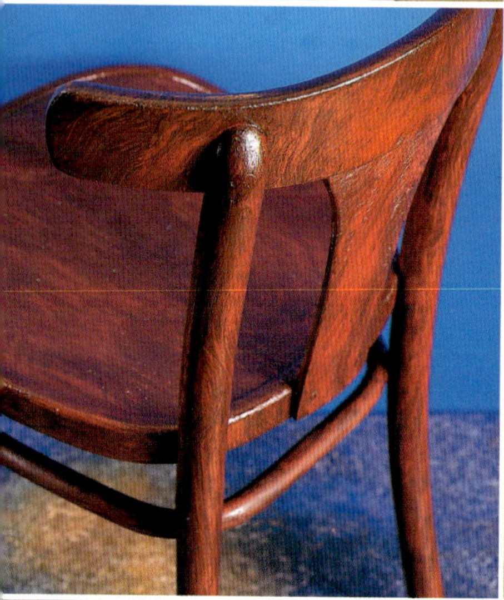
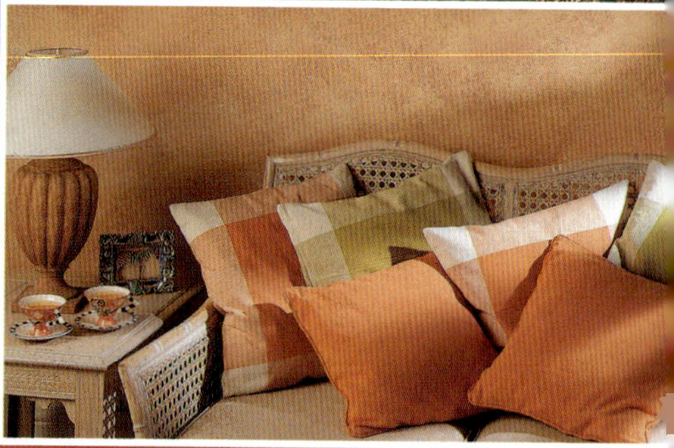

PAINT FINISHES

- Basic paint finishes
- Patterned paint effects
- Faux paint finishes

INTRODUCTION

For many people, decorating with paint means nothing more than applying solid colours to their walls, ceilings and woodwork, but there is so much more to be achieved with this material if a few techniques are learned and a little imagination applied. There are many types of paint to choose from, never mind a vast kaleidoscope of colours, and you may be surprised at the variety of effects that are possible. What's more, decorating with paint allows you to create unique, one-off decorative effects that you could never achieve with other materials, such as wallpaper. And, when the time comes for a new look, paint is the quickest to prepare and the easiest of materials to cover with something fresh.

There are many types of decorative paint effect to choose from, some being more difficult to create than others, but all are well within the scope of the determined and competent do-it-yourselfer. They can be applied to a variety of surfaces, but some lend themselves particularly to large areas,

ABOVE: Colourwashing is a simple technique for applying an overall pattern to a large surface area; it can be done with a brush or sponge.

LEFT: In roller fidgeting, two different colours are applied by the same roller in one operation to give an interesting two-tone effect.

LEFT: Some items of furniture can look particularly attractive if given a distressed appearance. This is easy to achieve with paint.

RIGHT: With care, it is even possible to use paint to re-create the appearance of wood grain. In this case, an oak finish has been applied.

such as walls, while others are more effective on smaller items, such as pieces of furniture.

Among the simplest of paint effects is the application of one colour over another in such a manner that the first can show through in some areas, usually in a random pattern. That pattern is created by using a variety of applicators – thick-bristled brushes, sponges or balls of cloth – and mixing additives into the paint that make it hold the marks that these leave.

More uniform patterns can be produced by using stencils or stamps to print motifs on the wall, or by masking certain areas before painting them. There are techniques, too, for painting surfaces to look like natural materials, such as wood or marble. These require a degree of skill, but can be achieved with practice and confidence.

Naturally, as with any painted finish, thorough preparation is crucial for any decorative paint effect; surfaces must always be sound and clean, while choosing the right tools is a must

RIGHT: Trompe l'oeil effects are intended to deceive the eye into thinking that a flat surface has depth. Clouds provide a tranquil backdrop.

(some effects require special tools). The type of paint you use is important too, since all have specific properties that make them suitable for particular situations. Knowing what you can and cannot do with a paint is vital.

In the following pages, not only will you learn about using specialist paint equipment, but also a variety of decorative techniques, ranging from simple sponging to complex wood-graining and marbling. Study them carefully and use your imagination to choose the right ones for your situation. If you follow the step-by-step techniques, you will be able to give your home a new look that reflects your personality in a unique manner.

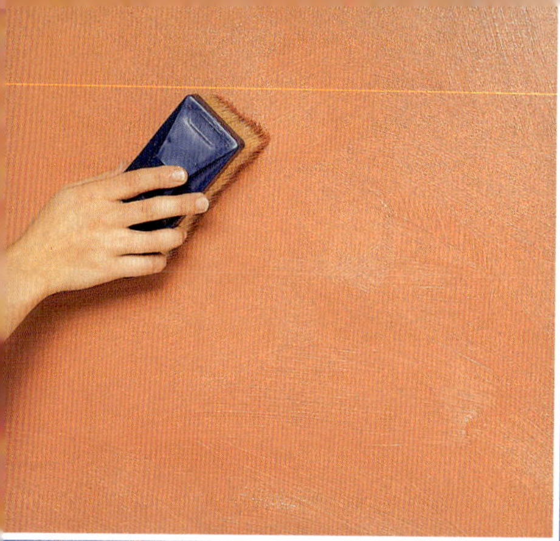

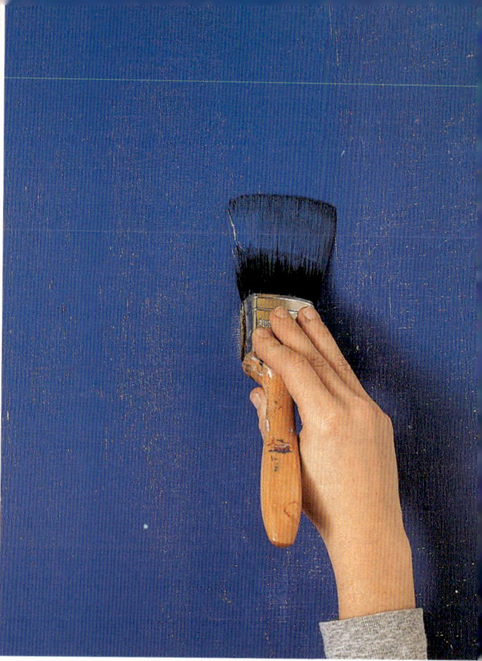

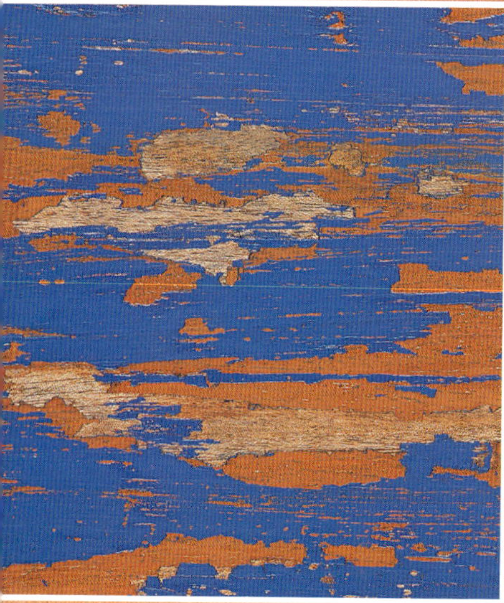

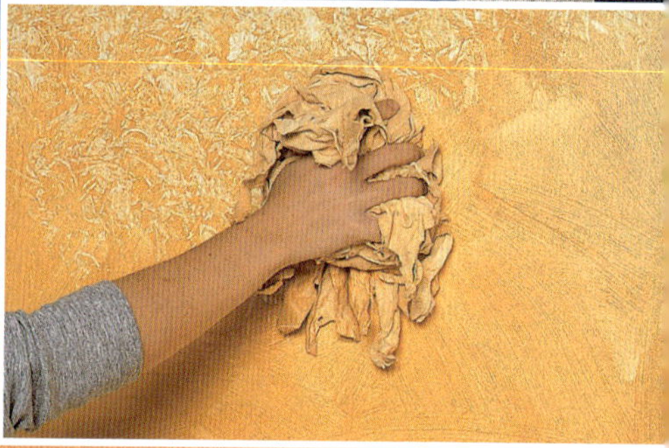

BASIC PAINT FINISHES

The techniques demonstrated in this section show you how to achieve a variety of traditional paint effects, most of which can be used to obtain an all-over impact. In the main, they are suitable for decorating large surface areas, such as walls, quickly and with ease. Several, such as distressing and wood washing, are ideal for putting your own personal stamp on furniture, while others – for example, applying crackle glaze – will enable you to transform small items and home accessories into something decorative and special. Spend some time practising the various techniques on pieces of scrap board until you are happy that you can achieve exactly the effect you want.

COLOURWASHING

You can dilute emulsion (latex) paint with water, wallpaper paste and emulsion glaze to make a mixture known as a wash. The effect varies depending on the consistency of the paint mixture and the method of applying the colour, but it is usually done with a broad brush.

In this instance, a large paintbrush has been used, but you could also employ a synthetic sponge to achieve a different effect.

Materials

emulsion (latex) paint	paint pot
wallpaper paste	large paintbrush

COLOUR EFFECTS

mauve

terracotta

lime green

stone blue

deep mustard

pale terracotta

1 Using a paint pot, mix 50 per cent emulsion (latex) paint with 50 per cent wallpaper paste (premixed to a thin solution). Using at least a 10cm (4in) brush (up to 15cm/6in), dip the tip into the mixture and wipe off the excess on the side of the pot. Add the first dashes on to the wall, well spaced.

2 Without adding more paint, brush out these dashes in random directions, using broad sweeping strokes. Continue working along the wall, adding a little more paint as you go and using quite a dry brush to blend the seams between areas of paint.

COLOURWASHING LAYERS

This is done in the same way as colourwashing one layer, but once the first layer is dry a second colour is applied on top. This layering will soften the overall effect of the brush or sponge marks. Experiment with different colour variations (contrasting and complementary) and layering combinations until you have achieved the effect you want, using a large piece of board as your "canvas".

Materials

emulsion (latex) paint in two colours
wallpaper paste
paint pot
large paintbrush

COLOUR EFFECTS

camel under cream

purple under mauve

jade green under pale green

blue under cream

terracotta under yellow

red under pale yellow

1 Mix the paint in a paint pot, using 50 per cent emulsion (latex) paint and 50 per cent wallpaper paste (premixed to a thin solution). Apply the paint to the wall with random strokes, varying the direction as you go. Continue until you have covered the whole surface.

2 When the first layer has been allowed to dry completely, repeat step 1, using a second colour of paint. Add more paint and soften the joins between areas. The overall colourwash effect will be much softer than when applying only one colour.

SPONGING

Large areas can be covered quickly and easily using the simple technique of sponging, perfect for beginners. Varied effects can be made by using either a synthetic sponge or a natural sponge. A natural sponge will produce smaller, finer marks, while heavier marks can be created with a synthetic sponge. Pinching out small chunks will avoid straight edges. You may find edges and corners are a bit tricky with a large sponge, so use a smaller piece of sponge for these.

Materials

emulsion (latex) paint   natural sponge

COLOUR EFFECTS

cream over terracotta

blue over lilac

mustard over white

grey over white

lime green over white

lilac over mauve

1 Pour the paint into a shallow container and dip the sponge into it; scrape off the excess paint on the edge of the container, ensuring that there are no blobs left on the sponge. Lightly dab the paint on to the surface, varying the angle of application to prevent a uniform appearance.

2 Add more paint to the wall, continuing to work over the surface until you have covered it completely. If necessary, fill in any gaps and make sure that the overall pattern is of similar "weight" – not too heavy in some areas or too light in others.

SPONGING LAYERS

The technique is the same as for sponging one layer, but the overall effect is deepened by the addition of one or more other colours. After the first has been applied and allowed to dry, you can proceed with the second, taking care not to put on too much paint, otherwise you will obliterate the colour below. Experiment with colour combinations, and perhaps try using a natural sponge for one layer and a synthetic sponge for another.

Materials

emulsion (latex) paint in two colours   natural sponge

COLOUR EFFECTS

turquoise and lime green

pale terracotta and yellow

purple and grey

cornflower blue and grey

orange, red and yellow

pale green, jade and grey

1 Apply a single layer by dipping the sponge into the paint, then scrape off the excess and dab on to the wall for an even pattern. Making the pattern even is not quite so important when applying two colours because the second layer will soften the effect. Allow the surface to dry completely.

2 Make sure the sponge is completely clean and dry. Dip it into the second colour paint, scraping off the excess as before and dabbing on to the surface. Do not apply too much paint, however, as you must make sure the first colour isn't totally covered.

DRAGGING

A special dragging brush is often used to achieve this effect, but it can also be done with a household paintbrush or even the end of a sponge. The technique is very simple – the brush is pulled down over wet paint in a clean line to produce a striped effect. These lines must be unbroken, so painting a full-height room may prove extremely difficult. To overcome this, a horizontal band can be added to break up the height of the room.

Materials

pencil	paint pot
rule	large paintbrush
emulsion (latex) paint	dragging brush
wallpaper paste	damp cloth

COLOUR EFFECTS

- terracotta
- brown
- stone blue
- yellow
- biscuit
- powder blue

1 Draw a horizontal baseline across the wall at dado (chair rail) level. Mix emulsion (latex) paint with 50 per cent wallpaper paste (premixed to a thin solution) in a paint pot and brush on in a lengthways band, slightly overlapping the baseline. Work on one small section at a time, about 15–25cm (6–10in) wide.

4 Drag straight over the join between the two areas of paint and carry on dragging. Continue in this way from one end of the wall to the other.

BASIC PAINT FINISHES • 63

2 Dampen the dragging brush with the wash before use, as initially it will take off too much paint if used dry. Then take the brush in one hand and flatten the bristles out with your other hand. Pull the brush down in as straight a motion as possible. This will create deep groove lines in the paint mixture.

3 Brush on another band of paint mixture, adjacent to the last one and overlapping it slightly. Do not cover too large an area at a time, otherwise the paint may become unworkable as it begins to dry.

5 Once this top section has been done, take a damp cloth and, pulling along the pencil line, remove the excess paint.

6 Drag in a horizontal motion across the bottom of the baseline, creating subtle stripes in a different direction.

STIPPLING

A delicate and subtle finish can be achieved by stippling. The technique consists of making fine, pinpoint marks over a wash of emulsion (latex) paint, and it creates a soft, mottled effect. However, it can be quite tiring to do, as the brush has to be dabbed over the surface many times, using firm, even pressure. Two people can speed up the process, one person applying the paint and the other stippling the surface.

Materials

emulsion (latex) paint
paint pot
wallpaper paste
household paintbrush
stippling brush

COLOUR EFFECTS

mid blue

lime green

mustard

green

lilac

orange

1 Mix a wash of 50 per cent emulsion (latex) paint and 50 per cent wallpaper paste, premixed to a thin solution, in a paint pot. Brush on a thin, even coat of the mixture, covering an area of about 0.2 sq m (2 sq ft).

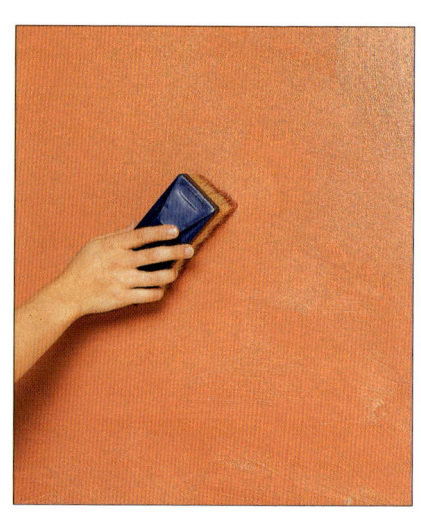

2 Take the stippling brush and dab over the surface with the tips of the bristles until the effect is even all over. Continue stippling the surface until there are no obvious joins (seams) and the whole effect looks soft and even.

BASIC PAINT FINISHES • 65

ROLLER FIDGETING

This is a quick and simple technique and consists of pouring two undiluted emulsion (latex) paint colours into a roller tray, one at each side. You will find that the two paints will sit quite happily together and do not instantly mix. Then, a long-pile masonry roller is skimmed over the surface of these colours until a good thick coat is applied. This is rollered on to the wall at varying angles.

COLOUR EFFECTS

red and camel

mid blue and grey

grey and cream

yellow and cream

pale mauve and dark mauve

mid blue and green

Materials

paint tray	long-pile masonry roller
emulsion (latex) paint in two colours	2.5cm (1in) household paintbrush

1 Pour two colours, one on each side of the pool of the roller tray. Apply a thick coat from here on to the roller so that it will create a two-tone effect. Apply the roller to the wall at varying angles, using short strokes.

2 Continue without applying more paint to the roller until the colours are slightly softened together. Keep the angles as random as possible. Go over the whole effect with the roller to soften it. Add more paint when starting another area.

RAGGING

There are two methods of ragging – ragging on and ragging off – and both techniques are as simple as they sound. With ragging on, you dab the rag into the paint, then dab on to the surface. The technique is similar to sponging, but leaves a sharper effect. The effect will vary depending whether you use a similar colour to the base or a strongly contrasting one. Make sure that the ragging is applied evenly.

Ragging off produces a stronger effect, like crumpled fabric. You brush paint on to the surface, then use a rag to remove some of the paint, leaving a ragged print. The recommended "rag" to use is a chamois, as it creates a definite print, although you can use most types of cloth for a particular effect.

When using either of the techniques, it is important to apply the rag to the wall with firm, but gentle, pressure. When you remove it, lift it cleanly from the surface without any vertical or sideways movement that might smear the paint and spoil the finished effect. The chamois leather should be squeezed out periodically.

Materials

emulsion (latex) paint	roller tray
wallpaper paste	large paintbrush
paint pot	chamois

RAGGING ON

1 Mix 50 per cent emulsion (latex) paint with 50 per cent wallpaper paste in a paint pot. Pour into a roller tray. Scrunch up a chamois, dip it into the paint and dab off the excess, then dab the "rag" on to the wall.

2 Continue re-scrunching the chamois and dipping it into the paint as before, then dabbing it on to the wall in a random manner. Carry on in this way until the surface has been covered evenly and completely.

BASIC PAINT FINISHES • 67

RAGGING OFF

1 Mix 50 per cent emulsion (latex) and 50 per cent wallpaper paste as before. Brush the wash over a large area.

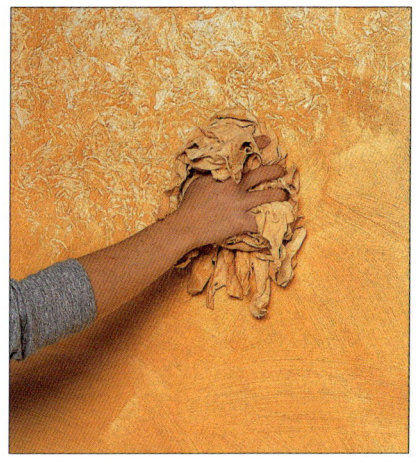

2 Take a chamois, scrunch it up and dab on to the wall to remove small areas of paint. Vary the angle with each dab.

COLOUR EFFECTS

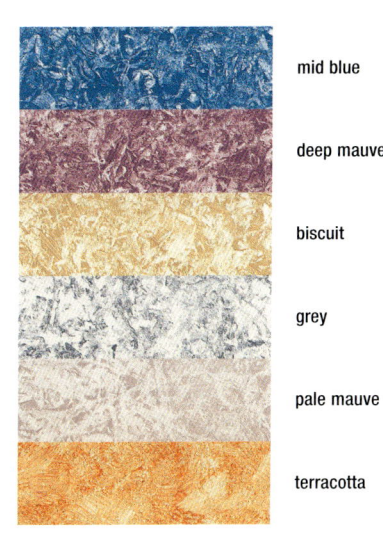

mid blue

deep mauve

biscuit

grey

pale mauve

terracotta

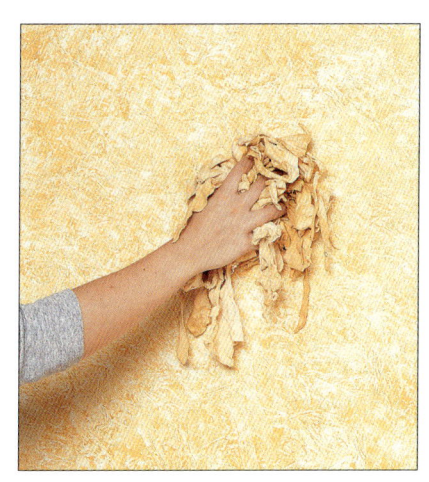

3 Continue working over the surface until the entire effect is even. If you find you are taking off too much paint, apply more immediately with a brush, then dab the chamois over the surface in the same manner as before.

DISTRESSING

This is a way of ageing paint to create chips and scratches that would occur naturally on a painted piece of furniture over a matter of time. The method shown here employs petroleum jelly and candle wax, but you can use just one or the other. This creates a barrier between the surface and the paint, so once the paint is dry it can be lifted away in certain areas where the medium has been applied.

Materials

petroleum jelly	paint scraper
artist's paintbrush	soapy water
emulsion (latex) paint	wax candle
household paintbrush	varnish

1 Using an artist's paintbrush, load it with petroleum jelly and apply long blobs in the direction of the grain of wood over a suitably coloured base coat. Even if the surface is not wooden, rub in a lengthways direction.

4 Wash down thoroughly with soapy water, as the paint that is sitting on top of the petroleum jelly will not actually dry and you will not be able to totally remove the petroleum jelly surface by using the scraper alone.

COLOUR EFFECTS

blue over yellow over wood

mauve over blue over wood

green over blue over wood

orange over yellow over wood

purple over red over wood

blue over burnt orange over wood

BASIC PAINT FINISHES • 69

2 Carefully paint the surface, making sure it is covered completely, but ensuring that the petroleum jelly is not dragged about too much, since it will spread readily under the action of the paintbrush. Allow the paint to dry thoroughly.

3 Once the paint has dried completely, carefully go over the surface with a paint scraper. This will lift off the areas of paint where the petroleum jelly has prevented contact between the top coat and base coat.

5 Once dry, rub over with a wax candle and then paint again, using a contrasting colour. (You could use another layer of petroleum jelly, following the same procedure as before, but the finished effect would not look as subtle.)

6 When the paint is dry, go over the surface once more with a paint scraper to lift off the areas over the candle wax. Wipe down to remove all the flakes of paint, then apply a coat of varnish to protect the surface.

WOOD WASHING

You can stain wood with a colour while allowing the beauty of the grain to show through, using wood washing (wood staining). The wood must be bare, either new or stripped of all traces of varnish, wax or previous paint. Depending on the product used, the surface may or may not need varnishing – read the manufacturer's instructions. Usually a matt (flat) finish looks appropriate for this technique.

Materials

specialist wood wash (wood stain)
paint pot
household paintbrush
cloth

COLOUR EFFECTS

yellow ochre

blue

Indian red

violet

cream

pale green

1 Pour the premixed wash (stain) into a paint pot. Then brush the wash evenly on to the wood, working in the direction of the grain. Keep a "wet" edge and do not overlap areas.

2 While wet, wipe off the excess with a cloth. This will even the effect and expose slightly more of the grain. Then leave to dry before varnishing if required.

BASIC PAINT FINISHES • 71

CRACKLE GLAZE

This technique reproduces the effect of old, crackled paint, but it can only work if you use a special crackle-glaze medium. A base coat is applied first, and when dry, a layer of crackle glaze is added. This is followed by a top coat of paint, which will not be able to grip the base coat while drying and subsequently will shrink and crack to produce a crackled effect. You can achieve some striking colour combinations with this technique.

Materials

emulsion (latex) paint in two colours

household paintbrush
crackle-glaze medium

COLOUR EFFECTS

mustard over red

navy over pale blue

mid blue over yellow

turquoise over lime green

lilac over purple

yellow over red

1 Apply a coat of base colour and leave to dry thoroughly. Then apply a second coat of base colour and allow to dry again. Apply a good solid coat of crackle-glaze medium. The timing for applying the various coats will vary according to the manufacturer, so follow the instructions given on the container.

2 Apply the top coat. Generally, the thicker the top coat of paint, the larger the cracks in the final effect. Make sure the top coat contrasts greatly with the one underneath so that the cracks are obvious. Do not overbrush when applying the top coat, as the effect occurs quite quickly and you could spoil it.

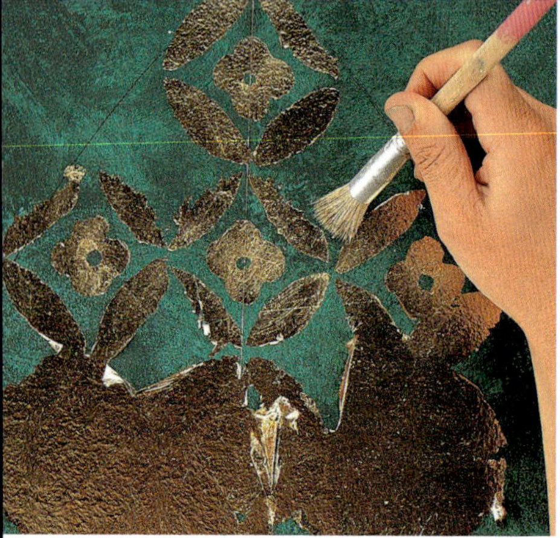
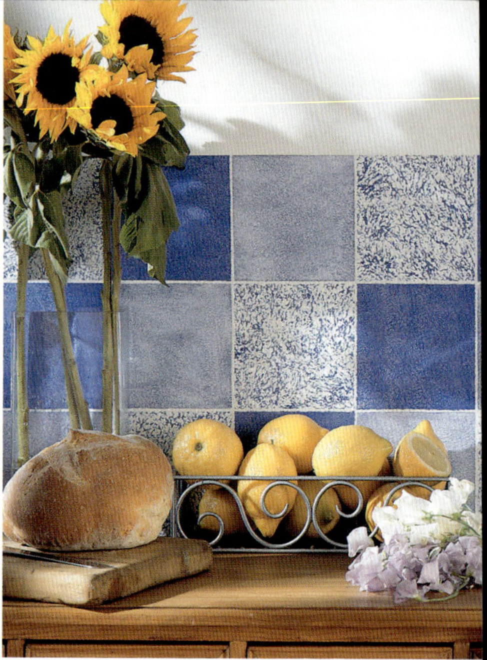
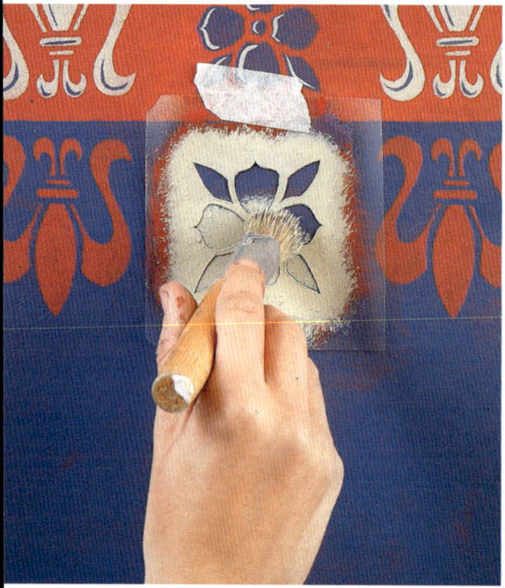
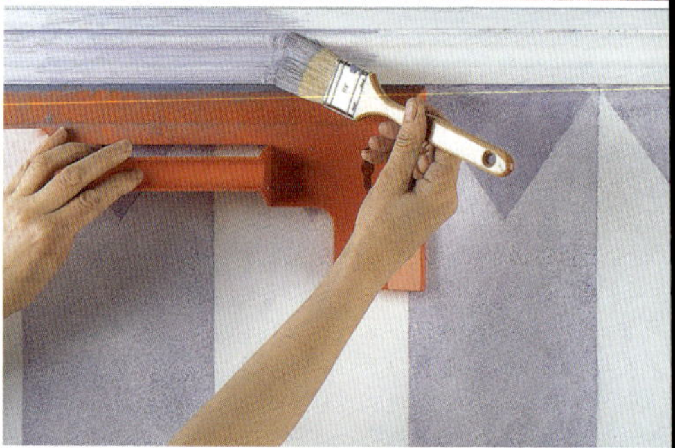
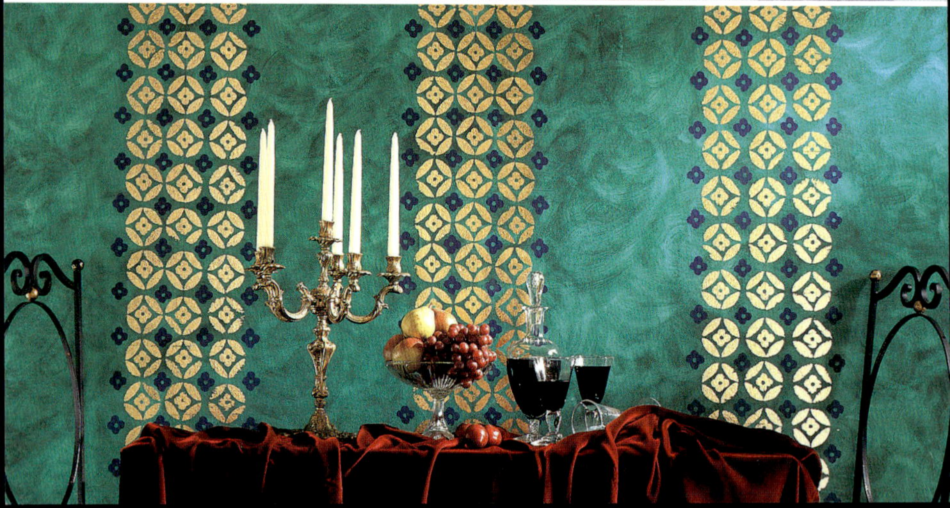

PATTERNED PAINT EFFECTS

There is a long tradition of using both simple and complex patterns as forms of decoration, but in the main these have been provided by wallpaper, which is a quick and convenient way of doing the job. However, using paint to make patterns allows you to create something quite unique. There are many ways of applying pattern as a decoration, whether freehand or using a template. With stencilling and stamping, you can add an individual touch to your schemes by choosing designs from a wealth that are available commercially or by drawing, cutting, and using your own stencils and stamps. Classic lines and stripes never seem to go out of fashion, and grid patterns are a fun way of combining colours.

STENCILLING

The decorative possibilities of stencilling are endless, so it is not surprising that it is one of the most popular of paint effects. It is an ideal way to create an interesting border or all-over pattern using motifs that relate to the theme of your room. Stencilling also enables you to co-ordinate furnishings and accessories by picking out details in similar or contrasting colours. Or you can use the patterns and colours of your stencilling as a starting point for the style and colours of your home. The fleur-de-lis and rose design shown here is typical of what can be achieved.

Materials

household sponge	masking tape
emulsion (latex) paint in three colours	spray adhesive
	tracing paper
rule	stencil card or acetate
spirit (carpenter's) level	two motif stencils
	stencil brush and fine lining brush
pencil	

1 Using a large sponge, rub the first emulsion (latex) colour on the wall. Leave to dry. Repeat using a second colour to cover the base. Using a rule and spirit (carpenter's) level, draw a line at dado (chair rail) height and place masking tape above it. Sponge your third colour below this.

4 When you have completed a line of motifs above the dividing line, make sure that the paint on the faces of the stencils is completely dry (or cut new ones), then flip the stencils over and position them as mirror images below the original motifs. Stencil the roses in the base colour and the fleur-de-lis in the second colour.

2 If necessary, cut stencils from stencil card or acetate. Secure the rose stencil above the dividing line and stencil in your third colour with a stencil brush. When dry, position the fleur-de-lis stencil next to the first and paint in the colour of the base coat. Alternate stencils around the room.

3 Make some highlighting stencils, using the originals as templates. Place them over the painted motifs and, with a stencil brush, add highlights in the base colour to the first stencilled design, and highlights in the third colour to the second design.

5 Allow the paint to dry, then go back and add highlights to the motifs as before, using base colour on the fleur-de-lis and the third colour on the roses. Again, make sure that there is no wet paint on the faces of the flipped stencils, since this could be transferred to the wall and spoil the overall effect.

6 Using a fine lining brush and the base colour paint, paint a narrow line where the two different colours on the wall meet. If you do not have the confidence to do this freehand, position two lines of masking tape on the wall, leaving a small gap between them. When the line of paint is dry, carefully remove the masking tape.

STAMPING

Like stencilling, stamping allows you to create your own decorative motifs. It is easy and inexpensive to cut out shapes in relief from high-density sponge and to use them to apply paint. However, you can also achieve quite sophisticated effects with this simple technique, and the steps here show how to add a special touch to a room by stamping panels with gold leaf. This is achieved by stamping the wall with gold size first, then rubbing on gold leaf, which will adhere to the tacky surface.

Materials

card (card stock)	household sponge
rule	plumbline
pencil	tape measure
scissors	small paint roller
high-density sponge	gold size
craft knife	Dutch Metal
emulsion (latex) paint	(simulated gold leaf)
in jade green and	soft brush
purple	

1 Fold a 30cm (12in) square piece of card in half, cut an arc from corner to corner and unfold to create a symmetrical arch template.

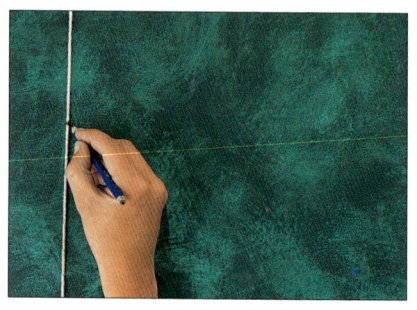

4 Using a plumbline as a guide, and beginning 23cm (9in) from a corner, mark a vertical line up the wall to a height of 1.8m (6ft). Use the plumbline to draw vertical lines every 60cm (2ft).

7 When the size is tacky, apply Dutch Metal (simulated gold leaf) by rubbing over the backing paper with a soft brush. Peel the backing away.

PATTERNED PAINT EFFECTS • 77

2 Transfer a design on to a piece of high-density sponge. Using a craft knife, cut away excess sponge from around the shape.

3 Apply jade green emulsion (latex) paint to the wall using a sponge and working in a circular motion. Allow the paint to dry.

5 Measure 15cm (6in) to each side of each line and draw two more vertical lines to mark the edges of the panels. Place the template at the top of each panel and draw in the curves.

6 Load the stamp with gold size and apply it to the areas within the outlined panels, beginning at the centre top and working down in horizontal lines. Reload the stamp as necessary.

8 Once the panel has been gilded completely, go over it with a soft brush to remove any excess gold leaf.

9 Using the centre of the stamp, fill in the spaces between the gold motifs with purple emulsion paint.

STRIPES

A classic design for decorating schemes, stripes are extremely versatile, as you can vary their width for any number of effects. If you are aiming for a symmetrical, formal look, it is important to measure out the available space accurately first so that you can be sure the stripes will fit. It is helpful to draw out the design in a small scale on a piece of paper to work out the correct balance.

Materials

emulsion (latex) paint in two colours	pencil
paint roller	masking tape
paint tray	acrylic scumble
paintbrushes	nylon stocking
	cardboard

1 Paint the walls. Mark the centre of the most important wall with a pencil. Make marks 7.5cm (3in) on each side of this, then every 15cm (6in). Continue around the room until the marks meet at the least noticeable corner.

4 Dilute some of the second colour with about 25 per cent water and 25 per cent acrylic scumble. Complete each stripe in two or three stages, blending the joins to achieve an even result.

7 Working on one stripe at a time, place masking tape between the top corners and the mark. Brush on the second colour, then dab the stocking over the wet paint. Leave to dry.

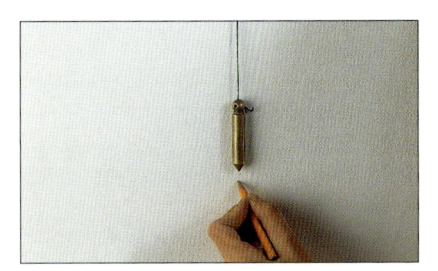

2 Hang a short length of plumbline from one of the marks, and mark with a dot where it rests. Then, hang the plumbline from this dot and mark where it rests. Continue down the wall. Repeat for each mark below the picture rail.

3 Starting in the centre of the wall, place strips of masking tape on alternate sides of the marked rows of dots to give 15cm (6in) wide stripes. Repeat until you have taped all the walls.

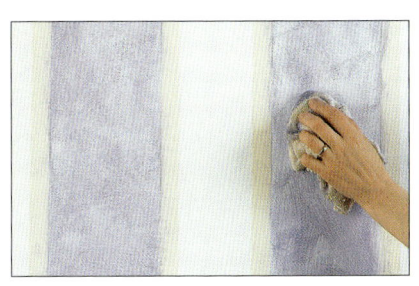

5 Dab the wet paint lightly with the stocking to smooth out the brush marks. Complete all the stripes, peel off the masking tape and leave the paint to dry.

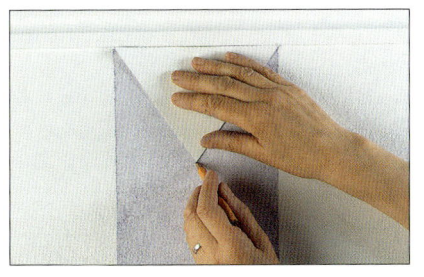

6 From a piece of cardboard, cut a triangle with a 15cm (6in) base and measuring 10cm (4in) from base to tip. Use this to mark the centre of each stripe.

8 Dilute some of the second colour paint with 20 parts water to one part paint. Brush this over the wall, working in all directions to give a hint of colour to the first colour stripes.

9 Add a little paint to the remaining diluted mixture to strengthen the colour. Using a paint guard or strip of card to protect the painted wall, brush the paint on to the picture rail.

PRINTED TILES

This is an inexpensive and clever way to create a tiled effect with simple painted squares. Fine tape separates the tiles and is removed when the effect is finished to give the illusion of grouting. Leave some of the squares plain, but add extra effects to others by sponging them or dabbing them with a nylon stocking. Experiment with different colours to create your own design, or leave some of the squares white as a contrast. You could also experiment with mosaic patterns by measuring and masking much smaller squares with fine lining tape before applying the second colour. You need not restrict yourself to creating squares either; you could try oblongs, triangles or diamonds, or perhaps even combinations of these shapes.

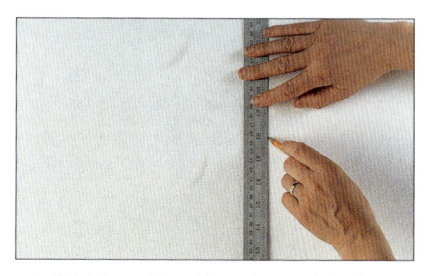

1 Paint the wall in white, using a paint roller to achieve an even texture. Decide on the width of your "tiled" panel. Mark the wall 45cm (18in) above your work surface and in the centre of the width measurement.

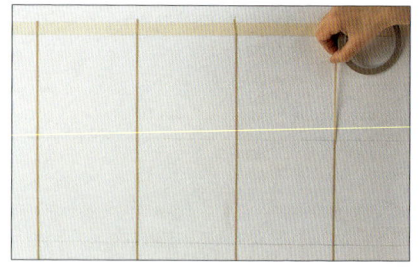

4 Place fine masking tape over the lines in both directions. Smooth the tape into place with your fingers, pressing it down well to ensure that paint does not seep underneath it.

Materials

emulsion (latex) paint in white and a second colour	standard, fine and low-tack masking tape
paint roller	sponge
paint tray	kitchen paper (paper towels)
paintbrush	
rule	nylon stocking
pencil	eraser
spirit (carpenter's) level	

PATTERNED PAINT EFFECTS • 81

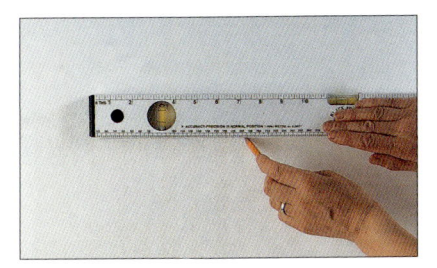

2 Draw a horizontal line across the wall at this height, using a spirit (carpenter's) level to make sure that it is straight and level. Apply a strip of standard masking tape to the wall above the line, making sure that it butts up to it accurately.

3 Mark dots along the tape at 15cm (6in) intervals on each side of the centre mark. Use the spirit level to draw vertical lines down the wall. Mark along the vertical lines at 15cm (6in) intervals and connect them with horizontal lines.

5 Place low-tack masking tape around one square. Pour the second colour into the paint tray and add 25 per cent water. Roll an even coat over the square. Repeat for all plain squares.

6 Mask off a square to be sponged. Dampen the sponge, dip it into the second colour and dab the excess on to kitchen paper (paper towels). Sponge the square. Repeat for other squares.

7 Mask off a square to be dabbed with the nylon stocking. Apply the paint with a brush, then use the stocking to blend it. Repeat for all the squares needing this effect.

8 Allow the paint to dry partially, then remove the tape while it is still soft. When the paint is completely dry, clean off all the pencil marks with an eraser.

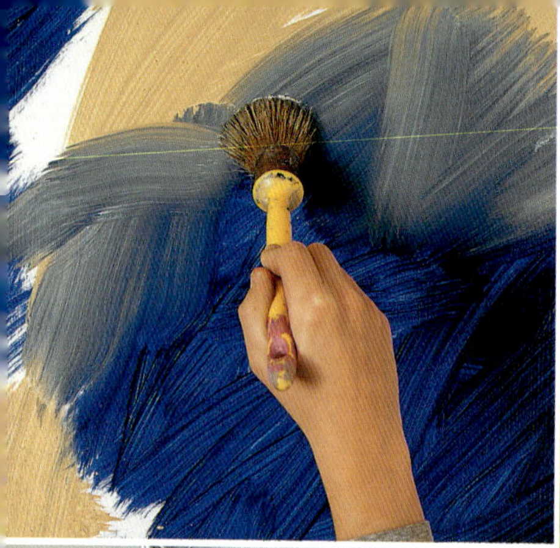
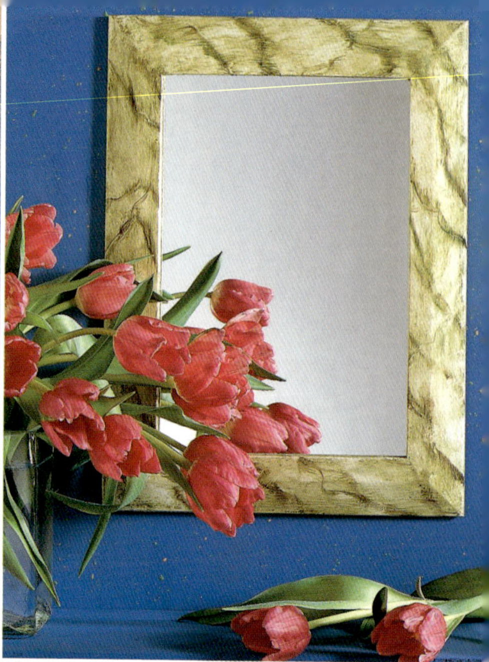
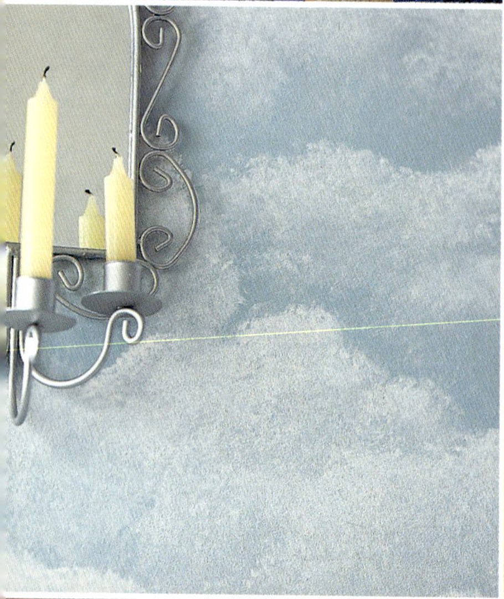
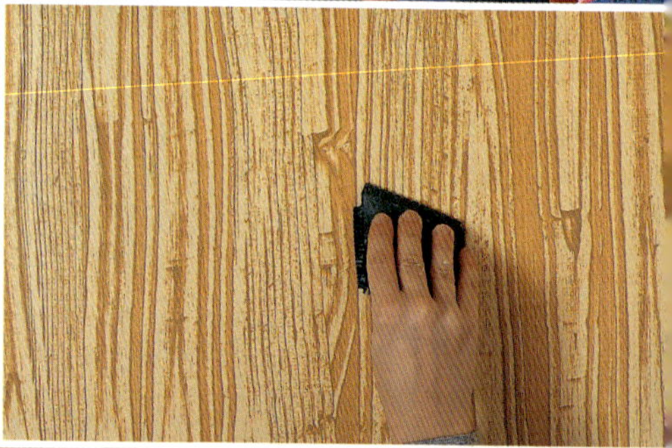
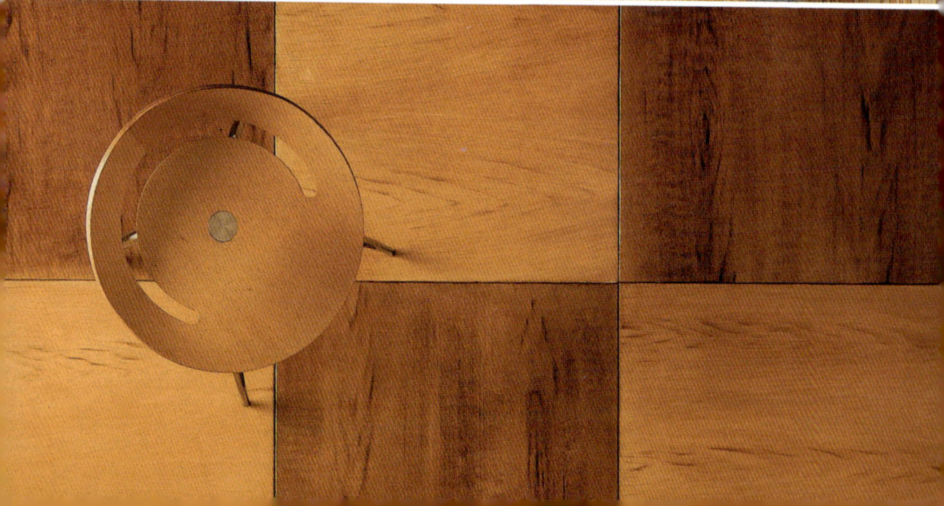

FAUX PAINT FINISHES

Techniques that reproduce the look of a particular surface or material are often very challenging, but they can be great fun too, and when done correctly they can produce very realistic and satisfying results. The following pages will show you how to achieve a number of wood and stone finishes that will allow you to create imaginative decorative effects throughout your home. Effects include pine, oak, mahogany, beech and marbling. Artist's oil colours are used, since their lengthy drying periods allow more time to work on the effect, and their colours are intense and translucent.

PINE

Woodgraining and wood effects can seem difficult and daunting to the beginner, but the right choice of colours and suitable base coats can be half the battle. The only specialist tools used are a heart grainer (graining roller) and comb, which are necessary as the patterns they create cannot be imitated in any other way. Both are relatively simple to use with a little practice and create convincing effects.

Look at pieces of real wood so that you can learn to replicate the grain accurately. Pine is readily available and you can use a pine effect surface in many locations throughout your home.

Materials

satinwood paint in pale yellow	white spirit (paint thinner)
household paintbrush	heart grainer (graining roller)
paint pot	comb
artist's oil colour paint in yellow ochre and burnt umber	large paintbrush varnish

1 Prepare the surface to be woodgrained in the normal manner. Brush on two coats of pale yellow satinwood paint, allowing each coat to dry thoroughly before proceeding.

4 Following the direction of the dragging, pull the heart grainer (graining roller) down gently, rocking it as you work, to create the effect. Butt one line straight over the other.

FAUX PAINT FINISHES • 85

2 Mix yellow ochre artist's oil colour paint with a tiny amount of burnt umber to dirty the colour slightly. Then mix with white spirit (paint thinner) to create a thick cream, and brush over the surface.

3 Drag the brush in a lengthways direction over the wet paint. This will allow streaks of the base colour to show through, which is the basis for the woodgrain effect.

5 Use the comb to make graduated cone shapes in random positions across the surface between the heart graining, slightly overlapping it in some areas.

6 Soften the surface while wet with a large dry brush, applying only light pressure and brushing in the direction of the effect. Varnish the finish when dry.

OAK

Perhaps nothing speaks more of a traditional style than solid oak wood furniture or panelling. Here is a way of disguising inexpensive white wood or modern pine and giving it the look of dark oak. If you are painting bare wood, remember to give it a coat of primer before starting the paint effect. This technique requires a heart grainer (graining roller) and a comb to re-create the details of the woodgrain, both of which can be bought from most good craft shops and specialist decorating shops.

Materials

gloss or satin paint in beige	paint pot
paintbrush	graduated comb
artist's oil colour paint in burnt umber	fine graduated comb
	heart grainer (graining roller)
white spirit (paint thinner)	cloth
	large paintbrush
	varnish

1 Prepare the surface to be woodgrained in the normal manner. Apply two coats of beige for the base coat in either gloss or satin finish, allowing each to dry thoroughly.

4 Use a heart grainer (graining roller) to start creating the detailed figuring of the grain. Do this by pulling the tool down gently over the surface with a slight rocking motion, to create the hearts with random spacings. Butt one line straight over the other as you go.

2 Mix burnt umber artists' oil colour paint with white spirit (paint thinner) in a small paint pot until it is the consistency of thick cream. Brush on and drag in a lengthways direction.

3 Using a graduated comb, pull down on the surface. Do not work in totally straight lines, but make them curve slightly, butting one up against the other.

5 When you are satisfied with the effect that the heart graining produces, take the fine graduated comb and go over all the previous combing. As the work progresses, you will begin to see the finish take on the appearance of genuine oak.

6 Wrap a piece of clean, lint-free cloth around the comb and dab it on to the surface in a random manner to create the angled grain, pressing it into the wet paint. Then soften the overall effect by going over the entire surface with a large dry brush. Varnish when dry.

MAHOGANY

This beautiful hardwood has a rich, warm colour that seems to suit most styles of home, whether traditional or modern. It was extremely popular during the Victorian era when it was complemented by deep-toned furnishings and fabrics. These days it is not ecologically desirable to use mahogany, and it is also hard to come by and expensive, so all the more reason to paint some for yourself. Practise on sample pieces first, then progress to larger furniture when you have more confidence in the technique.

Materials

satin or gloss paint in dusky pink	white spirit (paint thinner)
artist's oil colour paint in burnt sienna, crimson and burnt umber	paint pots
	paintbrushes in different sizes
	varnish

1 Apply two coats of dusky pink and leave to dry. Tint burnt sienna oil paint with crimson, adding white spirit (paint thinner) to make a thick creamy consistency. Brush on in long strips. Thin burnt umber to a thick cream. Fill gaps with long strips.

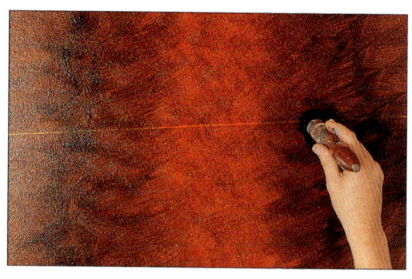

2 Stipple the surface gently with a dry paintbrush to soften the overall effect.

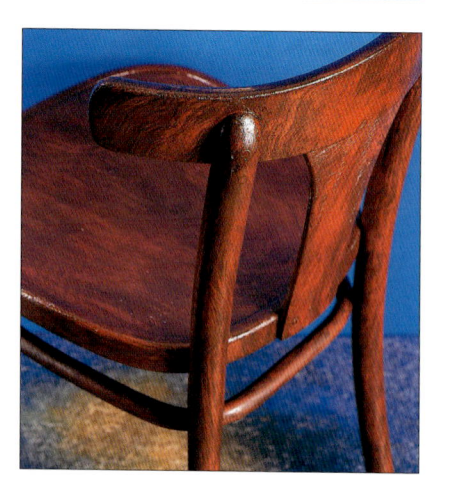

3 Starting at the bottom, with a 10cm (4in) paintbrush held almost parallel to the surface, drag through the wet paint in elongated arcs. Use the burnt umber area as the middle section. Before completely dry, soften in one direction using a large dry brush. Varnish when dry.

BEECH

In recent years, beech has become popular for both furniture and home accessories such as trays, and mirror and picture frames. It is a light-coloured, straight-grained wood, and its close patterning gives it a look of solidity. Its soft, warm colour and generally matt (flat) finish adds a quiet, but modern, tone to a room as well as helping to lighten it up. Like oak, beech is sometimes given a limed effect, so if this is what you require allow more of the base coat to show through when painting.

Materials

satinwood paint in white
household paintbrush
paint pot
artist's oil colour paint in Naples yellow and white
white spirit (paint thinner)
heart grainer (graining roller)
fine graduated comb
narrow comb
varnish

1 Apply two coats of white satinwood and leave to dry. Mix the yellow and white oils with white spirit (paint thinner) until a thick cream; brush on the surface. Drag in a lengthways direction.

2 Use a heart grainer (graining roller) to start graining, pulling it down gently and rocking it slightly, working in spaced lines. Do not butt them together. Use a graduated comb in the same direction to fill in between the heart graining.

3 Again, working in the same direction, soften the effect with a large dry brush. Now take a narrow comb and go over the entire surface in the same direction to add detail. Varnish when dry.

MARBLING

There are many specialist techniques for achieving a marble effect, but here is a very simple method. Types of marble vary greatly in colour and pattern, and it may be a good idea to use a piece of real marble as a reference source. Aim for a general effect of marbled patterning that is subtle in colour, with most of the veining softened to create depth.

Try colour variations of crimson and ultramarine; raw sienna and black; Indian red, yellow ochre and black; raw sienna, yellow ochre and Prussian blue; or Prussian blue and ultramarine.

Materials

satinwood paint in white	small paint pots
household paintbrush	white spirit (paint thinner)
artist's oil colour paint in ultramarine and yellow ochre	stippling brush
	swordliner brush
	gloss varnish

1 Paint a base coat of white satinwood paint on to the surface and leave to dry. Squeeze a long blob of ultramarine artist's oil colour paint into a paint pot and add some white spirit (paint thinner) to form a thick cream. Brush on patches of this.

4 Dip a swordliner brush into white spirit and drag it through the wet surface, applying no pressure, but just letting the brush stroke the surface of the paint. Slightly angle the bristles while you pull the brush down.

FAUX PAINT FINISHES • 91

2 Squeeze some yellow ochre artist's oil colour paint into a second paint kettle and dilute it with white spirit until it is the consistency of thick cream. Fill in the patches where the blue has not been painted with this mixture.

3 While the oil colours are still wet, take a stippling brush and work over the entire surface, blending them gently together. The idea is to make one colour fade gradually into the next without any hard lines.

5 Dip the brush back into the white spirit for each line. The white spirit will finally separate the oil glaze surface. Make sure there are not too many lines and only add the odd fork – the less complicated the pattern, the better the effect will be.

6 Dip the swordliner into the dark blue glaze remaining from step 1 and draw down the side of each painted line with a very fine line. When you are happy with the effect, allow the paint to dry completely, then coat with gloss varnish.

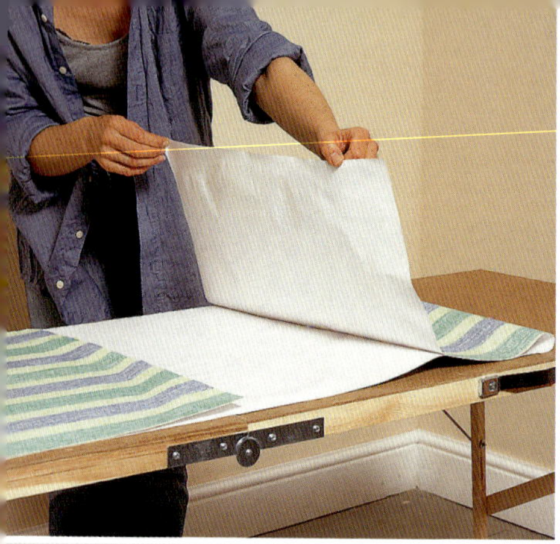
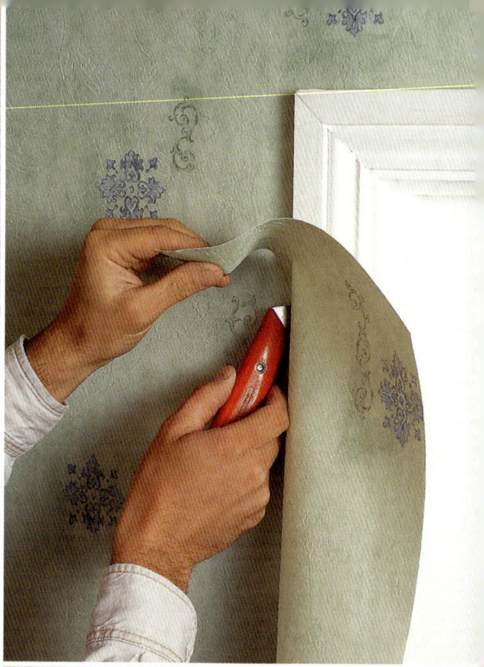
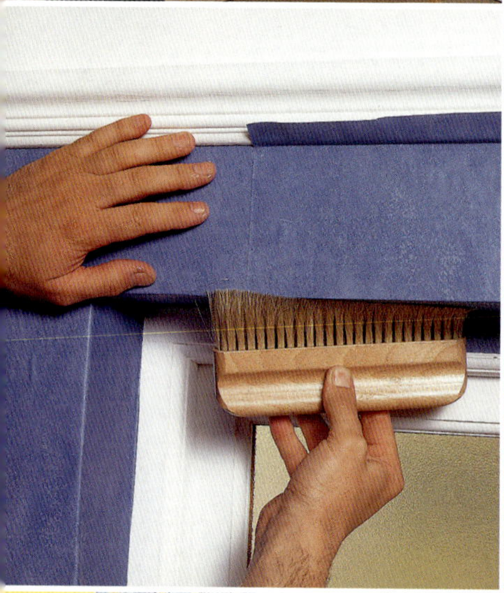
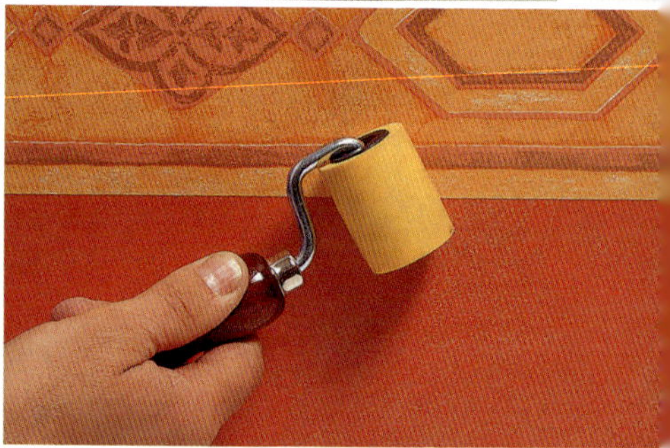

PAPERING WALLS & CEILINGS

- Wallcovering materials
- Wallcovering preparation
- Wallcovering techniques

INTRODUCTION

Fifty years ago, practically all of the rooms of almost every home would have had papered walls, and many would have had papered ceilings too. When decorating, few people would have even considered not hanging wallpaper; it was how things were done. In more recent times, however, the popularity of wallcoverings has diminished, and today many look upon them as a more luxurious finish to be reserved for the more important rooms in the home. That said, modern wallcoverings – not all of which are paper based – are far more versatile than their forerunners, offering not only a wide range of colours and patterns, but also in some cases high wear and moisture resistance, making them particularly suitable for kitchens, bathrooms and children's rooms, where traditional wallpapers would not be an ideal choice.

Many of today's do-it-yourselfers may be put off by the thought of hanging a wallcovering. But hanging wallcoverings is actually quite a straightforward task that, in the main, requires only care to achieve very professional-looking results.

While it is true that wallcoverings are not as popular as they once were, there is no doubt that a well-chosen example

LEFT: Hanging wallcoverings requires the use of a few specialized tools, which are readily available. You will also need an inexpensive folding pasting table and at least one set of sturdy stepladders.

ABOVE: When joining border papers that have intricate patterns, professional results can be achieved by cutting around a prominent shape in the pattern and butting the ends together.

While practically all wallcoverings are printed by machine, hand-printed examples are still available, often offering traditional patterns. Not surprisingly, they are expensive, but for the restoration of a period property they offer the perfect decorative solution.

You don't need many special tools for hanging wallcoverings, unlike many other do-it-yourself jobs: pasting and hanging brushes, some paperhanger's scissors and a pasting table, all of which are inexpensive. With this equipment, a roll of wallpaper and this chapter, you'll soon be giving your rooms a new look.

can give a far more impressive finish to a room than paint alone. Whether you want a subdued delicate pattern, a wildly flamboyant design, muted colours or bold tones, there will be a wallcovering to meet your needs. Moreover, you need not restrict yourself to flat coverings either, since there is a good choice of textured materials to be had. As with colours and patterns, textures may be light or heavy, and several can be over-painted, offering even greater decorative possibilities.

There are special finishes, too, that may be based on foils, fabrics and natural materials such as grasses. While these are more difficult to hang than conventional wallcoverings, they may be just what is required to add a final feature to a decorative scheme.

AVOIDING PASTE DRIPS

A length of string tied tightly across the top of a wallpaper paste bucket makes a handy brush rest. Use the string rather than the side of the bucket for removing excess adhesive from the pasting brush.

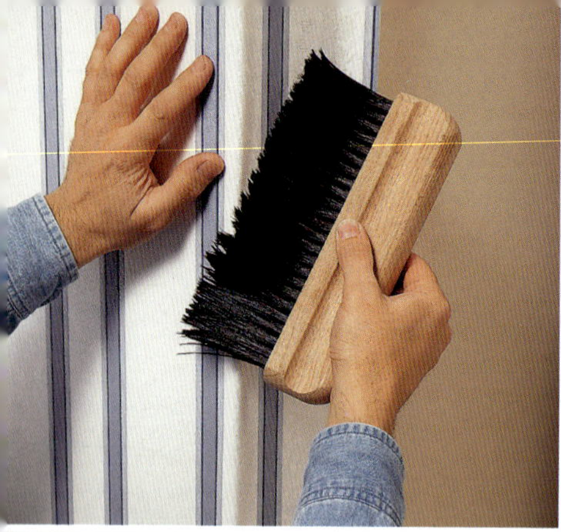

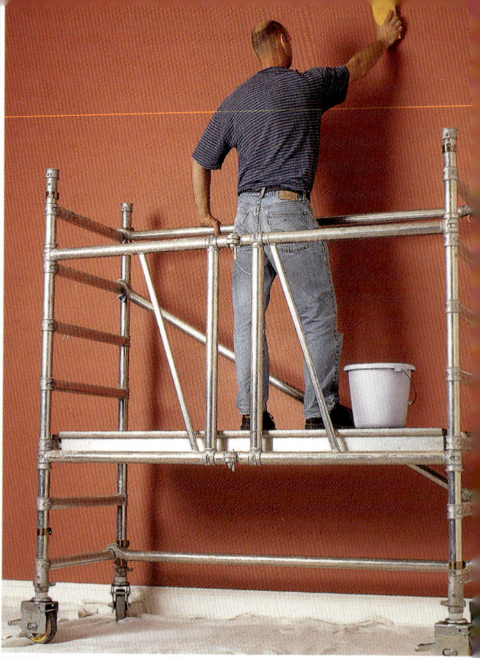

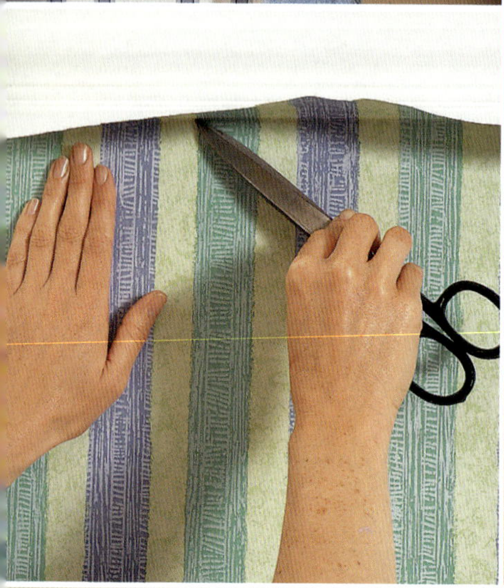

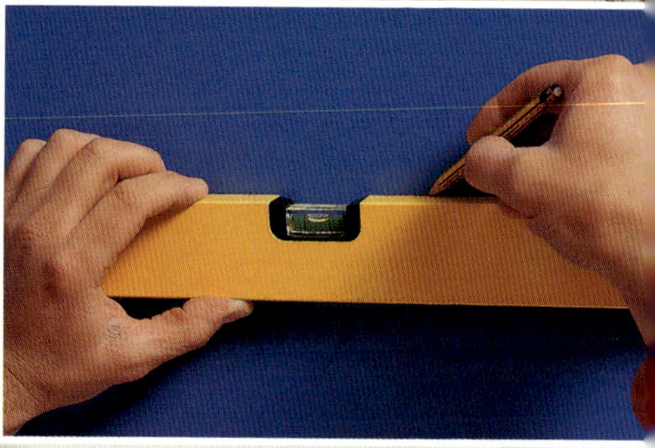

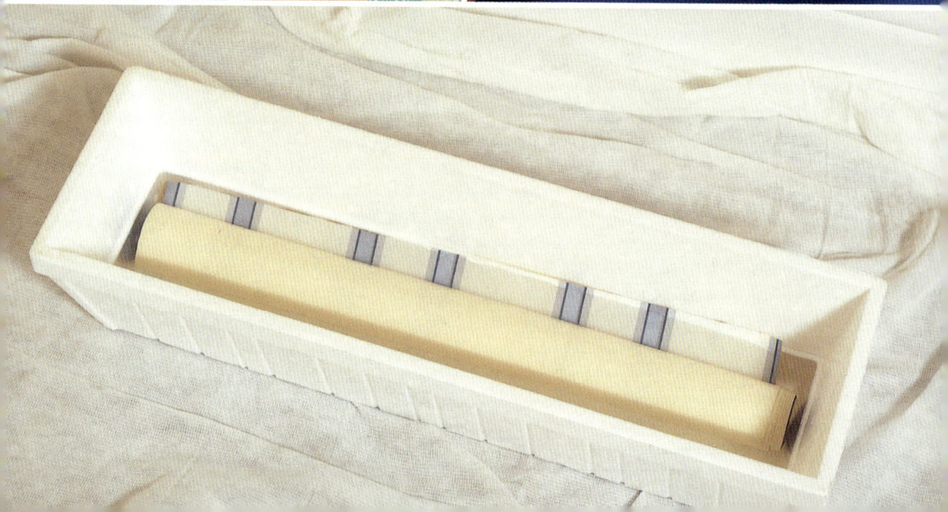

WALLCOVERING MATERIALS

These days, there are wallcoverings for every room in your home, offering a wide choice of colourways, patterns and textures. Some offer good wear resistance, and many are washable. So when considering this type of decorative finish, the first decision to make is what type of wallcovering suits your needs; then you can select from the colours and patterns on offer. Estimating quantities is important, as you don't want to end up with too many rolls; equally, too few could cause problems, as subsequent rolls you buy may come from later batches and display colour differences. Fortunately, estimating is a simple task. You will need some special tools and equipment, but these are widely available.

CHOOSING WALLCOVERINGS

Wallcoverings offer a wide range of patterns and colourways, from very traditional to the most modern designs. Choose with care, particularly if you are new to hanging wallpaper, as some will be much easier to hang than others. Check the manufacturer's guidelines before buying to determine the suitability of the paper.

BUYING WALLCOVERINGS

When shopping for wallcoverings, ask for a large sample of any design that catches your eye so you can examine it in the room that is to be decorated. Look at the samples in both natural and artificial light, near a window and in a dark corner, as some colours and patterns alter dramatically when viewed in different lights.

Test a sample for durability by moistening it under a tap. If it tears easily or the colours run when rubbed lightly, the paper could be difficult to hang and maintain. Avoid thin papers, particularly if you are an inexperienced decorator, as they are likely to tear when moistened by the paste and may be difficult to hang.

Never skimp on the number of rolls you buy, and check that the batch number on all rolls is the same, as there may be a slight colour variation between batches that may not be noticeable on the roll, but could become obvious after hanging. However, the batch system is not infallible, so check rolls again for a good colour match before cutting and hanging. It is also worth buying at least one extra roll. Many retailers offer a sale-or-return service.

CHOOSING A PATTERN

Take a critical look at the room you plan to decorate and make a note of any aspects that could make hanging a wallcovering difficult. Uneven walls and

ABOVE: A freematch wallpaper or one with a continuous pattern, such as stripes, will not need an allowance for pattern matching.

ABOVE: A straight-match pattern has the same part of the pattern running down each side of the paper, making the cutting of drops simple.

ABOVE: An offset pattern has motifs staggered between drops, which must be taken into account when cutting and measuring the paper.

awkward corners, for example, can make pattern matching particularly problematic, while some types of wallcovering will conceal a poor surface better than others.

Regular patterns, such as vertical stripes, checks and repetitive geometric designs, will emphasize walls that are out of true, whereas random florals and paint-effect papers will not encourage the eye to rest on any one point and, therefore, will help to disguise awkward angles. Trimming can also ruin the appearance of a large pattern, so in a room that has a sloping or uneven ceiling, or several windows, cabinets and doors, a design with a small pattern may be a better choice. If a poor surface is the problem, avoid thin or shiny wallcoverings, which will highlight every blemish.

If you are not an experienced decorator, avoid complicated patterns, as any mismatching will be obvious; instead consider using one of the many easy-to-hang, freematch designs that are readily available.

BELOW: Wallcoverings are available in many different designs and finishes, so choose with care.

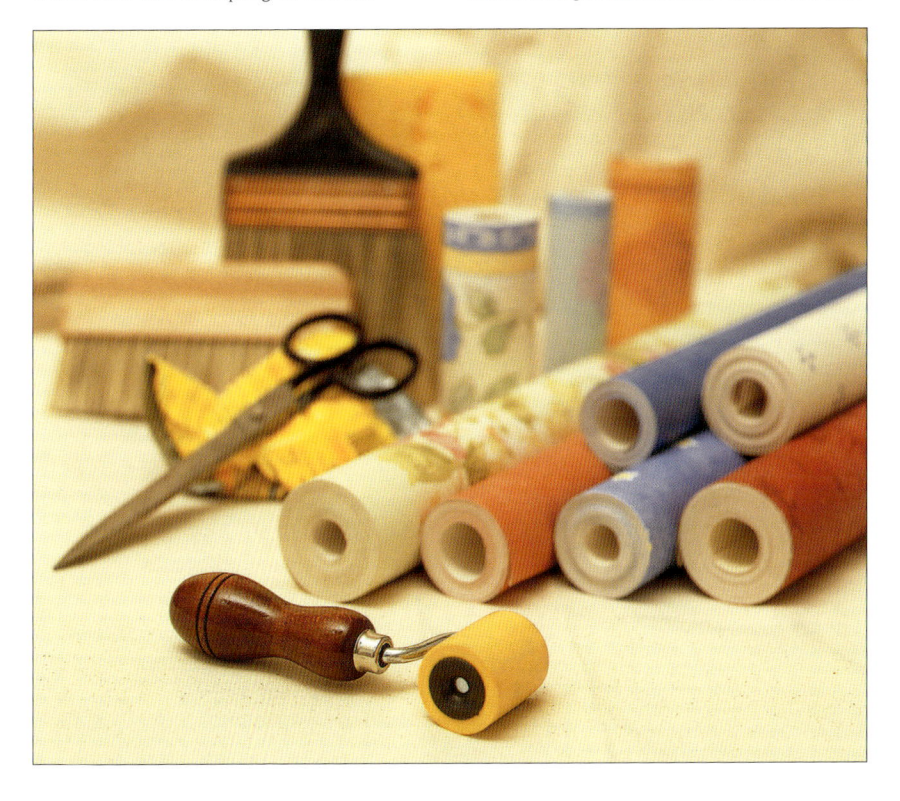

ESTIMATING QUANTITIES

Standard wallcoverings are sold in rolls that measure approximately 10m long by 530mm wide (33ft x 21in). Use the tables to calculate the number of rolls that you require for walls and ceilings, remembering to add 10 per cent for waste, especially if the design has a large pattern repeat. Lining paper is usually 560mm (22in) wide and is available in standard 10m (33ft) and larger roll sizes.

You can calculate the number of rolls required from the tables, but there is no need to add any extra for a pattern repeat. For walls, measure around the room and include all the windows and doors in your calculation, except for very large picture windows and patio doors. It is easier to measure the perimeter of the floor to calculate the size of a ceiling.

Depending on where they were manufactured, you may find papers in non-standard sizes, so do check. This could well be the case with handmade wallcoverings. These often have the added complication of an unprinted border down each edge, which must be removed before hanging, although some suppliers may be able to do this for you. In the USA, wallcoverings vary in width and length, but are usually available in rolls sized to cover specific areas.

In fact, it is not that difficult to calculate your requirements for a non-standard wallcovering. When papering walls, measure the height of the wall first and divide the length of a single roll by that figure. This will give you the number of drops you can cut from a single roll. Multiply that number by the width of the roll to determine the width of wall that will be covered by a roll. Then divide the total width of all the walls to be covered by that figure. This will give you the total number of rolls needed. As before, include windows and doors and add 10 per cent for waste.

If in any doubt, approach your supplier; many will be happy to make the calculation for you.

CALCULATING THE NUMBER OF ROLLS NEEDED FOR A CEILING

MEASUREMENT AROUND ROOM		NUMBER OF ROLLS
10m	(33ft)	2
11m	(36ft)	2
12m	(39ft)	2
13m	(43ft)	3
14m	(46ft)	3
15m	(49ft)	4
16m	(52ft)	4
17m	(56ft)	4
18m	(59ft)	5
19m	(62ft)	5
20m	(66ft)	5
21m	(69ft)	6
22m	(72ft)	7
23m	(75ft)	7
24m	(79ft)	8
25m	(82ft)	8

LEFT: Measuring up for wallcovering. Measure the height of the walls and their total width. Then refer to the tables to determine the number of standard-size rolls required. There is no need to deduct the area of doors and windows, unless they are very large. If you want to paper the ceiling, it will be easier to measure the floor to calculate the area.

CALCULATING THE NUMBER OF ROLLS NEEDED FOR WALLS

WIDTH OF WALLS	HEIGHT OF ROOM FROM SKIRTING (BASEBOARD)							
	2–2.25m (6ft 7in–7ft 5in)	2.25–2.5m (7ft 5in–8ft 2in)	2.5–2.75m (8ft 2in–9ft)	2.75–3m (9ft–9ft 10in)	3–3.25m (9ft 10in–10ft 8in)	3.25–3.5m (10ft 8in–11ft 6in)	3.5–3.75m (11ft 6in–12ft 4in)	3.75–4m (12ft 4in–13ft 1in)
	NUMBER OF ROLLS							
10m (33ft)	5	5	6	6	7	7	8	8
11m (36ft)	5	6	7	7	8	8	9	9
12m (39ft)	6	6	7	8	8	9	9	10
13m (43ft)	6	7	8	8	9	10	10	10
14m (46ft)	7	7	8	9	10	10	11	11
15m (49ft)	7	8	9	9	10	11	12	12
16m (52ft)	8	8	9	10	11	11	12	13
17m (56ft)	8	9	10	10	11	12	13	14
18m (59ft)	9	9	10	11	12	13	14	15
19m (62ft)	9	10	11	12	13	14	15	16
20m (66ft)	9	10	11	12	13	14	15	16
21m (69ft)	10	11	12	13	14	15	16	17
22m (72ft)	10	11	13	14	15	16	17	18
23m (75ft)	11	12	13	14	15	17	18	19
24m (79ft)	11	12	14	15	16	17	18	20
25m (82ft)	12	13	14	15	17	18	19	20

BASIC WALLCOVERINGS

When choosing a wallcovering, it is important to take into consideration how practical it will be in the room you wish to decorate. Each room in your home has very different requirements and by choosing the right type of wallcovering, you will be sure of a decorative surface that will wear well and look good for years to come.

LINING PAPER

This provides a smooth base for wallpaper or paint on walls and ceilings. It is made in several grades from light 480 grade, suitable for new or near-perfect walls, to extra-thick 1200 grade for use on rough and pitted plaster. A good-quality lining paper will be easier to handle than a cheap, thin paper and less likely to tear when it has been moistened by paste.

WALLPAPERS FOR PAINTING

Woodchip paper is made by sandwiching particles of wood between two layers of paper. The thicker grades are easy to hang and cover uneven surfaces quite well, but woodchip paper is not easy to cut and can be difficult to remove, while the thinner grades tear easily. Woodchip paper is a budget buy, but it is not particularly attractive or durable.

Relief wallpaper is imprinted with a raised, decorative surface pattern and is available in a wide choice of designs, as well as pre-cut dado (chair) rail panels and borders. It is quite easy to hang, although the thinner grades can tear when wet. It hides blemishes well and is durable once painted.

Textured vinyl has a deeply embossed surface pattern that masks flaws and is uncrushable, so it is suitable for hardwearing areas such as the hall (lobby) and children's rooms. It is more expensive than relief wallpaper, but is very easy to hang and usually dry strippable.

Embossed wallcovering comes in rolls and pre-cut panels made from a solid film of linseed oil and fillers fused on to a backing paper. It requires a special adhesive and will crack if folded. It is very expensive, but is extremely hardwearing and durable, and the deeply profiled, traditional designs are particularly suited to use in older and period properties. It can also be painted over.

IMPORTANT CONSIDERATIONS

While woodchip and relief papers are ideal for disguising minor blemishes and irregularities in the wall surface, they cannot be used to hide a poor-quality surface. This should be borne in mind when choosing the wallcovering, and steps should be taken to make good any substantial damage, or an unstable surface, before hanging.

In addition, the heavier types of embossed wallcovering require special hanging techniques that may, in the long run, make it preferable to repair the wall and use a more conventional wallcovering. For example, some types may require the wall to be covered with

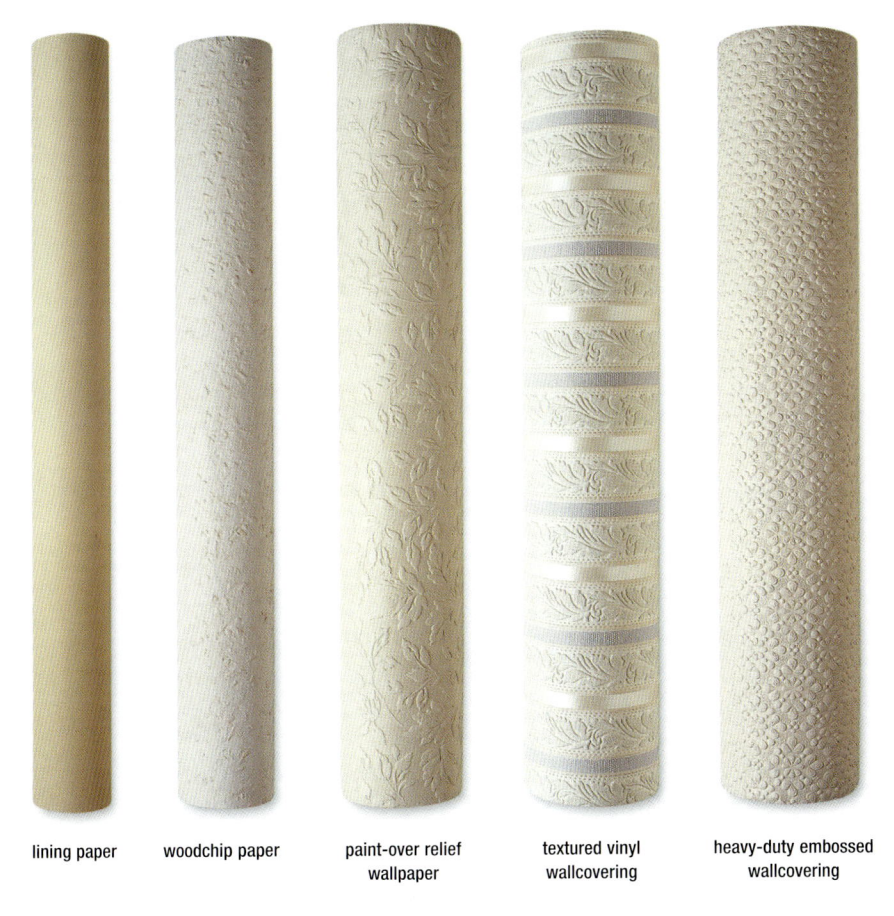

| lining paper | woodchip paper | paint-over relief wallpaper | textured vinyl wallcovering | heavy-duty embossed wallcovering |

lining paper first, and soaking times can be quite long. The back of some papers must be thoroughly soaked with hot water before applying paste. These papers are very stiff and must be handled with care; they cannot be folded, as this would break the relief pattern, leaving a permanent mark.

A seam roller cannot be used, as this would flatten the edges between drops, damaging the relief pattern and making the joins between drops really obvious. Instead, careful work with a paperhanger's brush is required to ensure that edges are pressed down. Because the papers cannot be folded, they cannot be brushed around internal and external corners. Therefore, drops must be cut to fit exactly up to the angles; at an external corner, the join must be disguised by applying a small amount of conventional cellulose filler (spackle) once the paper has dried.

PRINTED WALLCOVERINGS

Printed wallcoverings offer a wide variety of designs and finishes to suit every situation in your home. Choose them with care.

PATTERNED WALLCOVERINGS

Printed wallpaper is available in an extensive choice of patterns and colours. The cheapest are machine-printed, but top-price designs are hand-printed and often untrimmed, so hanging is best left to the professionals. Printed wallpaper can be sponged, but is not particularly durable and is best used in rooms where it will not be subjected to much wear. The thinner grades tear easily when pasted.

Washable wallpaper also comes in a good choice of designs, but is more durable and has a thin plastic coating that allows the surface to be washed clean when necessary. It is priced competitively, is fairly easy to hang and in some cases is dry strippable.

Vinyl wallcovering has a very durable surface layer of PVC that creates a hardwearing, often scrubbable, finish that resists steam, moisture and mould. There is a good choice of colours and patterns, as well as pearlized and embossed textured designs. Vinyl wallcovering is usually ready-pasted and dry strippable; paste-the-wall ranges are also available.

Sculptured vinyl is a thick, very hardwearing vinyl imprinted with a decorative design or tile effect. The waterproof finish resists steam, condensation, grease and cooking splashes, so it is a good choice for kitchens and bathrooms. It requires a heavy-duty adhesive, but is easy to hang and is dry strippable.

When buying wallcoverings, check the labels carefully to determine whether the covering you like will be suitable for the situation in which you want to hang it. If in doubt, seek the advice of your supplier. He or she will also be able to tell you if any special adhesives or hanging techniques will be required for what you have in mind. Be wary of opting for "fashionable" patterns, particularly if they are flamboyant, as they may soon lose their appeal.

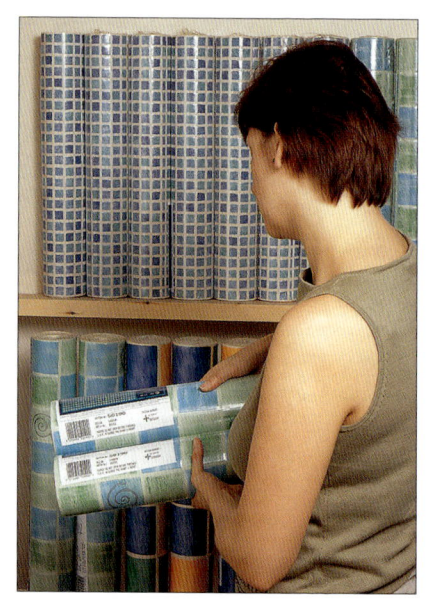

ABOVE: Some wallcoverings are more hardwearing than others. Bear this in mind when choosing a pattern and material.

WALLCOVERING MATERIALS • 105

printed wallpaper

vinyl wallcovering

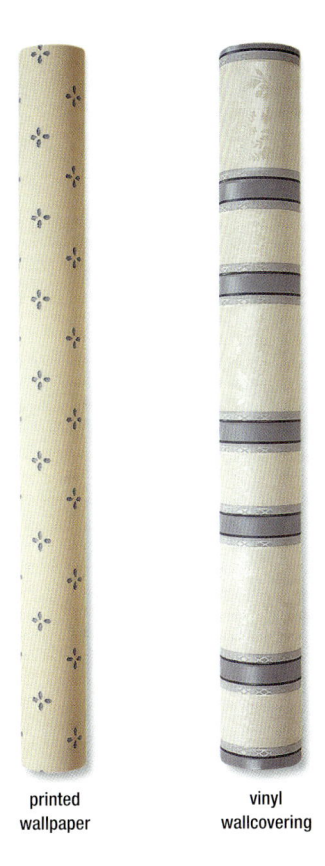

paste-the-wall wallcovering

sculptured vinyl wallcovering

SPECIAL WALLCOVERINGS

Metallic foils and wallcoverings made from natural materials such as cork, silk and grasscloth can often be ordered from dedicated decorating outlets. They are expensive and difficult to hang, so employing a professional is advisable. In general, they are hard to clean, so they are best for low-wear areas of the home.

Some special wallcoverings will actually hide minor imperfections in the wall surface; others will highlight them, so choose with care.

special metallic wallcoverings

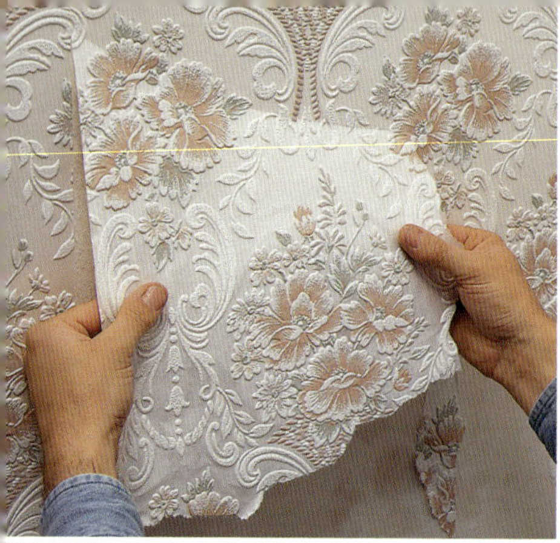

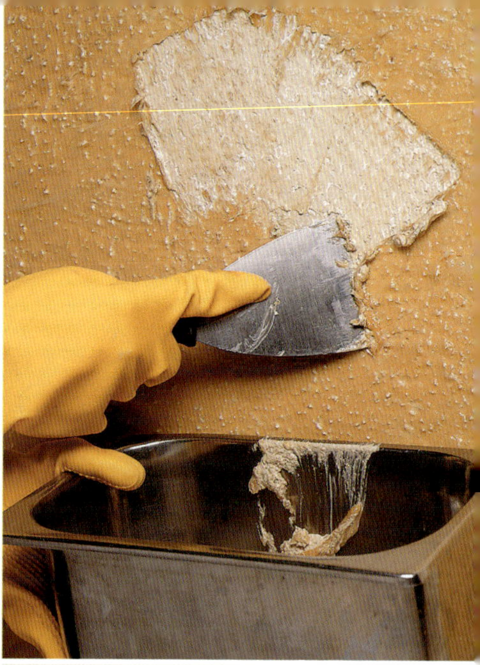

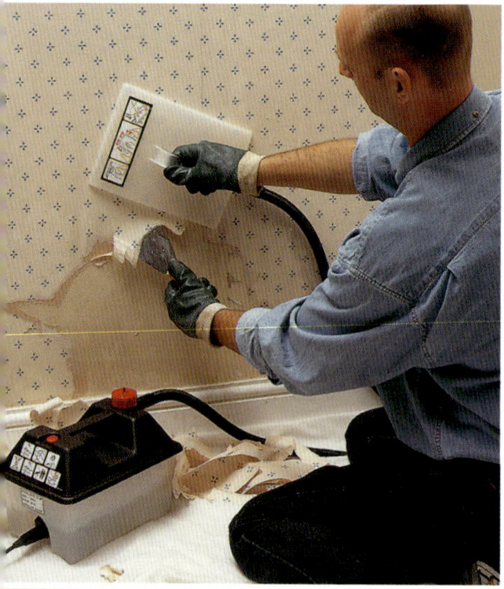

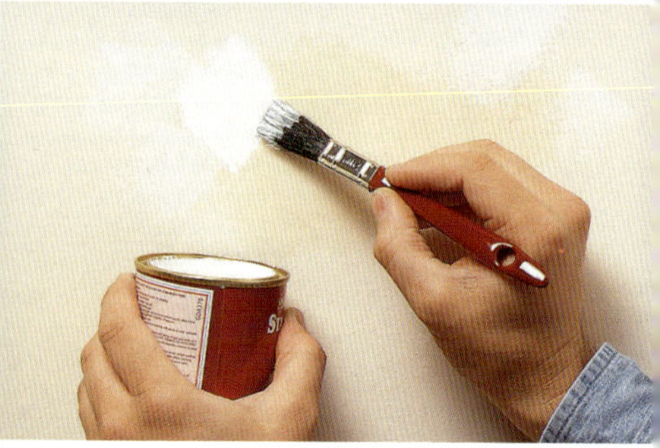

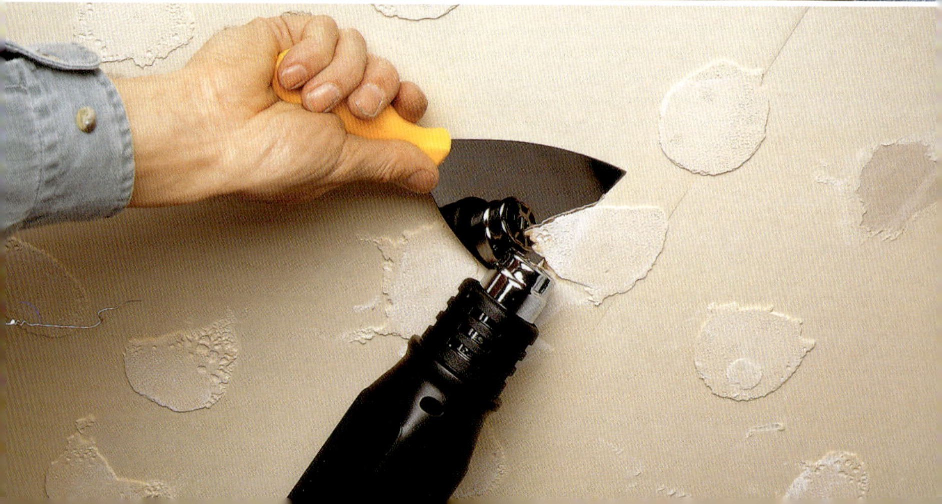

WALLCOVERING PREPARATION

As with any decorative scheme, wallcoverings rely on the quality of the surface to which they are applied for their final appearance. While some papers and vinyls are thick and will disguise minor irregularities in a wall or ceiling, most will not, so it is essential to repair all surface defects if you want the finish to look its best. Although an existing sound papered finish can be papered over, it is far better to remove the old covering and apply the new one to a clean surface. And if that surface is dusty, it should be washed off and sealed so that the wallpaper paste can adhere well. For some wallcoverings a lining paper should be hung on the wall first to provide the best finish.

REMOVING TEXTURED FINISHES

If the wall or ceiling to be given a new covering is painted or wallpapered, preparing the surface for its new finish is quite straightforward. However, if it was previously covered with materials such as texture paint, ceramic or polystyrene (Styrofoam) tiles or wall panelling, more work will be needed to remove the old finishes and return the surface to its original condition.

Textured finishes are tackled in different ways, depending on their type. Texture paints are basically thick water-based paints, normally used to create relatively low-relief effects, and can be removed with specially formulated paint removers. Some textured effects formed with a powder or ready-mixed compound are best removed with a steam wallpaper stripper, which softens the compound so that it can be scraped from the wall.

Never attempt to sand off a textured finish. There are two reasons. The first is that it will create huge quantities of very fine dust; the second is that older versions of this product contained asbestos fibres as a filler, and any action that might release these into the atmosphere as inhalable dust must be avoided at all costs.

PRACTICAL CONSIDERATIONS

Whichever method you use for stripping old texture paint, it will be messy, so you must take steps to protect yourself and areas of the room that you are not working on. Preferably wear overalls; at the very least old clothes. Rubber gloves are a must, as is some form of eye protection if you are working on a ceiling, while the latter is also essential when using a chemical stripper. A hat will keep your hair clean.

Ideally, remove all furniture from the room, but if you can't or don't want to do this, place it all together in the centre of the room and cover it with dust sheets (drop cloths). When working on a ceiling, you will have to move the furniture to another part of the room at some stage. Cover the floor with dust sheets, too, and provide yourself with a supply of plastic bags for collecting the paint scrapings. Bear in mind that chemical strippers can give off toxic fumes, so open windows to ensure good ventilation, but close doors to other rooms to prevent the fumes from spreading through your home. Make sure you clean up before leaving the room to prevent tracking paint scrapings through the house.

Always follow the instructions given with a chemical stripper, allowing the required soaking time before scraping off the softened paint. In some areas, you may need a second application of stripper to remove all the paint. Don't cover too large an area at one time, as this will cause an unnecessary build-up of fumes. You should be able to get into a rhythm of scraping one area while the stripper soaks into the next. Make sure you wash off all traces of stripper before hanging your paper.

REMOVING TEXTURED FINISHES

1 Strip off old texture paint by brushing on a generous coat of a proprietary texture paint remover using an old paintbrush. Stipple it well into the paint and leave it to penetrate for the specified amount of time.

2 When the paint has softened, scrape it off with a broad-bladed scraper. At all times, wear gloves and also safety goggles as protection against splashes.

3 Once the bulk of the coating is removed, use wire (steel) wool dipped in the paint stripper to remove any remaining flecks of paint.

4 Remove powder-based or ready-mixed types using a steam stripper, which will soften the finish. Never try to sand off this type of finish.

REMOVING TILES AND PANELLING

For tiles and wall panelling, complete removal or a cover-up with plasterboard (gypsum board) are the two options available. The former will leave a surface in need of considerable renovation, while the latter will cause a slight loss of space within the room, as well as some complications at door and window openings. If you are faced with removing a layer of ceramic tiles from a wall, it is unlikely that you will be able to do so without causing a fair amount of damage to the surface below. In this situation, it will be better to add a skim coat of fresh plaster to the entire surface, rather than try to make good individual areas of damage. Unless you are confident that you can achieve a perfectly flat finish, entrust this work to a professional plasterer.

REMOVING WALL PANELLING

1 The last board to be attached will have been nailed to the fixing grounds through its face. Use a hammer and nail punch to drive the nails right through the board and free it. Lift it off the wall.

REMOVING CERAMIC TILES

1 On a completely tiled wall, use a hammer to crack a tile and create a starting point for the stripping. On partly tiled walls, start at the tile edge.

2 Use a broad bolster (stonecutter's chisel) and a club (spalling) hammer to chip the old tiles off the wall.

2 The other boards will have been secret-nailed through their tongues. Use a crowbar (wrecking bar) to prise them away from their grounds, taking care not to cause too much damage to the wall.

3 Finally, prise the grounds off the wall. Use a claw hammer with some protective packing to lever them out of the wall. Some nails may come away with the grounds; others may be left in the wall.

REMOVING POLYSTYRENE (STYROFOAM) TILES

1 Lever the tiles away from the ceiling with a scraper. If the tiles were fixed with a continuous coat of adhesive, consider fitting a new ceiling.

2 If the tiles were stuck in place with blobs of adhesive, use a heat gun to soften the old adhesive so it can be removed with a scraper.

REMOVING OLD WALLPAPER

Although a sound wallcovering can be papered over, it is far better to remove all traces of it.

REMOVING WALLPAPER
Ordinary wallpaper is not difficult to remove and requires only wetting and soaking for 10–15 minutes before stripping with a broad-bladed scraper. Adding wallpaper stripper or a few drops of washing-up liquid (dishwashing detergent) to the water will help it to penetrate the paper. Wallpaper that has been over-painted or has a washable finish needs scoring with the edge of a scraper before soaking, but hiring a steam stripper is the easiest method, and you are less likely to damage the plaster surface.

If walls are faced with plasterboard (gypsum board), take care not to saturate the surface or hold a steam stripper in place for too long. Dry-strippable papers can simply be peeled from the wall, leaving the backing paper in place. If this is still adhering well and remains intact, a new wallcovering can be hung over the top, but if it tears, the backing should also be removed.

PREPARING SURFACES
Once all the old paper has been removed, walls should be washed thoroughly with a solution of sugar soap (all-purpose cleaner) to remove dust, grime and traces of old adhesive. Rinse and allow the surface to dry. Cracks and gaps should also be repaired, and any stains that remain after cleaning should be sealed. For settlement cracks between walls and the ceiling or woodwork, use a flexible decorators' filler, and seal stains with an aluminium primer or proprietary aerosol stain block.

New porous plaster and old walls that are dusty will require sealing. A PVA adhesive (white glue) solution of one part PVA to five parts water is ideal for sealing these surfaces and will stabilize them before papering. A coat of size or heavy-duty wallpaper paste ensures good adhesion of the wallcovering and allows paper to be manoeuvred freely on the wall.

PREPARING WALLS

1 Use abrasive paper wrapped around a sanding block to remove any remaining "nibs" of wallpaper.

WALLCOVERING PREPARATION • 113

ABOVE: Stubborn wallpaper will be easier to remove with a steam stripper. You can hire one if you don't expect to be doing much stripping.

ABOVE: Vinyl wallcoverings can usually be stripped dry and will peel off the wall, leaving the backing behind; strip this off if it tears.

2 Repair any cracks with cellulose filler (spackle) and seal persistent stains with a stain block or aluminium paint.

3 A coat of size will make the wallpaper easier to hang on new plaster; it prevents moisture being absorbed too quickly from the paste.

HANGING LINING PAPER

Lining paper helps to disguise surface blemishes and provides a good surface for decorating. It is usually hung horizontally so that the joints do not coincide with those of the decorative paper, but hanging vertical lengths will be easier in narrow alcoves and where there are wall fixtures such as pipes. On poor walls, two layers of lining paper may be necessary; the first layer should be hung vertically, and the second horizontally.

The basic paperhanging techniques shown on the following pages can also be used for lining paper, but it should be left to soak for only five minutes to become pliable. Treat each surface separately and trim the paper to fit into internal and external corners. Do not use a ceiling as a guideline, expecting it to be level; mark a horizontal guideline for the lower edge of the first length (immediately below the ceiling) with a spirit (carpenter's) level and long straightedge. If you are lining both walls and ceiling, start with the ceiling, working from one end of the room to the other.

Work from right to left if right-handed and left to right if left-handed, folding each length of lining paper concertina-fashion to make it manageable. Allow a slight overlap on to the adjacent wall at each end and on to the ceiling if this is uneven. When the paper has been brushed out, crease these overlaps with the back of the scissors, peel back and trim to the crease before brushing back. Work down the wall, trimming the last length so that it butts against the top edge of the skirting (baseboard).

1 Normally, lining paper is hung in horizontal lengths across each wall, preventing the joints from coinciding with those of the decorative paper, as this could cause them to open up as the paste dries.

TIPS

- Allow at least 24 hours for lining paper to dry out completely before hanging the final wallcovering.
- Lining paper may shrink as it dries. Fill small gaps between lengths with fine surface filler and sand smooth. In corners, use a bead of flexible filler (spackle) and smooth with a wet finger.

2 Lining paper can be hung vertically in narrow alcoves or behind pipework, however, if this makes the job easier. It should also be hung vertically if you intend over-painting it, as the joins will be less obvious.

3 To line a ceiling, work across the longest dimension of the room, marking an initial guideline. You may find it easier if someone else holds the concertina of pasted paper while you brush it into place.

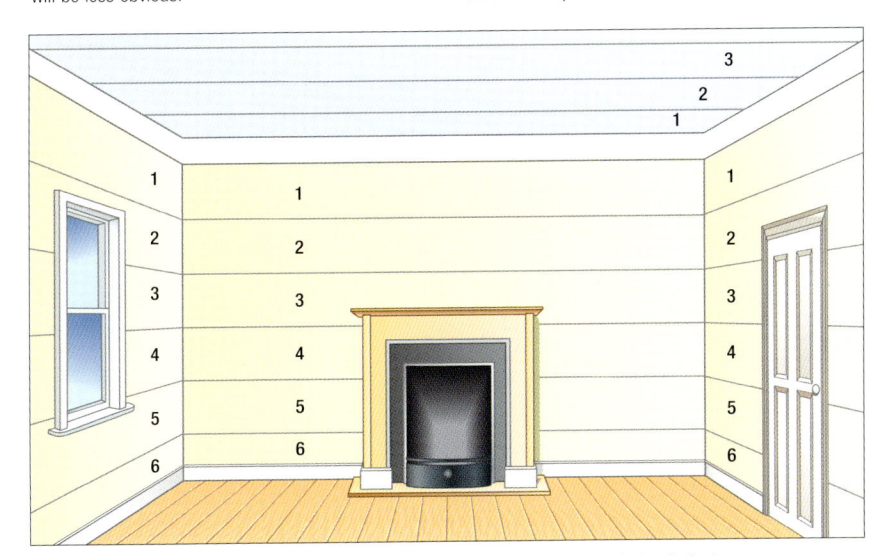

ABOVE: The correct sequence of work when hanging lining paper: for a wall, begin just below the ceiling and move downward; for a ceiling, work across the longest dimension from one end of the room to the other. In each case, trim the last length to width.

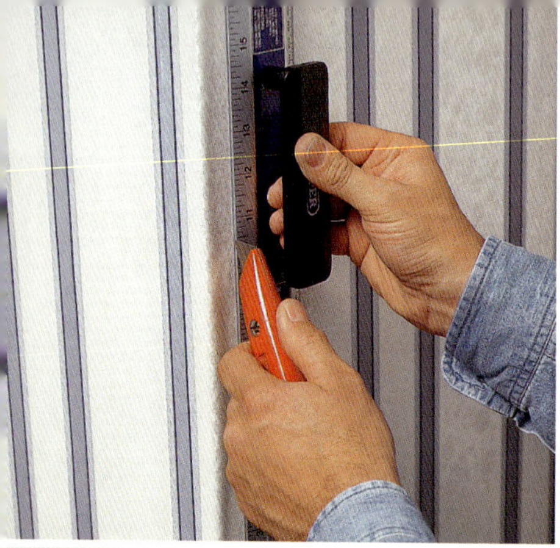
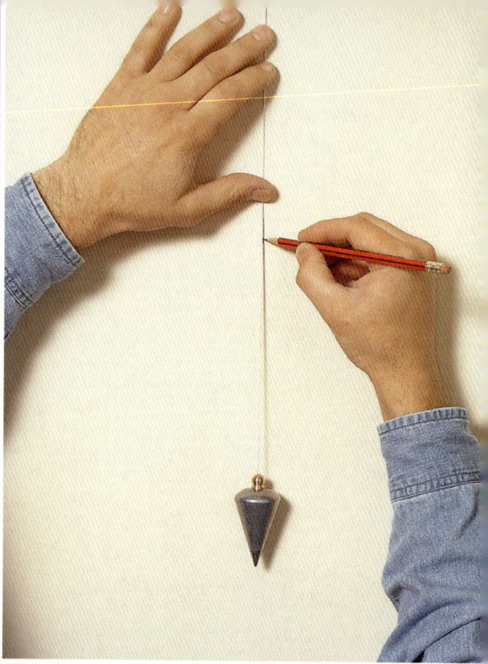
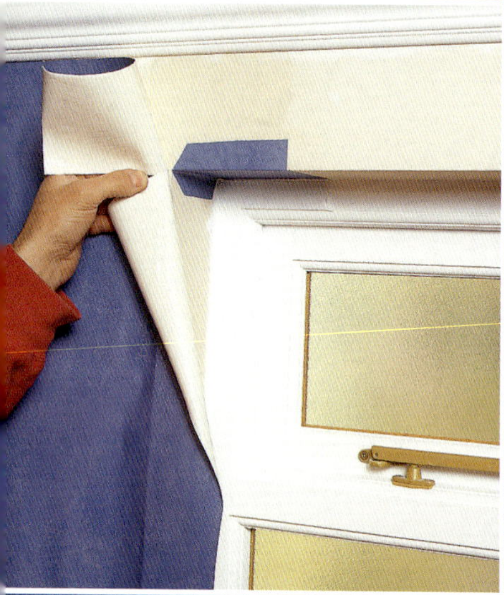
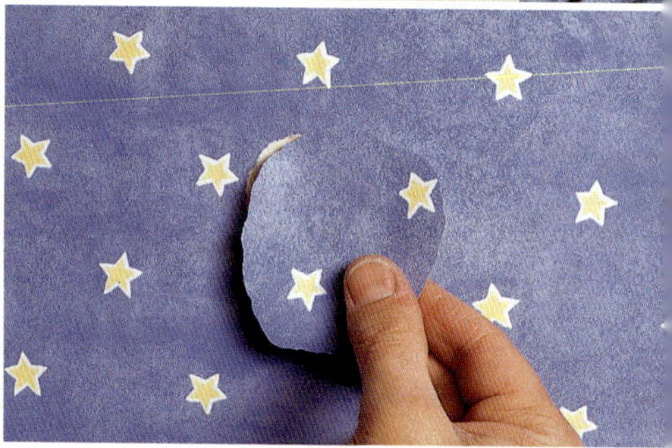
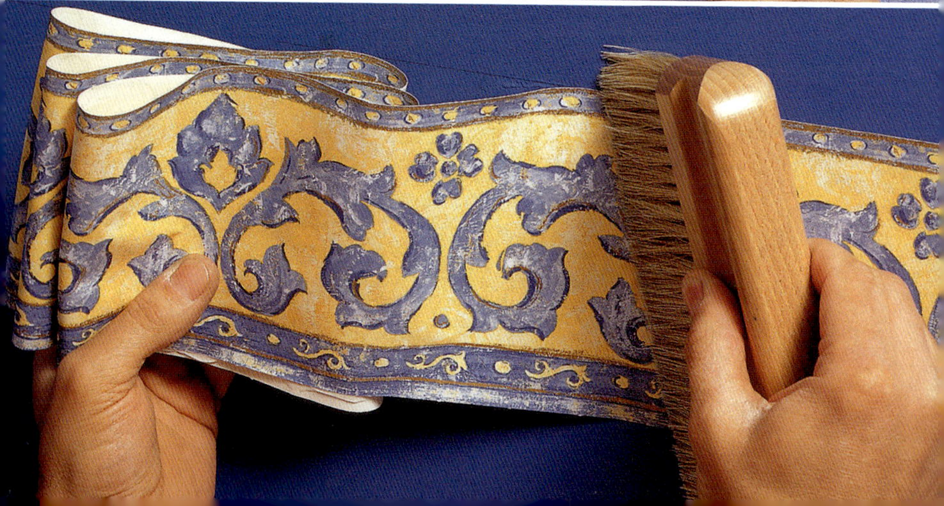

WALLCOVERING TECHNIQUES

Contrary to what many people think, hanging wallpaper is actually quite a simple process. You do need to take care, though, since you will be dealing with long strips of wallcovering, which in practically all cases will be covered in sticky paste on one side. The potential for mishaps is quite high, so work in an unhurried, logical manner, keeping the work area tidy. The following pages show you all the techniques you need to know to paper walls and ceilings successfully, and how to cope with difficult areas, such as corners, doors, windows and alcoves. Common problems are described, together with the methods for overcoming them.

PREPARING WALLPAPER

Wallpaper can be hung using one of three methods, depending on whether you are using a ready-pasted, paste-the-wall or traditional unpasted paper. However, the most important step with any paperhanging task is to prepare fully before cutting the paper by carefully measuring the lengths and making an allowance for pattern matching to avoid mistakes.

PREPARING UNPASTED PAPER

Measure the height of the wall from the ceiling to the top of the skirting (baseboard) and add 100mm (4in) for trimming the top and bottom. Measure and cut the first drop to length. To ensure a square cut, lay the paper flush with the long edge of the pasting table and use a straightedge to mark the cutting line.

If the ceiling is quite level, you can cut a number of lengths. Match the pattern of each length dry off the roll against the first cut length to avoid problems with pattern matching as the job progresses.

Use the paperhanger's brush to weigh one end down, and line up the edge of the paper with the edge of the pasting table, then apply a thin, even coat of paste brushing outward toward the edges.

Fold the ends of the pasted length in to the centre and leave it to soak, checking the manufacturer's guidelines for the exact length of time. Long lengths of paper should be lightly folded concertina-style.

READY-PASTED PAPER

To activate ready-pasted papers, fill a trough two-thirds with water and put it on the floor at the end of the pasting table. Roll a length of paper with the decorative face inside and immerse for the recommended soaking time. Draw it on to the pasting table, patterned side down so that excess water can drain into the trough.

For paste-the-wall papers, apply a coat of paste to an area wider than the paper – it can be hung directly from the roll or using cut lengths.

PREPARING PRE-COATED WALLCOVERINGS

You can buy many wallcoverings pre-coated with adhesive. The adhesive is activated by soaking a length of paper in a trough of cold water. Once immersed and soaked for the recommended length of time, drain the paper into the trough. Mix ordinary paste to recoat any dry edges.

CUTTING, PASTING AND FOLDING WALLPAPER

1 Measure carefully, allowing for pattern matching, and cut the paper to length. Cut several more drops from the same roll and to the same length, marking their tops.

2 Brush on an even coat of paste, working out from the centre to the edges. Align each edge with the table edge in turn to prevent paste from getting on to the table.

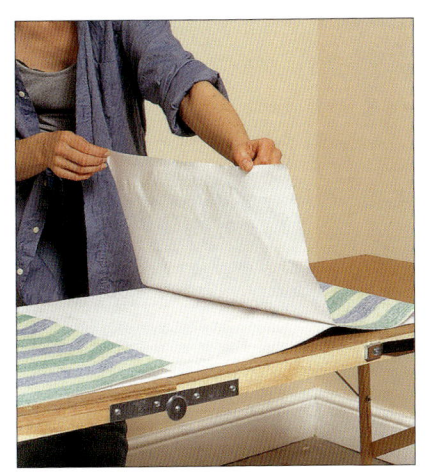

3 When you have pasted about half of a short drop, fold the pasted end into the middle. Then slide the paper along the table and paste the rest. Fold the end in to meet the first.

4 Fold longer lengths of wallpaper concertina-fashion to make them more manageable. Leave the folded drops of paper for the required time so that the paste soaks in.

HANGING THE FIRST LENGTH

In a room with no focal point, work clockwise around the room. Start and finish near the least obtrusive corner so that any pattern mismatch will not be obvious.

To ensure the end result is well balanced, centre a pattern over a chimney breast (fireplace projection) or other prominent feature and work outward in both directions.

WHERE TO START

Use a plumbline and spirit (carpenter's) level to mark a guideline on the wall. The distance from a corner to the guideline should be one roll width less 25mm (1in), and the first length should be hung so that you are working away from (and not into) the corner.

HANGING THE PAPER

Place the first length next to the guideline, then adjust the top so that there is 50mm (2in) of paper lapping on to the ceiling and slide the vertical edge into its final position.

Lightly brush out the top half of the paper, working downward to expel air bubbles and firmly push the top trimming allowance into the angle with the ceiling. Make sure that the vertical edge is aligned with the guideline then continue to work down the wall, brushing outward from the centre of the length.

Crease the paper into the junction between wall and ceiling by running the blunt edge of the scissors along the paper, then gently peel back the paper and trim neatly to fit along the creaseline. Brush the trimmed edge firmly back into position.

Ease the bottom half of the paper away from the wall and smooth it into place. Make sure that it is aligned with the guideline, then crease the bottom edge of the paper into the skirting (baseboard) and trim to fit, as before, using scissors.

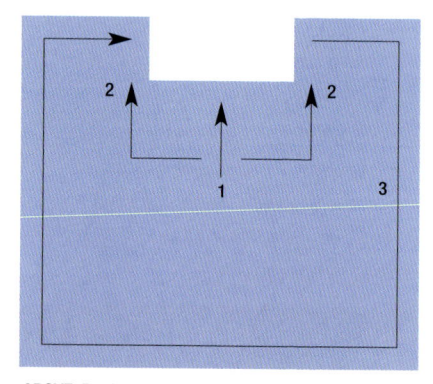

ABOVE: Begin by centring a pattern over a prominent feature, then work outward in both directions.

TIPS

- Hang papers with a large design so that any loss of pattern occurs at floor level, not at the ceiling.
- Agitate pre-pasted papers during soaking to expel any air bubbles and ensure that all the paper comes into contact with water. Make sure the paper is loosely rolled.
- Edges can dry out during trimming – keep a little extra paste handy.

WALLCOVERING TECHNIQUES • 121

1 Place the edge of the first drop against the vertical guideline, making sure that it is aligned accurately. When you are happy, begin brushing the paper on to the wall.

2 Brush out the top half of the length and push it into the angle with the ceiling, using a dabbing action with the paperhanger's brush. Make sure you brush out all air bubbles.

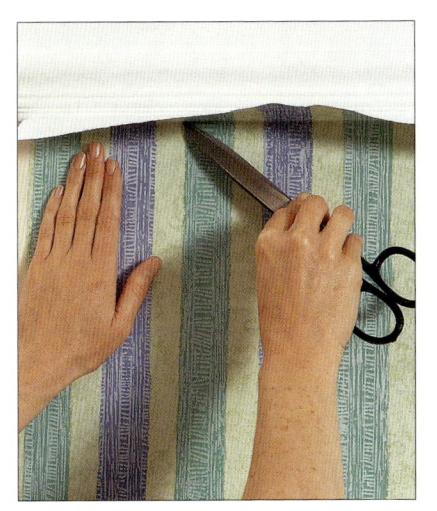

3 Using the back edge of the scissors blade, run along the wall/ceiling angle to crease the paper into it. This will provide an accurate trimming line.

4 Gently peel back the paper and cut along the crease line to remove excess paper. Then brush the end of the drop back into place. Repeat at the skirting (baseboard).

EXTERNAL CORNERS

Corners are unlikely to be completely square, so never try to hang a full width of wallpaper around them as it will not hang straight. Hanging two separate lengths of paper and overlapping them slightly at the corners will produce a far better result, although some small loss of pattern will be inevitable on walls that are not perfectly true.

PAPERING AN EXTERNAL CORNER
Hang the cut length as usual, matching the pattern down the full length, then lightly brush the paper around the corner. Do not apply too much pressure, as the paper could tear, but make sure that there are no bubbles and the paper has adhered well along the edge of the corner.

Use scissors to make a release cut top and bottom where the wall meets the skirting (baseboard) and ceiling. This will allow the paper to be smoothed on to the wall on both sides of the corner and trimmed along the skirting and ceiling. Using a craft knife, trim the length vertically to leave an overlap of about 25mm (1in) brushed around the corner. Discard the waste.

Cut another length and hang this to a vertical guideline on the second wall so that it overlaps the strip of paper brushed around the corner, with its edge about 12mm (½in) from the corner and the pattern matching as closely as possible.

To do this, you may need to hang the new length so that it overlaps the previous length substantially. The width of the pattern will determine how much the two lengths may have to be overlapped. Make a vertical cut with a craft knife through both layers, from ceiling to skirting. Pull away the waste strip of the overlapping drop, then carefully peel back the edge of that drop until you can remove the waste strip of the overlapped drop. If necessary, add a little more paste, then brush back the paper to leave a neat butt join between the two drops. Finally, trim to fit the top and bottom as normal.

When working with a very thin paper, especially if it has a white ground, you can simply leave one drop overlapping the other at an external corner. This will not be very noticeable. However, if you are hanging a vinyl wallcovering, you must make the vertical cut through both drops to produce a butt join, as the pasted overlapping drop will not adhere to the vinyl surface of the drop below, unless you use special overlap adhesive.

If the wall is not completely square, the pattern may not match exactly along the full drop where the two lengths cross over. This cannot be avoided and should be taken into account when planning the order of the work. Always aim for the overlap to be where it is least noticeable. On a chimney breast (fireplace projection), for example, the overlaps should be on the side walls, not the face.

1 Hang the last drop on the first wall and brush the wallpaper smoothly around the external corner.

2 Make vertical release cuts at the top and bottom, into the skirting (baseboard) and ceiling junctions.

3 Trim off the excess paper to leave an overlap of about 25mm (1in). Make sure the edge is brushed down firmly.

4 Hang the first drop on the second wall so that it overlaps the turned paper and the pattern matches as closely as possible.

5 When working with a thick paper or a vinyl wallcovering, make a single cut down through both layers using a sharp knife. Keep the cut as straight as possible.

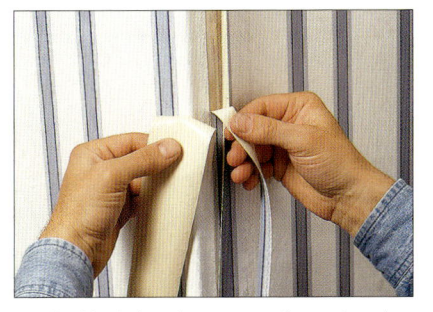

6 Peel back the edges, remove the waste and brush the edges back into place. You should be left with a neat butt join and minimal disruption to the pattern.

INTERNAL CORNERS

As with external corners, internal corners should be papered with two separate pieces of wallpaper, overlapping them slightly.

Hang the last full-width length, then measure the distance from the edge of the paper into the corner, taking measurements from the top, centre and bottom of the wall. Add a 12mm (½in) overlap allowance to the widest measurement and cut a strip of this width from the next full length. Do not discard the offcut (scrap) – put it to one side for use later.

Hang the cut length, brushing the overlap allowance on to the adjacent wall. Make sure the paper is brushed firmly into the corner by dabbing the wallpaper into the angle with the tips of the brush bristles.

Measure the width of the offcut and use a plumbline to mark a vertical guideline on the adjacent wall that distance from the corner.

If the internal corner is badly out of true, take measurements from the top, centre and bottom of the wall, and adjust the guideline for the offcut so that it will not overlap on to the previous wall.

Hang the offcut against the guideline, overlapping the strip of paper turned on to the wall. Although there will be a slight mismatch of the pattern, it should not be too noticeable. Trim the top and bottom of the length neatly with scissors. Treat a vinyl in the same manner as for an external corner, or use overlap adhesive.

1 When you come to an internal corner, hang the last full-width drop, then measure from the edge of the wallcovering into the corner at the top, middle and bottom.

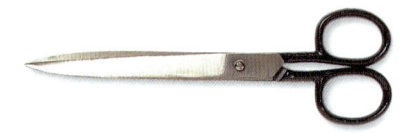

TIPS

- If an overlap allowance puckers in an internal corner, make small horizontal cuts in the paper so that it lays flat.
- Keep a tube of overlap adhesive handy to ensure that overlapping edges of vinyl wallcoverings adhere properly.
- Paper with a straight-match pattern can be difficult to align in an internal corner. Hold a spirit (carpenter's) level horizontally across the corner to check that the design is level.

WALLCOVERING TECHNIQUES • 125

2 Using the widest of the three measurements, and adding an allowance to turn around the corner, cut a strip from the next pasted length of paper. Do not discard the waste length.

3 Hang the strip of paper, butting its edge up to the last drop hung and brushing the overlap allowance on to the facing wall. Make sure to brush it well into the corner.

4 Measure the width of the waste length cut from the drop and make a mark at this distance out from the corner. Use a plumbline to position a vertical guideline at this point.

5 Hang the offcut against the line, overlapping the strip turned around the corner and making sure that the edge is brushed down well. Trim at top and bottom.

AROUND DOORS

If you follow the correct sequence for hanging and trimming the lengths of wallpaper, you should be able to paper around a door frame with little trouble.

Mark out the walls in roll widths first so that you know exactly where each length falls. Thin strips beside a door or window will be difficult to hang and are likely to peel, so adjust the starting point if necessary, perhaps moving it half a roll's width in one direction or the other. When you are happy that you will not be left with awkward strips on either side of the door, begin hanging full drops in the normal manner. Continue until you have hung the last full drop before the door.

Hang a full length so that it overlaps the architrave (trim), matching the pattern to the last length hung. Lightly brush the paper on to the wall where possible, and then use the bristle tips of the brush to press the paper into the top of the architrave. Take great care not to tear the wallcovering at this point, particularly if you are using a thin paper.

Locate the external corner of the door frame and make a diagonal release cut into this point with scissors. As you cut toward the corner, press the paper against the wall to prevent it from tearing. Smooth the paper down the wall and brush the vertical overlap of paper into the edge of the architrave. Brush out the section of paper above the door frame, pressing it into the wall/ceiling angle and the angle between architrave and wall.

Make sure the paper does not separate from the previous length as you do this. Crease the paper against the architrave with the back of the scissors, then ease the paper away from the wall and cut along the creases, or trim with a craft knife held at a 45-degree angle to the wall. Trim the top of the door frame first, cutting inward from the outer edge of the architrave. Brush the paper back into place against the side and top of the architrave. Then crease the paper against the ceiling and trim it to fit. Wipe the paste from the woodwork and the paper. Hang the next drop in a similar manner, butting it against the last drop above the door and making a release cut so that it will fit around the frame. Trim and brush into place.

TIPS

- Lightly smooth the pasted paper on to the wall before trimming so that it does not tear under its own weight when it is damp.
- The junction between wall and door frame is rarely even; trimming the paper so that it overlaps the frame slightly will create a much neater finish.
- If the sides of a reveal are uneven, trim overlapping paper to 50mm (2in) and make horizontal release cuts down the length so that it lies flat, then cut a separate strip to fit.
- Complete all cutting and trimming around doors and windows first, leaving the trimming at the top and bottom of each length until last.

WALLCOVERING TECHNIQUES • 127

1 Hang the drop on the wall, butting it up to the last full drop hung. Then drape the paper over the frame and brush it gently into the top of the architrave (trim).

2 Take the paperhanger's scissors and make a diagonal release cut through the paper into the external corner of the frame. Be careful not to tear the damp paper.

3 Brush the resulting flaps of paper into the side and top of the architrave, using a dabbing action with the bristles of the paperhanger's brush. Crease them with the scissors.

4 Trim the paper flush with the architrave using a sharp craft knife, or pull it back gently and cut it with the scissors. Hang the next drop around the other side of the frame.

AROUND WINDOWS

Hanging wallpaper around a window that is set flush in the wall with a decorative frame around it requires a similar technique to that used for papering around a door. However, many windows are set into the wall to leave a shallow recess that must be tackled in a slightly different manner. Fortunately, any small mishaps or irregularities in the papering around a window can often be concealed by curtains or blinds (drapes or shades).

Hang the first length overlapping the window, matching the pattern to the last length hung. Smooth the paper on to the wall, then make horizontal cuts into the corners of the reveal – the first level with the top of the window sill, and the second level with the top of the reveal.

Locate the corners of the window sill and make diagonal release cuts toward these points so that the paper can be eased around the shape of the sill. Brush the paper below the sill on to the wall, and trim to fit. Brush the remaining flap of paper around the corner into the reveal and trim to fit against the window frame. Make sure air bubbles are expelled, but do not apply too much pressure. If the overlap is not deep enough for the reveal, hang a narrow strip to fit between its edge and the window frame.

Cut an oversized patch to fit the head of the reveal, matching the pattern to the paper above the reveal. Make a release cut in the outer corner, then slip the pasted patch into place. Tuck

1 Drape the paper over the window reveal, and make horizontal cuts at top and bottom so that the paper can be brushed into the reveal. Cut only as far as the corners of the reveal.

the edges of the patch under the paper above and inside the reveal, and trim through both layers with a wavy stroke. Peel back the paper to remove the waste and brush down firmly – the joint should be almost invisible. Complete the rest of the window in the same way, hanging short lengths above and below the reveal. Lengths above the window can be brushed into the reveal complete, provided that it is not deep and the edge is square. With a deep reveal, or one where the edge is not square, cut strips to fit the reveal, turning them slightly on to the face of the wall, then overlap their edges with drops hung on the face. Make a wavy cut through both layers, as before, remove the waste and brush flat.

WALLCOVERING TECHNIQUES • 129

2 Cut along the top of the window sill and make diagonal release cuts around the sill.

3 Brush the remaining flap of wallpaper into the reveal and trim to fit.

4 Ease back the paper, and cut and fit a patch in the corner of the reveal.

5 Cut through both layers and remove the waste to create an unobtrusive butt join.

6 Hang short lengths above and below the window, matching the pattern.

7 Cut lengths long enough to be brushed into the reveal at the top.

AROUND SWITCHPLATES

Before wallpapering around sockets and switches, turn off the electricity supply and hang the paper over the fitting. Press it firmly against the faceplate so that you can see a clear impression and make a pencil mark 6mm (¼in) in from each corner. Make diagonal cuts to each pencil mark with scissors, trimming the flaps of paper 6mm (¼in) in from the outer edge of the faceplate.

Loosen the screws of the faceplate and ease it from the wall, then use a paperhanger's brush to gently push the flaps of paper behind the faceplate. Push the faceplate back into position and tighten its screws. Wipe off any adhesive from the fitting and allow the paste to dry before restoring the power.

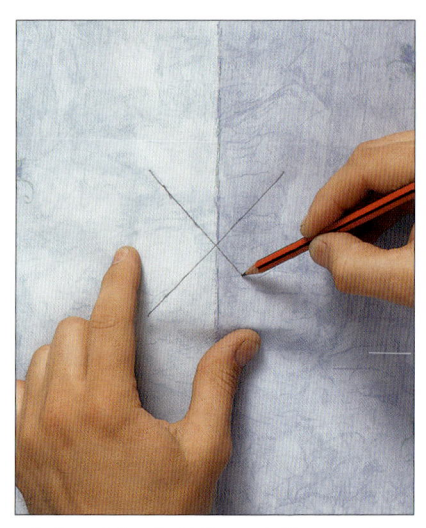

1 Turn off the electricity supply. Use a pencil to mark the corners on the paper where it overhangs the fitting.

2 Make a diagonal cut from the centre to each corner of the faceplate. Loosen the screws and pull the faceplate back.

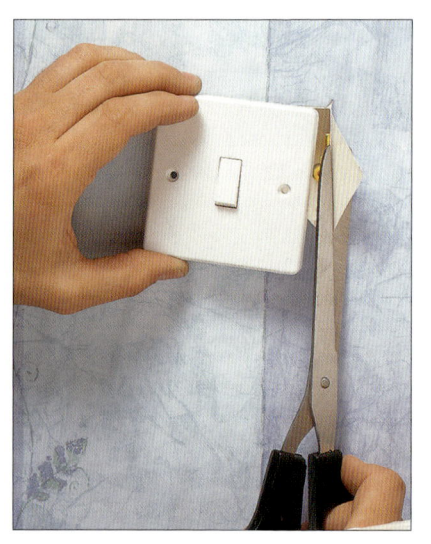

3 Trim the flaps of paper and push them under the edges of the loosened faceplate. Retighten the screws.

AROUND LIGHT FITTINGS

If there is a ceiling rose, turn off the electricity supply before brushing the paper over the casing and then locate its exact centre with your finger. Make a small cut in the paper at this point and gently pull the pendant through the cut, taking care not to tear the paper.

Ease the paper around the shape of the rose by making a series of small radial cuts from the centre of the rose to the edge of the casing. Smooth the paper into place on the ceiling around the rose and finish hanging the rest of the paper. Crease the paper into the edge of the rose before restoring the electricity supply. The paper can be trimmed neatly with a knife once the paste has dried but turn the electricity supply off again before doing this. Where there is a large ceiling centrepiece, it is easier to hang and trim the paper if you plan your starting point so that a join runs through the middle of the fitting. Make radial cuts as for a normal rose to fit the paper up to the edges of the centrepiece.

WALL LIGHT FITTINGS

Turn off the electricity supply and remove the fitting. Bind the wires with electrical insulating or masking tape. Hang the paper to the cable, mark its position on the paper and make a small incision. Feed the cable through the hole, taking care not to tear the paper. Finish hanging the drop and allow the paste to dry before replacing the fitting.

1 Turn off the electricity supply. Make a series of cuts in the paper toward the edge of the ceiling rose. Brush down.

2 Crease the paper around the edge of the rose, then trim neatly with a knife. Finally, brush the paper smooth.

AROUND FIREPLACES

Fireplaces come in a variety of forms; some are very simple and rectangular in outline; others are very ornate. When faced with papering around a simple fireplace, you can use the same techniques as you would for papering around a door frame – make diagonal cuts to the corners and brush the paper into the angles between the fireplace and the wall. However, an ornate frame will require a little more effort.

Hang a full length so that it drapes over the fireplace and match the pattern above the mantel shelf to the last length hung. Lightly brush the paper into the junction of the wall and shelf and trim. Cut inward from the outer corner of the mantel shelf, and support the rest of the length to prevent it from tearing.

Press the paper against the wall at the point where the corner of the shelf meets the wall, gently easing the paper around the contours with your fingers. Make a series of small cuts to allow the paper to lie flat, then use the tips of a paperhanger's brush to mould the paper into the precise shape. Trim each small flap of paper, then crease and trim the paper down the side of the fireplace and wipe any adhesive from the surface.

In some cases, the mantel shelf may span the entire chimney breast (fireplace projection), in which case you need only paper down to the shelf, then cut strips to fit at the sides, making release cuts as necessary to match the shape of the fireplace. You could also use this technique for a fireplace that has a very complex shape to the sides.

1 Hang the drop above the fireplace, draping the paper over the mantel shelf. Brush it into the angle and trim along the back edge.

2 Ease the paper around the contours of the mantel shelf by making small release cuts. Brush it into place and trim off the excess.

BEHIND RADIATORS

If a radiator is too heavy to remove, turn it off and allow it to cool completely. Measure and make a note of the position of each wall bracket from the outer edges and top of the radiator, then hang the paper on the wall so that it drapes over the radiator. Match the pattern with the last length hung.

Measure out the position of the wall bracket and make a pencil mark on the wallpaper at this point. Make a vertical slit with scissors from the bottom edge of the paper up to the mark, and use a radiator roller to feed and smooth the paper down on each side of the bracket. Trim the paper neatly along the skirting (baseboard) and wipe off any adhesive left on the face of the wallpaper, skirting and radiator. Repeat for the other bracket.

WALL FITTINGS

When removing wall fittings, mark the position of each screw hole with a wooden match and carefully press the tip through the pasted paper before it is smoothed into place.

1 Use paperhanger's scissors to make a vertical cut from the bottom of the paper in line with the radiator bracket.

2 Carefully feed the paper down behind the radiator with a radiator roller, smoothing it on to the wall at the same time.

HANGING BORDERS

A decorative border can add the finishing touch to a wallpaper or paint scheme. You can choose from a wide variety of patterns, colourways and sizes, all of which are quick and easy to hang. The key to a professional-looking result is to make sure that the border is absolutely straight and hung against accurate guidelines, and that all the joins are neat.

BASIC TECHNIQUES

Use a spirit (carpenter's) level to mark the position of the border on the walls at 300mm (12in) intervals, joining the pencil marks with a long straightedge. Measure from one corner of the wall to the other and add 50mm (2in) for trimming. Paste by brushing out from the centre, and fold concertina-style, leaving the paper to soak for ten minutes. Brush the back of a ready-pasted border with tepid water, rather than immersing it in a trough. A self-adhesive border needs to be re-rolled so that the decorative face is facing outward.

To hang, place 300mm (12in) of the border against the guideline at a time, allowing the folds to drop out as you work. If using a self-adhesive border, peel away the backing paper and smooth it into place. Before cutting and hanging the next length, match the pattern on the roll. Do not attempt to hang a continuous length of border around an external or internal corner; instead use the same technique as for hanging conventional paper.

DEALING WITH CORNERS

1 Draw a guideline for the border on the wall using a spirit (carpenter's) level.

TIPS

- Hang a border by working from right to left if you are right-handed, and left to right if left-handed.
- Positioning a border is easier if the guideline is above a horizontal border, and on the inner edge around windows and doors.
- Hang a border below an uneven ceiling and paint the gap to match.

If you have to use more than one length on a wall, a butt join can be used for borders with a simple repeat pattern. For more complex designs, overlap the two lengths so that the pattern matches exactly and carefully cut around a motif through both layers. When the waste paper has been removed and the cut edges smoothed into place, the join should be almost invisible. Use a seam roller to press down the edges.

WALLCOVERING TECHNIQUES • 135

2 Fold a pasted border concertina-style so that it is ready to hang and easy to handle.

3 Match the pattern in a corner using a dry length, before cutting and pasting.

CREATING A BUTT JOIN

1 Form a butt join between two lengths of a border that has a simple pattern.

2 Use a seam roller to press edges and joins down firmly.

CREATING AN INVISIBLE JOIN

An intricate pattern gives you the option of disguising a join between lengths of border. Simply overlap the end of one length over the other, matching the patterns accurately, then cut through both layers, following the outline of part of the pattern. Remove the waste and brush down; the join will disappear.

DIVIDING A WALL WITH A BORDER

A border will allow two different wallpaper patterns to be applied to a wall, one above and one below, by concealing the joint between them. Mark a guideline on the wall, approximately 900mm (3ft) from the floor, and hang a length of each design at the same time so that it overlaps the pencil line by 50mm (2in). Before hanging the next lengths, hold a long straightedge on the guideline and cut through both layers of paper with a knife. Remove the waste strips and smooth down the cut edges to form a neat butt join.

When the room has been papered, the border can then be hung. Centre it over the butt join using an overlap adhesive for vinyl wallcoverings.

AROUND A WINDOW OR DOOR

Draw a horizontal guideline to the full width of the border above the frame, and then mark a vertical guideline down each side. Cut the horizontal length 50mm (2in) longer than required and hang it, making sure that it overlaps the side guidelines evenly.

Add the vertical lengths, overlapping the horizontal strip squarely at the corners. Use the trimming allowance on the vertical lengths to adjust the border so that you will be cutting through the busiest part of the design. Holding a steel rule at a 45-degree angle, cut through both layers of paper from the external to internal corner of the border, using a craft knife. Peel back the cut edges and remove the waste paper from the wall. Brush the border back into place to create a neat mitred join at each corner.

You can use this technique of making mitred right-angled joins between lengths to allow for changes in floor or ceiling level, or to use the border to

DIVIDING A WALL

1 Hang a drop of each patterned paper so that they overlap the pencil guideline. Work on one pair of drops at a time.

MITRING A CORNER BORDER

1 Mark out horizontal and vertical guidelines for the lengths of border, using a spirit (carpenter's) level.

outline other features such as fireplaces or perhaps even pictures.

In some cases, you might want the border to run along the wall above the stairs. In this situation, the technique of making an angled cut through both layers of the border where they overlap is the same, but the actual angle will be shallower. You need to mark the wall with a pencil guideline that runs parallel to the flight of stairs, then hang the border. Where it overlaps at the top and bottom of the stairs, cut from corner to corner as before and brush flat.

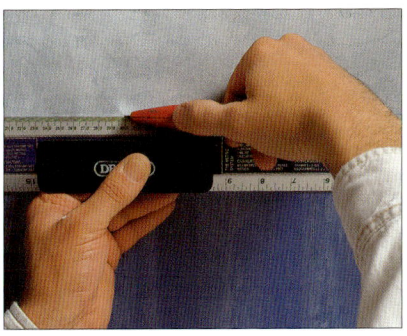

2 Brush the ends of the paper flat, trim through both layers along the guideline and remove the waste. Brush the ends back.

3 When you have completed the wall, centre the border over the butt join between the two papers and wipe away any traces of adhesive.

2 Overlap the ends of the lengths of border and cut through both layers from corner to corner, using a straightedge and sharp knife.

3 Remove the waste pieces of paper and smooth down the cut edges to form a neat mitred join.

PAPERING CEILINGS

Wallpapering a ceiling is not as difficult as it may appear. The techniques used are the same as for walls and there are few obstacles or awkward angles to deal with. Although the job will be easier with two people, it is possible to achieve good results on your own. Adequate access equipment, however, is essential and will make the job very much easier.

ACCESS EQUIPMENT

Before tackling this job, it is important to consider how you plan to reach the ceiling safely. Access equipment will be needed that allows you to hang a full length across the room. Scaffold boards supported at either end by sturdy stepladders or trestles will create a flat, level walkway spanning the full width of the room, and can be adjusted to a working height to suit you. Use two boards tied together for a distance of more than 1.5m (5ft) and provide support in the centre.

PAPERING SEQUENCES

Plan the papering sequence so that a paper that has a definite pattern is centralized across the room. A sloping ceiling can be papered either to match the ceiling or the walls, but do not attempt to hang a single length down the sloping surface on to the wall below. Treat the wide angle between the two surfaces as an internal corner.

HANGING THE FIRST LENGTH

Assemble your work platform across the main window of the room. Ceilings should be papered by hanging lengths across the room parallel to the window, working away from the light so that you are not in your own shadow and daylight will not emphasize the joins between lengths.

To mark a guideline for the first length, measure one roll width less 25mm (1in) out from each corner and drive in a nail at each point. Tie a taut, chalked length of string between the nails, then snap the string against the ceiling to create a guide for the first length. If hanging paper on a white ceiling, make sure you use coloured chalk to coat the string. ▶

HANDLING PAPER

As long lengths of paper are often needed for a ceiling, fold these concertina-style after pasting. When papering, they are easier to handle if you support them with a spare roll of wallpaper.

1 Measure out from each corner to a distance equal to the width of a roll and mark the positions with nails.

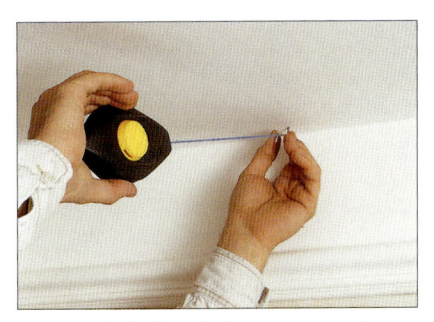

2 Tie a chalked length of string between the nails, making sure it is taut. Snap it against the ceiling to leave a chalk guideline.

3 Hang the first length against the chalk line, brushing it into place as you go. If possible, have someone else support the folded paper.

4 Use the bristles of a paperhanger's brush to ease the paper into the angle between the wall and ceiling.

5 Use the back of the scissors blade to crease the paper. Then pull it back from the ceiling and trim along the long edge. Brush the cut edge back into place firmly. Treat each end of the length in the same manner.

Cut the first strip of paper to length, allowing an extra 100mm (4in) for trimming, then paste and fold it concertina-style. Place one end so that about half of the trimming allowance laps on to the wall and the edge of the paper is aligned with the chalk line, then brush it firmly into place.

If you are papering around a bay window or alcove, make diagonal release cuts at the external corners to allow the paper to lay flat. Brush the paper into the side wall of the recess and trim the edges to fit along the edge of the ceiling.

Once the first length of wallpaper is in position, crease and trim the long edge into the angle between the wall and ceiling first, followed by each end, using normal wallpapering techniques. Continue hanging lengths of paper across the ceiling, trimming their ends where they meet the walls. Finally, cut the last length roughly to the width required, making sure you allow 25mm (1in) for trimming along the edge of the paper. Hang and trim it in the same manner as the first length.

DEALING WITH PROBLEM AREAS

If you are faced with papering around a bay window or an alcove, make diagonal release cuts in the paper at the external corners of the recess to allow the paper to lay flat against the ceiling. Brush the paper into the side walls of the recess, crease it and trim it to fit along the edges of the ceiling.

PAPERING AN ALCOVE

ABOVE: Paper into a bay window or an external corner by making a diagonal cut to ease the paper around the external angle.

A SLOPING CEILING

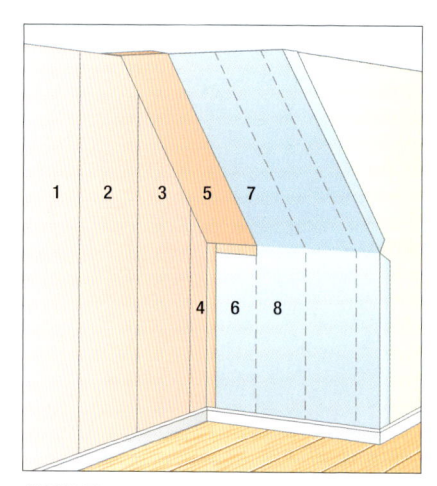

ABOVE: The sequence for papering a wall and a sloping ceiling. Do not try to hang a complete length on the sloping surface and down the wall.

PAPERING ARCHES

If possible, arrange your starting position on the wall containing the arch so that you will be left with an even width to fill between the arch and each full-width drop on each side of it. This will ensure a balanced appearance. Hang the paper so that it overlaps the arch, matching the pattern to the last length hung, then trim off the waste to within 25mm (1in) from the edge of the arch. Brush the trimming allowance on to the inner face of the arch, making right-angled cuts into the paper every 12mm (½in) around the curve of the arch so that it lays flat. Paper across the rest of the arch, length by length, using the same method of cutting to cope with the curved edge.

For the inner face, cut a strip of paper 35mm (1¼in) wider than the arch. If the paper has a definite pattern, use two strips with a butt joint at the highest point. Align the manufactured edge of the cut strip with one edge of the arch and trim the other edge with a knife once the paper has been smoothed into place.

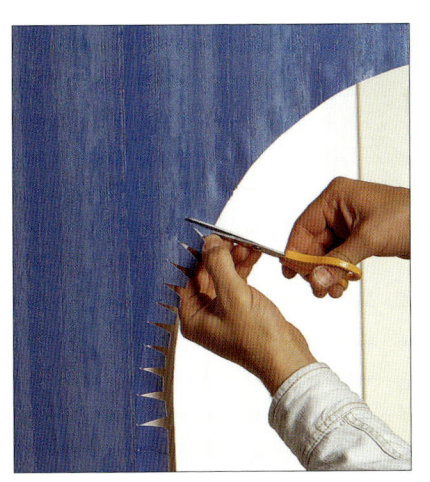

1 Trim away excess paper from the arch to leave a trimming allowance of 25mm (1in).

2 Make right-angled cuts to ease the paper around the curve of the arch.

3 Paper the inner face of the arch last, joining strips at the highest point.

PAPERING STAIRWELLS

When working in stairwells, safety is the main priority. Access equipment suitable for use on stairs may be hired, but you can also construct your own safe work platform.

ORDER OF WORK

Hang the longest length first, and work upward from the foot of the stairs.

Hang the top half of each length, but leave the rest of the folded length hanging while you move the work platform out of the way. Then smooth the lower half of each length into place.

When measuring lengths for a well wall, make sure that you allow for the gradient of the stairs.

Tackle the head wall next, hanging the top portions of the two or three drops needed, leaving the remainder of the folded lengths hanging. Adjust the work platform so that the planks rest on a stair or ladder and are supported by a ladder at the bottom. Smooth the lower portions of the lengths on to the head wall, and trim neatly in line with the hallway ceiling. Hang lengths along the lower head wall from the foot of the stairs.

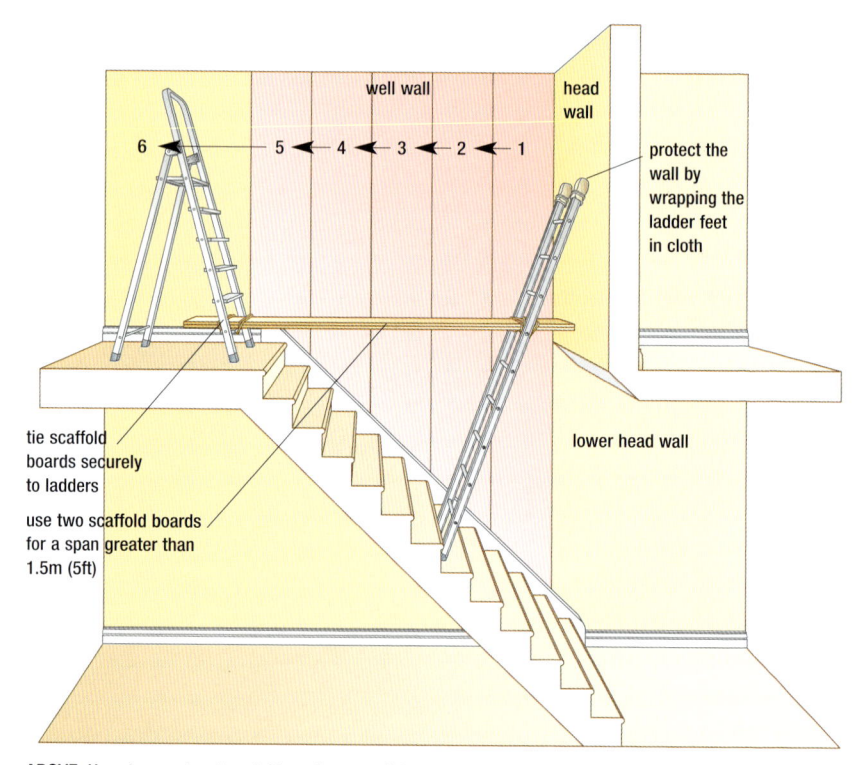

ABOVE: How to construct a platform for a straight staircase and order of papering for the well wall.

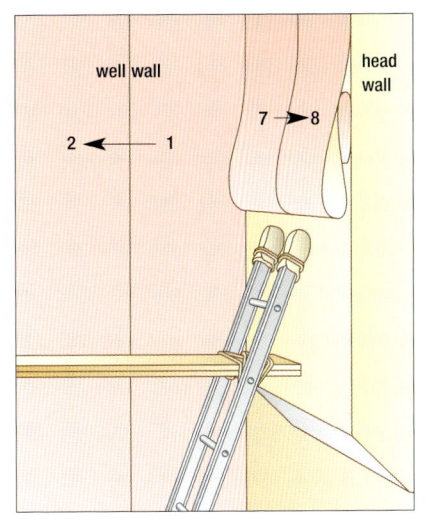

ABOVE: The order of papering for the head wall of a stairwell. Note that the ends of the straight ladder have been padded to prevent damage to the wall. Adjust the access equipment before brushing the lower half of the wall.

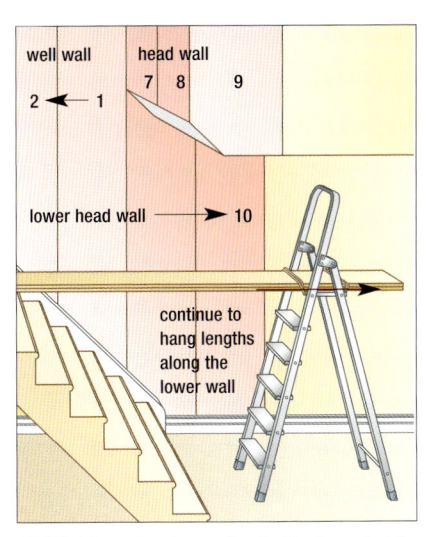

ABOVE: The order of papering for the lower head wall of a staircase. Work off the foot of the stairs, using a scaffold board and stepladders as necessary. Trim the paper neatly at the angles between ceiling, stairs and wall.

ABOVE: Be especially careful to take accurate measurements. Mistakes can be costly when working with very long lengths.

ABOVE: Hang the longest length first and work upward from the foot of the stairs. Hang the top half of each length first.

COMMON PROBLEMS

Inadequate preparation and poor papering techniques, rather than faults with the paper itself, are the cause of most wallpapering problems. Some minor mistakes such as air bubbles are quite easy to remedy, but if the problem is extensive, it is better to strip off the affected area and start again.

DEALING WITH BUBBLES

Bubbles that remain after the paste has dried are caused by not allowing the paper to soak for long enough, not having brushed out the paper properly, or by poor preparation, which prevents the paper from sticking to the wall.

With a small bubble, you may be able to cut a slit in the paper and inject a little paste behind it with a syringe. Then press the paper down and carefully wipe off any excess paste.

For a larger bubble, make two diagonal cuts with a sharp knife. Carefully peel back the flaps and use a small paintbrush to apply paste to the back of each. Press the flaps back against the wall and brush flat, again wiping off any excess paste.

REPAIRING A BUBBLE

1 When faced with the occasional large bubble in a papered surface, make diagonal cuts across its face with a sharp knife. Then peel back the resulting flaps.

2 Apply more paste to the wall or the backs of the cut flaps of paper. Press back into place and brush down firmly. If there are lots of bubbles, it may be better to replace the drop.

REPAIRING TEARS

Often, tears are not as bad as they look. If the tear is small, carefully apply some overlap adhesive to the torn piece and ease it back into place with the tips of a brush.

When faced with a large tear in wallpaper, remove loose and damaged paper by tearing it gently from the wall. Tear, rather than cut, a patch from a new piece of paper so that the pattern matches the surrounding area, then feather the edge by tearing away a 6mm (¼in) strip from the back. Paste the patch and lightly brush it into place.

With a vinyl wallcovering, cut a patch so that the pattern matches the surrounding area and tape it to the wall over the damage. Cut through both layers to form a square, remove the damaged vinyl from the wall, then paste and fit the patch.

REPAIRING DAMAGED WALLCOVERINGS

1 Carefully tear away any loose or damaged wallpaper, feathering the edges.

2 Make a matching patch by carefully tearing the paper. Feather the edges and stick it down.

REPAIRING VINYL

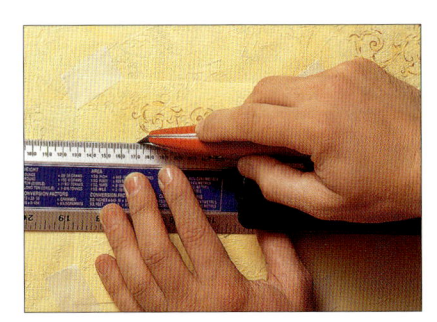

1 Cut out damaged vinyl and a new patch taped on to the wall to match in one go.

2 Remove the old vinyl from within the cut square and apply the patch.

OTHER WALLPAPERING TIPS

By and large, hanging a wallcovering is a straightforward process which, in most cases, will go without a hitch. However, now and again you may come across a difficult situation that needs overcoming. Some of the most common problems are covered here, and if you follow the techniques you will be able to give your decorative scheme a professional-looking finish.

LONG LENGTHS

In the stairwell the drop from ceiling to floor will be considerable in places. Get someone to support the weight of the wallcovering while you hang the top portion.

BULKY OVERLAPS

Overlapped edges can create bulky seams in relief and embossed wallpapers. Feather the trimming allowance by carefully tearing down the edge, then flatten the torn paper with a seam roller before hanging the overlapping length.

GAPS IN SEAMS

Paper shrinking as it dries, due to poor pasting technique or poor butt joins, can cause gaps at the seams. To avoid this, disguise the gaps with a fine felt-tipped pen, paint or crayon in a similar shade to the base colour.

CURLING EDGES

These are caused by inadequate pasting, paste drying out during hanging or, on overlapped vinyl, the wrong paste having been used. Lift the edge of the paper with the back of a knife blade and apply a small amount of paste with a fine brush. Smooth the paper firmly into place with a damp sponge. For overlapping edges on vinyl wallpaper, use vinyl overlap adhesive.

POOR PATTERN MATCH

Usually the result of inaccurate cutting and hanging, patterns not matching may also be caused by variations in the paper along the seams. Check the whole batch and return faulty rolls to the retailer. Straight-match patterns can be difficult to match, especially in internal corners where the edge has been trimmed. Use a level to check that prominent motifs are level across the corner.

SHINY PATCHES

Brushing matt (flat) finish wallpapers too vigorously can cause shiny patches. Normally, they cannot be removed, but rubbing gently with a piece of fresh white bread may disguise them. Bread is also useful for removing greasy fingermarks from non-washable papers.

STAINS ALONG SEAMS

Paste that has been allowed to dry on the face of the paper can result in stains. These are difficult to remove, but if the paper is washable, try wiping with a sponge and a solution of mild detergent. Bear this in mind while working and sponge off splashes before they have a chance to dry.

WALLCOVERING TECHNIQUES • 147

ABOVE: Supporting the weight of long lengths will help prevent the wallpaper tearing.

ABOVE: Feather the edge of relief wallpaper at external and internal corners.

ABOVE: Disguise gaps with a felt-tipped pen, a crayon or watercolour paint.

ABOVE: Apply wallpaper adhesive to curling edges with a fine brush.

ABOVE: Use a spirit (carpenter's) level to check that motifs are level across a corner.

ABOVE: Rubbing with a ball of white bread may make shiny patches less obvious.

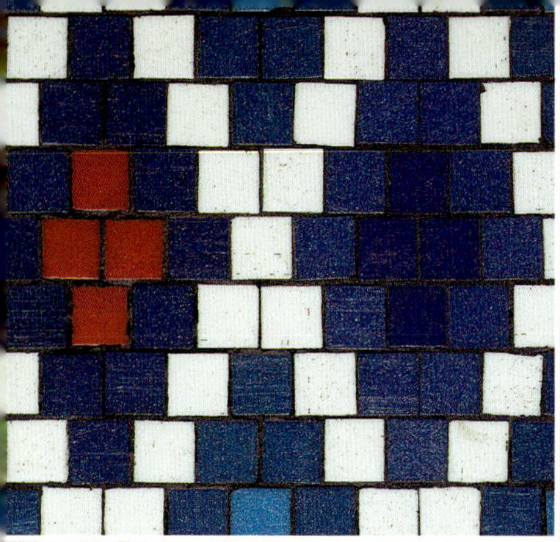

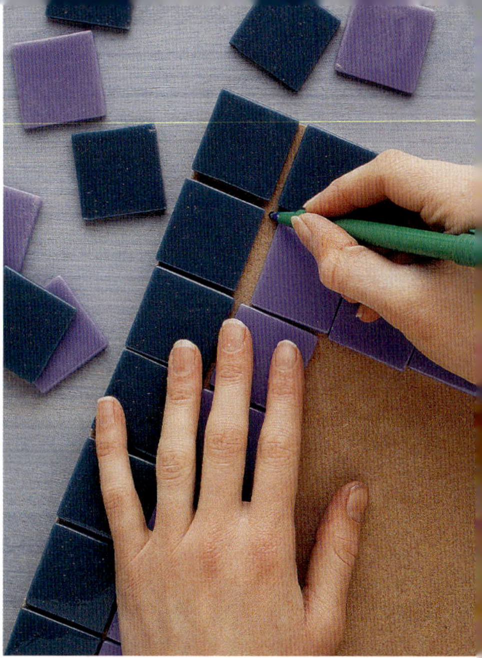

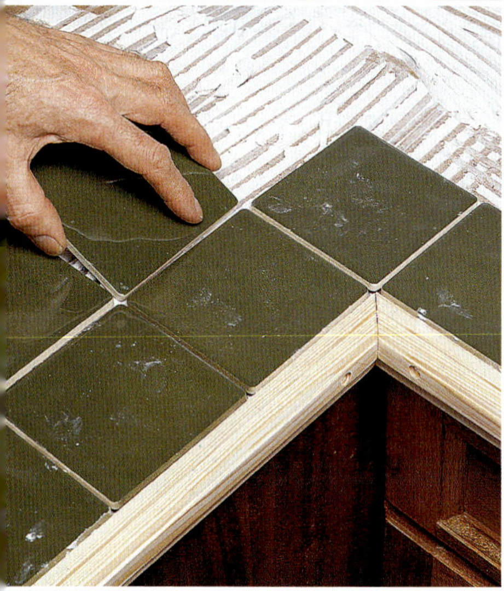

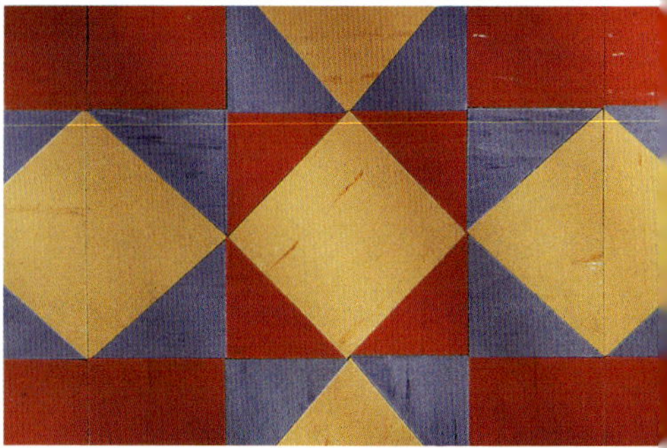

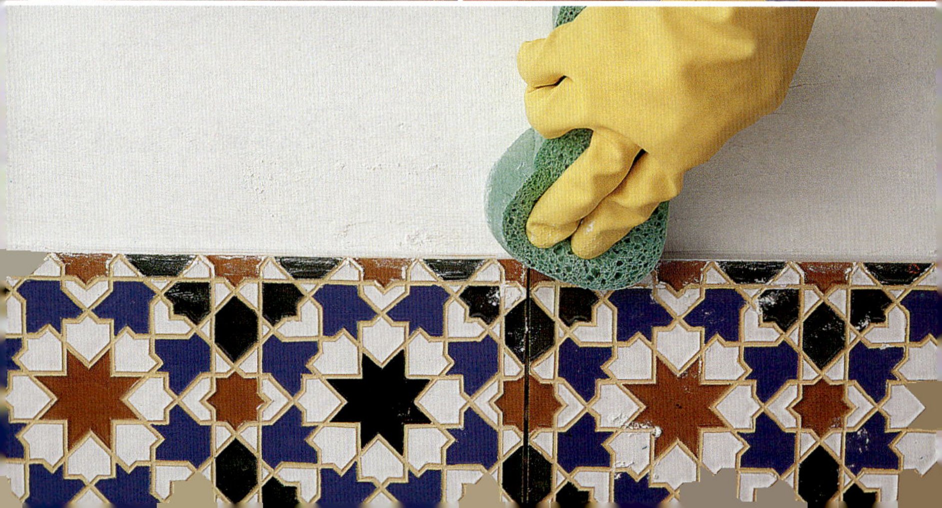

HOME TILING

- Tiling materials
- Tiling preparation
- Tiling techniques
- Decorative tiling layouts

INTRODUCTION

Tiles have a long pedigree in the interior decoration business. Faience (glazed earthenware) plaques have been found in Cretan buildings dating from around 1800 BC, and a tradition of ceramic wall and floor decoration was established soon after this farther east in Syria and Persia (now Iran). Mosaic wall and floor decorations, incorporating stone (usually marble), glass and ceramic tesserae, were a major feature of Roman interiors. The technique spread to North Africa and thence to Spain, and the Renaissance soon led to widespread use of decorative tiling all over Europe.

Probably the most important centre of ceramic tile making in Europe was Holland, where the creation of individually hand-painted tiles in a unique blue-grey colour soon made Delft famous in the early 17th century. From there, the use of tiles spread rapidly, and it was not long before mass production was introduced.

The end product is the familiar ceramic tile we use today. The manufacturing and printing technology may have changed, and the adhesives and grouts used may have improved, but the result would be familiar to a 17th-century Dutchman.

The 20th century brought new kinds of tile, notably vinyl, linoleum and cork tiles, which owe their existence to advances in plastics and resins technology. They offer a combination of properties that make them useful alternatives to ceramics in a wide range of situations, and they are generally much less expensive.

Here in the 21st century there is a huge range to choose from – in every style imaginable – but the techniques for working with them remain the same.

INTRODUCTION • 151

The following pages concentrate on working with ceramic wall tiles, since these are the most popular of the types available. A wide range of situations is dealt with, from splashbacks to whole walls, including information on working around obstacles such as door and window openings and on creating special effects with tiled borders and feature panels. There are also sections on using other types of wall tiles, and on tiling floors.

ABOVE: Tile friezes and panels have been used to clad walls since the Renaissance, and can make a stunning focal point in a garden or courtyard.

LEFT, BELOW AND OPPOSITE: Tiles have never before been available in such a profusion of styles and designs. These range from highly glazed plain types to more rustic versions with matt (flat) or textured surfaces, and patterns that look as though they have been hand-painted.

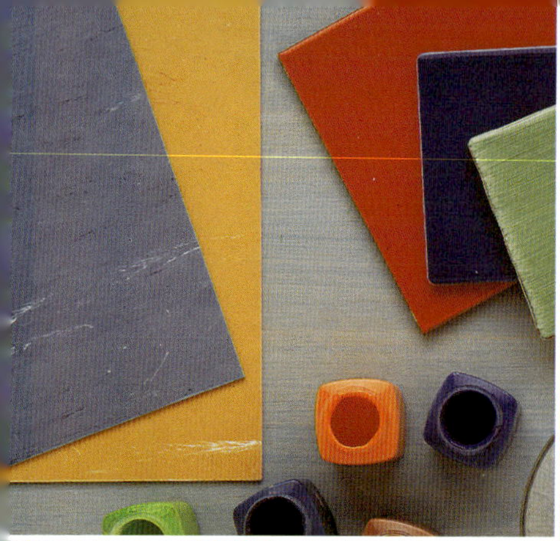
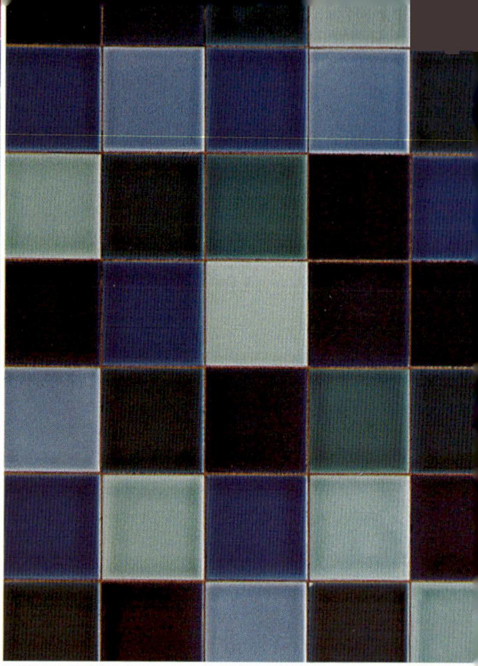
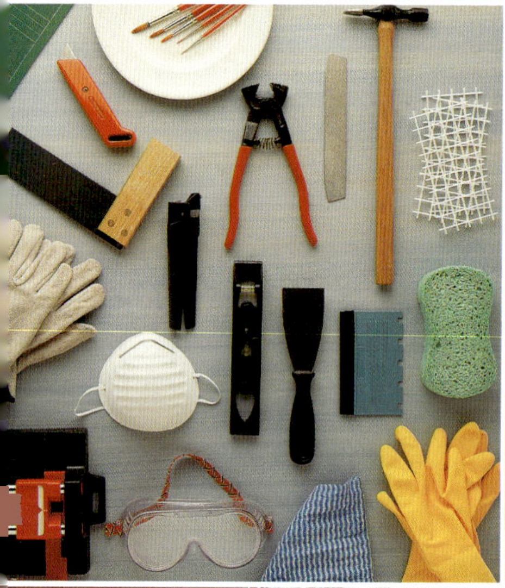
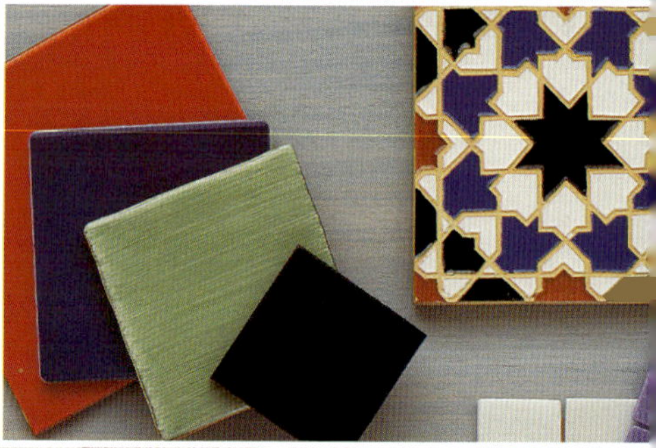
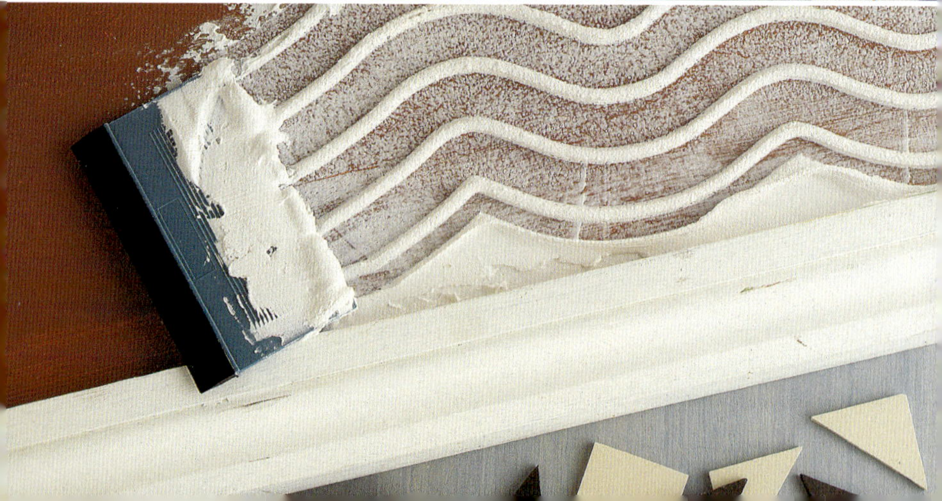

TILING MATERIALS

Ceramic tiles provide the most durable of all finishes in the home, whether for walls, floors or worktops, and there has never been a bigger choice of colours, designs, shapes and sizes. Vinyl, lino and cork floor tiles offer an alternative floor finish to ceramics, and offer the advantages of ease of laying combined with a surface finish that is warmer to the touch and also less noisy underfoot than ceramic tiles. For a hard-wearing and attractive floor, there are also quarry tiles, ideal for areas that receive a lot of foot traffic. For most tiling jobs, you will need tools for measuring, spacing and cutting the tiles, and adhesive and grout for attaching the tiles. Notched spreaders and grout finishers are usually sold with adhesives and grouts.

WALL TILES

In today's homes, the surfaces that are tiled more often than any other are walls, especially in rooms such as kitchens and bathrooms, where a hard-wearing, water-resistant and easy-to-clean decorative finish is required. Often the tiling protects only the most vulnerable areas such as splashbacks above wash basins and shower cubicles; but sometimes the whole room is tiled from floor to ceiling.

Tiles used for wall decoration are generally fairly thin, measuring from 4 to 6mm ($^3/_{16}$ to $^1/_4$in) thick, although some imported tiles (especially the larger sizes) may be rather thicker than this. The commonest kinds are square, measuring 108mm (4$^1/_4$in) or 150mm (6in) across, but rectangular tiles measuring 200 x 100mm (8 x 4in) and 200 x 150mm (8 x 6in) are becoming more popular.

Tile designs change with fashions in interior design, and current demand seems to be mainly for large areas of neutral or small-patterned tiles interspersed with individual motif tiles on a matching background. Plain tiles, often with a simple border frame, are also popular, as are tiles that create a frieze effect when laid alongside one another. Some sets of tiles build up into larger designs (known as feature panels), which can look quite striking when surrounded by an area of plain tiling.

The surface of ceramic wall tiles is no longer always highly glazed, as it was traditionally. Now there are semi-matt finishes, often with a slight surface texture that softens the harsh glare produced by a high-gloss surface.

Tile edges have changed over the years too. Once, special round-edged tiles were used for the exposed edges of tiled areas, and plain ones with unglazed square edges elsewhere. Nowadays, tiles are either the universal type or the standard square-edged variety. Both types usually have two adjacent edges glazed so they can be used as perimeter tiles, and sometimes all four edges are glazed.

LEFT: Wall tiles can be used to make eye-catching schemes, mixed geometrically or at random.

MOSAICS

Mosaics are just tiny tiles – usually plain in colour, sometimes with a pattern – that are sold made up in sheets on an open-weave cloth backing. These sheets are laid like larger tiles in a bed of adhesive, and all the gaps, including those on the surface of the sheet, are grouted afterwards. Square mosaics are the most common, but roundels, hexagons and other interlocking shapes are also available. Sheets are usually square and 300mm (12in) across, and are often sold in packs of five or ten. The best way of estimating quantities is to work out the area to be covered and to divide that by the coverage figure given on the pack to work out how many packs to buy. Note that wall and floor types are of different thicknesses, as with ordinary ceramic tiles.

ABOVE AND BELOW: Mosaic tiles are regaining the popularity they enjoyed in times past, but laying them is definitely a labour of love.

FLOOR TILES

Although less widely used than wall tiles, ceramic floor tiles are a popular choice for heavy traffic areas such as porches and hallways. They are generally thicker and harder-fired than wall tiles, to enable them to stand up to heavy wear without cracking. Again, a wide range of plain colours, simple textures and more elaborate designs is available. Common sizes are 150mm (6in) and 200mm (8in) squares and 200 x 100mm (8 x 4in) rectangles; hexagons are also available in plain colours, and a popular variation is a plain octagonal tile that is laid with small square coloured or decorated inserts at the intersections.

Quarry tiles are unglazed ceramic floor tiles with a brown, buff or reddish colour, and are a popular choice for hallways, conservatories and country-style kitchens. They are usually laid in a mortar bed, and after the joints have been grouted the tiles must be sealed with boiled linseed oil or a recommended proprietary sealer. Common sizes are 100mm (4in) and 150mm (6in) square. Special shaped tiles are also available for forming upstands at floor edges.

Terracotta tiles look similar to quarry tiles, but are larger and are fired at lower temperatures, so they are more porous. They are sealed in the same way as quarry tiles. Squares, ranging in size between 200 and 400mm (8 and 16in), and rectangles are the commonest shapes, but octagonal versions with small square in-fill tiles are also popular.

Cork tiles come in a small range of colours and textures. Their surface feels warm and relatively soft underfoot, and they also give some worthwhile heat and sound insulation – particularly

FAR LEFT: Ceramic floor tile with a painted medieval design.

MIDDLE: Ceramic tiles provide a durable and waterproof surface for bathroom floors.

LEFT: Quarry tiles provide a durable and attractive floor covering, and are especially suited to kitchens and conservatories.

useful in bathrooms, kitchens, halls and even children's bedrooms. The cheapest types have to be sealed to protect the surface after they have been laid, but the more expensive vinyl-coated floor types can be walked on as soon as they have been stuck down. They need little more than an occasional wash and polish to keep them in good condition. However, even the best cork floor tiles are prone to damage from sharp heels and heavy furniture, for example.

Vinyl tiles come in a very wide range of plain and patterned types, and generally resist wear better than cork, so they can be used on floors subject to fairly heavy wear. However, they are a little less gentle on the feet. Some of the more expensive types give very passable imitations of luxury floor coverings such as marble and terrazzo. Most are made in self-adhesive form and very little maintenance is needed once they have been laid.

Modern lino tiles, made from natural materials rather than the plastic resins used in vinyl tiles, offer far better performance than traditional linoleum. They come in a range of bright and subtle colours and interesting patterns, often with pre-cut borders.

All these types generally come in 300mm (12in) squares, although larger squares and rectangles are available in some of the more expensive ranges. They are generally sold in packs of nine, covering roughly 0.84 sq m (1 sq yd), although many kinds are often available singly.

ABOVE LEFT: Cork is the warmest of tiled floor coverings underfoot, and when sealed is good-looking and durable too.
MIDDLE: The more expensive types of vinyl floor tile offer superb imitations of other materials, such as wood, marble and terrazzo.
ABOVE RIGHT: Lino tiles offer a warm, attractive and durable alternative to cork and vinyl floor coverings in rooms such as kitchens and hallways.

ADHESIVE AND GROUTING

Both adhesive and grout for wall tiling are now usually sold ready-mixed in plastic tubs complete with a notched plastic spreader. For areas that will get the occasional splash or may suffer from condensation, a water-resistant adhesive and grout is perfectly adequate, but for surfaces such as shower cubicles, which will have to withstand prolonged wetting, it is essential to use both waterproof adhesive and waterproof grout. Always use waterproof grout on tiled worktops; ordinary grout will harbour germs. Some silicone sealant or mastic (caulking) may also be needed for waterproofing joints where tiling abuts baths, basins and shower trays.

ADHESIVE

Ceramic floor-tile adhesive is widely available in powder form as well as ready-mixed. It is best always to use a waterproof type (plus waterproof grout), even in theoretically dry areas.

Special water-based adhesive is the type to choose for both cork and lino tiles; solvent-based contact adhesives were formerly the first choice, but their fumes are extremely unpleasant and also dangerously inflammable, and they are no longer recommended. For vinyl-coated cork tiles, a special vinyl acrylic adhesive is needed. For vinyl tiles, an emulsion-type latex flooring adhesive is the best choice.

It is important that you allow adhesive to dry for at least 24 hours before applying grout.

GROUTING

Grout is generally white, but coloured grout is on sale and will make a feature of the grout lines (an effect that looks best with plain or fairly neutral patterned tiles).

Adhesive and grout are both sold in a range of quantities, sometimes labelled by weight, sometimes by volume; always check the coverage specified by the manufacturer on the packaging when buying, so as not to buy too much or run out halfway through the job.

TOOLS FOR ADHESIVE AND GROUTING

Notched spreaders are used for creating a series of ridges in the adhesive, allowing it to spread when the tile is pressed home, and ensuring that an even thickness of adhesive is applied. They are available in various sizes. Grouting tools include a grout spreader, grout finisher and grout remover.

OTHER MATERIALS

A damp sponge or cloth is needed to remove excess grout from the faces of the tiles, and a clean, dry cloth is needed to polish the tiles afterwards.

For protection, a face mask, safety goggles and leather gloves should be worn, especially when cutting and smoothing tiles, and when handling cut tiles. Rubber gloves should be worn when using tile adhesive, grout and grout colourant. If your skin is very sensitive, use a barrier cream also.

adhesive

small notched adhesive spreader

large notched adhesive spreader

grout finisher

grout

grout remover

grout spreader

polishing cloth

rubber gloves

sponge

RENEWING GROUT

Over the years, the grout in an existing tiled surface may become discoloured or cracked, which could cause serious problems in a shower. Fortunately, it can be renewed without having to strip off all the tiles. However, being very hard, it is difficult to remove and you will need a proper grout remover. This has a hardened, sharp serrated blade.

If the grout is only discoloured, it can be removed to a depth of about 3mm ($\frac{1}{8}$in), then new grout applied on top; if it is cracked, however, go to the thickness of the tile before regrouting.

Take care when using a grout remover, as it may chip the glaze along the edges of the tiles, which will be difficult to disguise and may lead to water penetrating the tiled surface.

A grout remover is also useful for removing a damaged tile prior to replacing it. After raking out all the grout around the damaged tile, chip out the tile carefully with a hammer and cold chisel. Wear safety goggles and thick leather gloves to protect your eyes and hands from flying shards of tile, which will be sharp.

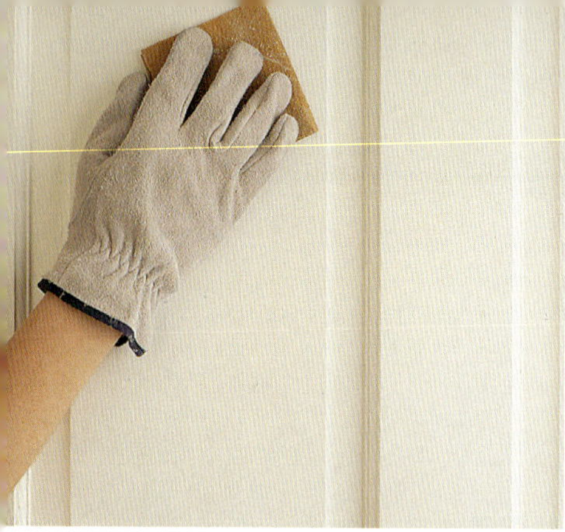
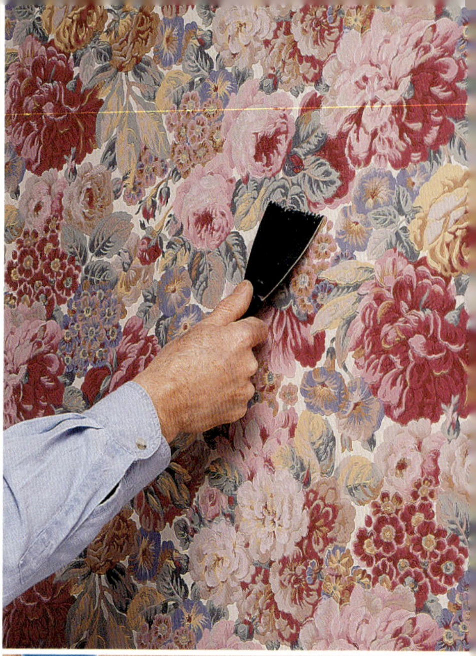
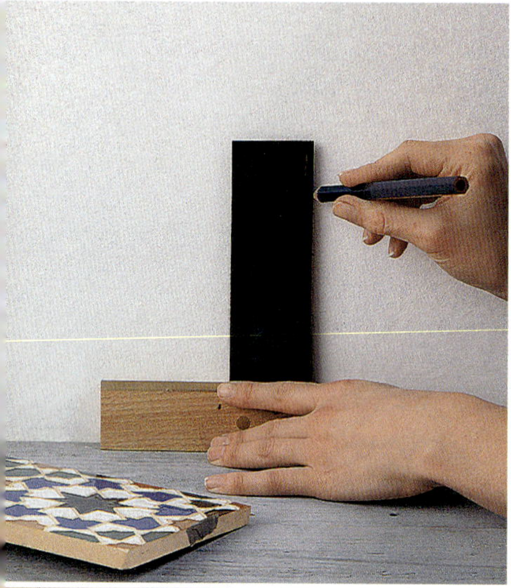
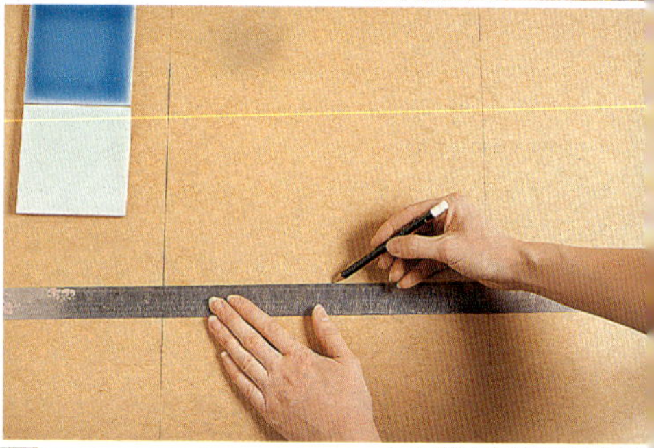
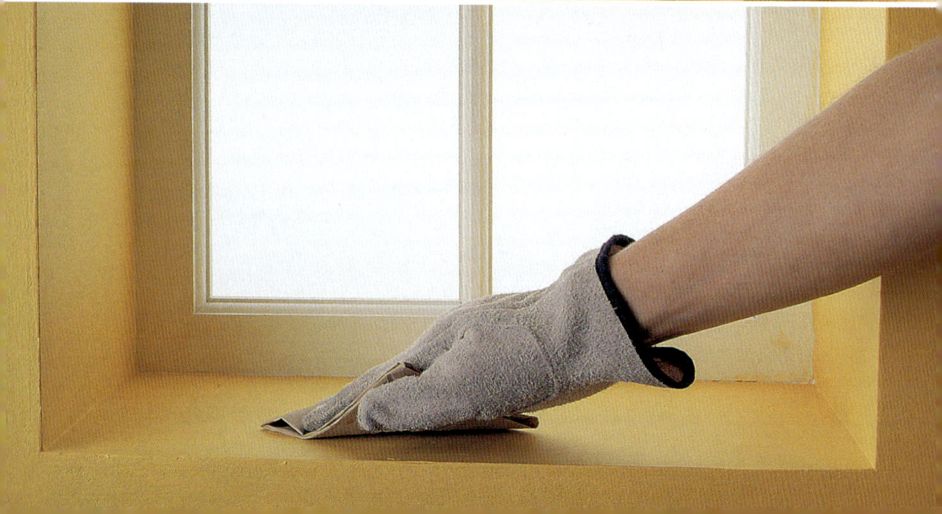

TILING PREPARATION

The best way to practise tiling skills is to begin by covering just a small area such as a washbasin splashback, where setting out the tiles so that they are centred on the area concerned is a simple job, and there is very little tile cutting to do. For a larger area – a whole wall, or perhaps even a complete room – exactly the same techniques are used. The big difference is the sheer scale of the job, which makes the preliminary setting-out by far the most important part. The problem is that walls are seldom blank surfaces, and there may be a number of obstacles to tile around. Care must be taken to get the best fit with these inflexible tile squares, without needing to cut impossibly thin slivers to fill in gaps.

PLANNING

The most important thing to do is to plan precisely where the whole tiles will fall. On a flat, uninterrupted wall this is quite easy; simply find the centreline of the wall and plan the tiling to start from there. However, there will probably be obstacles such as window reveals, door openings and built-in furniture in the room, all competing to be the centre of attention, and it will be necessary to work out the best "centre-point" while all the time trying to avoid having very thin-cut tile borders and edges.

It is best to use a device called a tiling gauge – a batten (furring strip) marked out in tile widths – to work this out. The gauge is easy to make from a straight piece of timber about 1.2m (4ft) long, marked off with pencil lines to match the size of the tile. Use this to ensure that the tiles will be centred accurately on major features such as window reveals, with a border of cut tiles of equal width at the end of each row or column of tiles.

The next stage is the actual setting-out. With large areas of tiling, two things are vitally important. First, the tile rows must be exactly horizontal; if they are not, errors will accumulate as the tiles extend across the wall, throwing the verticals out of alignment with disastrous results. When tiling right around a room, inaccurate levels mean that rows will not match up at the start and finish points. Second, the tiles need some support while the adhesive sets; without it, they may slump down the wall.

The solution is to fix a line of battens across the wall – or right around the room – just above the level of the skirting (baseboard), securing them with partly-driven masonry nails (tacks) so that they can be removed later when the adhesive has set. The precise level will be dictated by setting-out with the tiling gauge, but usually will be between half and three-quarters of a tile width above the skirting. Do not rely on this being level; it may not be. Draw the line out in pencil first, using the spirit (carpenter's) level, then pin the battens up and check the level again. If everything is straight, it is time to start tiling.

ESTIMATING QUANTITIES

When working out how many tiles you will need, first select the tile size. Then set out the area to be tiled on the wall and use the setting-out marks to count how many tiles are needed in each horizontal row and each vertical column. Count cut tiles as whole tiles, then multiply the two figures together to obtain the total required. Always add a further 5 per cent to the total to allow for breakages and miscalculations.

NUMBER OF TILES NEEDED

TILE SIZE	NO/SQ M	NO/SQ YD
108 x 108mm (4¼ x 4¼in)	86	71
200 x 100mm (8 x 4in)	48	41
150 x 150mm (6 x 6in)	43	36

MAKING AND USING A TILING GAUGE

1 Use a pencil and one of the chosen tiles to mark up a length of wood for use as a tiling gauge. Allow for the width of tile spacers if they are to be used.

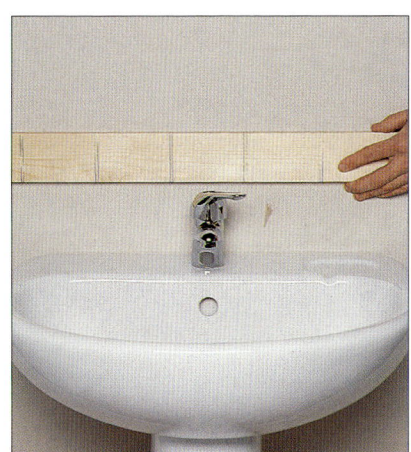

2 Hold the tiling gauge horizontally against the wall to see how many tiles each row will take, and also to centre the tiling on a wall feature or window opening.

3 Similarly, hold the gauge vertically to assess how many tiles will fill each column, and where best to position any cut tiles that may be needed at top or bottom.

SETTING OUT TILED WALLS

Careful setting-out is essential to the success of any tiling job. The object is to obtain a balanced look to each tiled surface, with the rows of tiles being centred on the wall itself or on some prominent feature, much like you would centre a wallpaper pattern. This will ensure that any cut tiles at the margins or around a feature are of equal size.

Doors and window openings particularly can cause problems and often require quite a bit of thought.

TILING AROUND A DOOR

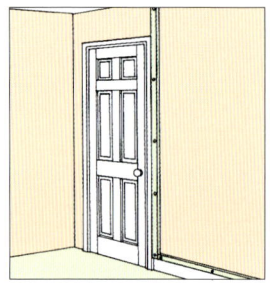

1 If the door is close to the room corner, start with whole tiles next to the frame. Use a vertical tile guide if the architrave (trim) is not truly vertical (it may not be).

2 Tile the whole of the main wall area, adding cut tiles next to the room corner and at ceiling level. Remove the tile supports when the adhesive has had time to set.

3 Fit a tile support above the door, in line with the tile rows, and another between it and the other room corner, just above skirting (baseboard) level.

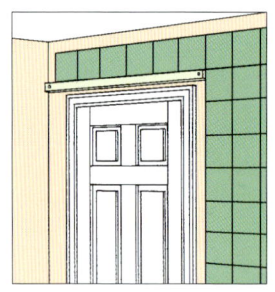

4 Carry on placing whole tiles above the door opening, filling in with cut tiles at the room corner and at ceiling level, as in step 2.

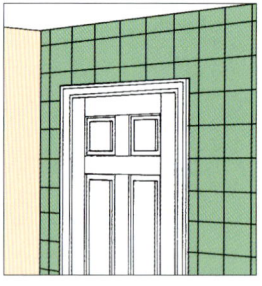

5 Remove the tile support above the door opening and fill in all around it with cut and whole tiles as required. Grout the tiles when the adhesive has set.

6 If the door opening is near or at the centre of the wall, centre the tiling on it and fix tile support battens (furring strips) as required.

TILING AROUND A WINDOW

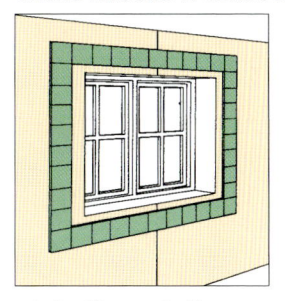

1 For tiling a wall with a window opening, first decide on where to centre the tiling. On a wall with one window, centre the tiling on a line drawn through its centre.

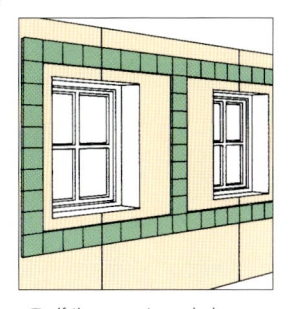

2 If there are two window openings in a wall, centre the tiles on a line drawn through the centre of each window, provided an exact number of whole tiles will fit between them.

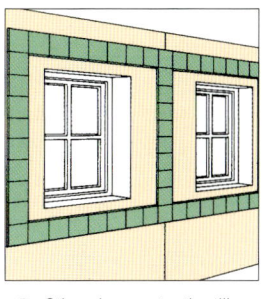

3 Otherwise, centre the tiling on a line drawn midway between the windows. Always work across and up the wall, placing whole tiles up to window-sill level, then up the wall at each side of the window. Fit a tile support above the opening to support whole tiles there.

4 Remove the support strips and cut tiles to fit on the face wall at each side and across the top of the window. To tile a window reveal, place whole tiles so they overlap the edges of the tiles on the wall face. Then fill in between these and the frame with cut tiles.

POSITIONING CUT TILES FOR PANELS

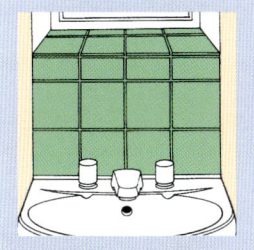

If the height of a tiled splashback is determined by a feature such as a mirror or window, position a row of cut tiles along the top of the panel. Make sure their top edges are overlapped by any tiles in a window recess.

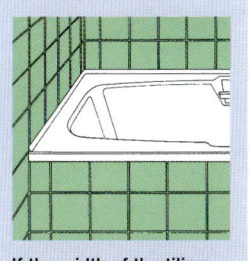

If the width of the tiling is defined, as with a bath panel, always position cut tiles of equal size at each side.

SETTING OUT TILED FLOORS

Tiled floors need careful setting-out if the end result is to look neat and professional. This is especially important with glazed ceramic and quarry tiles and also patterned vinyl and lino tiles, but matters rather less with plain vinyl or cork tiles where the finished effect is of uniform colour and the joints between the tiles are practically invisible.

Fortunately the necessary setting-out is much easier with floor tiles than wall tiles, since the tiles can be dry-laid on the floor surface and moved around until a starting point is found that gives the best arrangement, with cut border tiles of approximately equal size all around the perimeter of the room.

In a regularly shaped room, start by finding the centre-point of the floor by linking the midpoints of opposite pairs of walls with string lines. In an irregularly shaped room, place string lines as shown in step 2 so that they avoid obstructions, then link the midpoints of opposite pairs of strings to find the room's centre. Now dry-lay rows of tiles out toward the walls in each direction, allowing for any joint thickness, to see how many whole tiles will fit in and to check whether this results in over-narrow border tiles or awkward cuts against obstacles. Move the rows slightly to improve the fit if necessary, then chalk the string lines and snap them against the floor to mark the starting point.

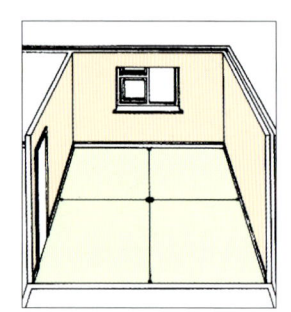

1 In a regularly shaped room, find the centre by linking the midpoints of opposite pairs of walls with string lines.

2 In an irregularly shaped room, use string lines that avoid obstacles, and link their midpoints to find the centre.

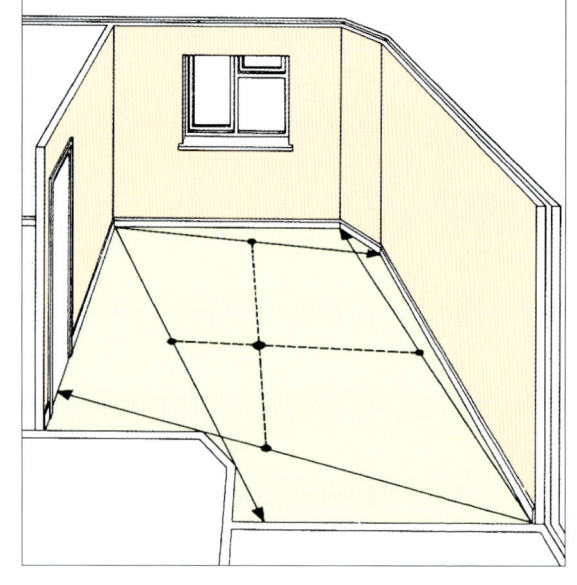

TILING PREPARATION • 167

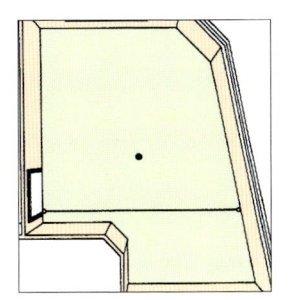

3 To ensure that tiles will be laid square to the door threshold if the walls are out of square, place a string line at right angles to the door opening across the room to the opposite wall.

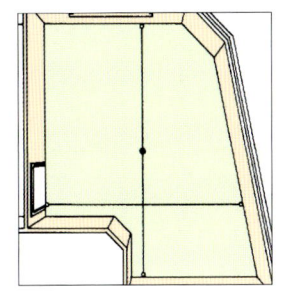

4 Place a second string line at right angles to the first so that it passes through the room's centre-point.

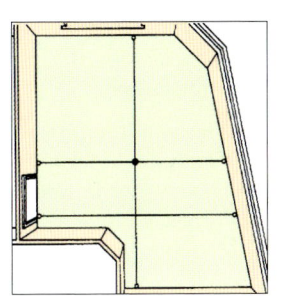

5 Place a third string line at right angles to the second, again passing through the centre-point, to complete the laying guide.

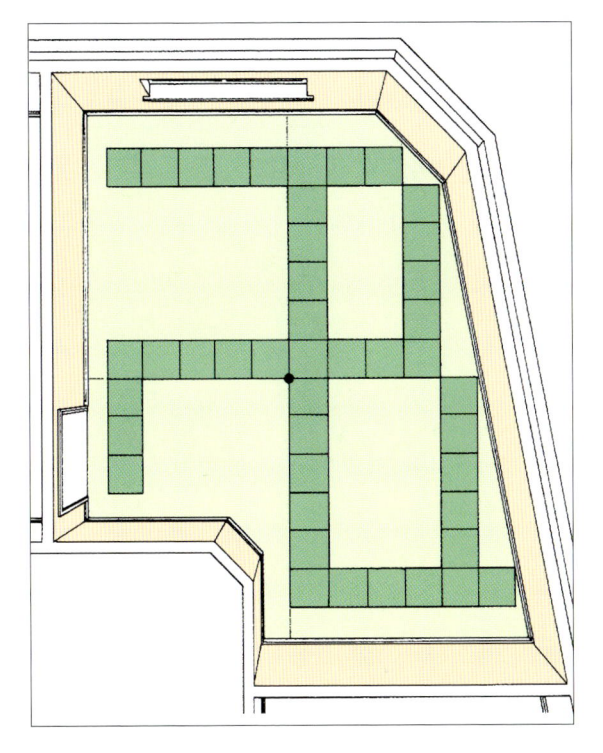

6 Dry-lay rows of tiles out from the centre of the room toward the walls, allowing for the joint width, as appropriate, to determine the width of the border tiles and the fit of the tiles around any obstacles.

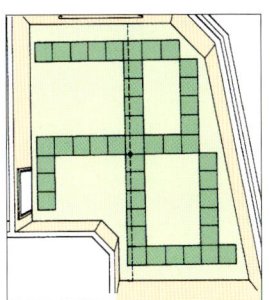

7 Adjust the string lines to obtain the best possible fit, chalk them and snap them against the floor to mark the laying guidelines.

PREPARING A SURFACE FOR TILING

The surface for tiling should be clean and dry. It is possible to tile over painted plaster or plasterboard (gypsum board), but old wallcoverings should be removed and brick walls must be rendered. Note that modern tile adhesives allow tiling over existing tiles, so there is no need to remove these if they are securely bonded to the wall surface. There is also no need to fill minor cracks or holes; the tile adhesive will bridge these as it is applied to the wall surface. Printed wallpaper can easily be removed because it will absorb water splashed on it immediately; other types will not. With paper-backed fabric wallcoverings, it is often possible to peel the fabric away from its paper backing; try this before turning to other methods.

REMOVING WALLPAPER

1 To strip printed wallpaper, wet the surface with a sponge or a garden spray gun. Wait for the water to penetrate, and repeat if necessary.

WASHING WALLS AND CEILINGS

Wash wall surfaces down with sugar soap (all-purpose cleaner) or detergent, working from the bottom up, then rinse them with clean water, working from the top down. Wash ceilings with a floor mop or squeegee, after disconnecting and removing light fittings. Again, rinse off with clean water.

4 After removing the bulk of the old wallpaper, go back over the wall surface and remove any remaining "nibs" of paper with sponge/spray gun and scraper.

2 Using a stiff wallpaper scraper – not a filling knife (putty knife) – start scraping the old paper from the wall at a seam. Wet it again while working if necessary.

3 Turn off the power before stripping around switches and other fittings, then loosen the faceplate screws to strip the wallpaper behind them.

5 To strip a washable wallpaper, start by scoring the plastic coating with a serrated scraper or toothed roller, then soak and scrape as before.

6 For quicker results, use a steam stripper to remove washable papers. Press the steaming plate to the next area while stripping the area just steamed.

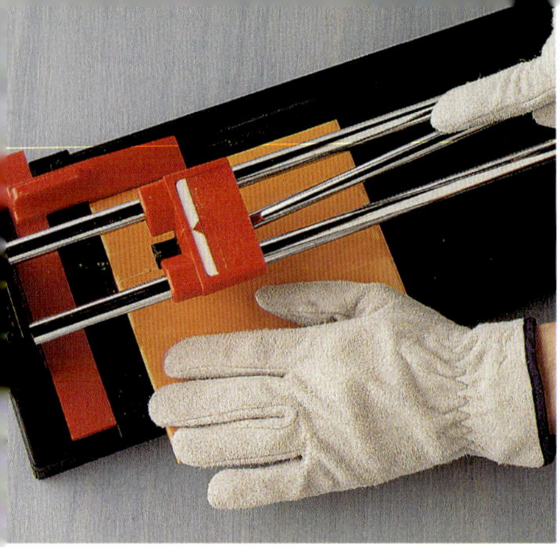
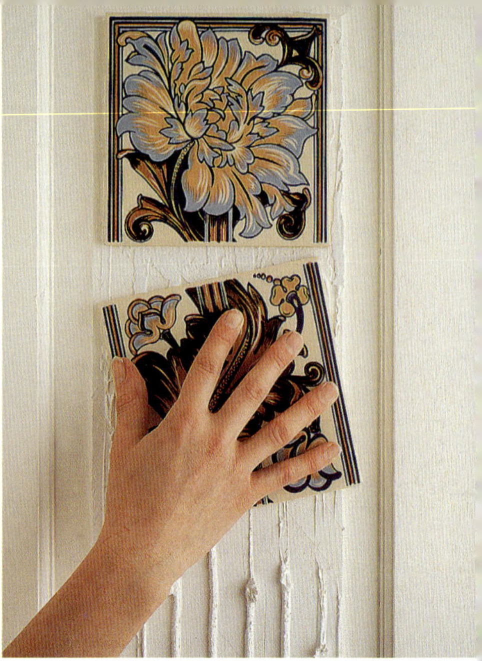
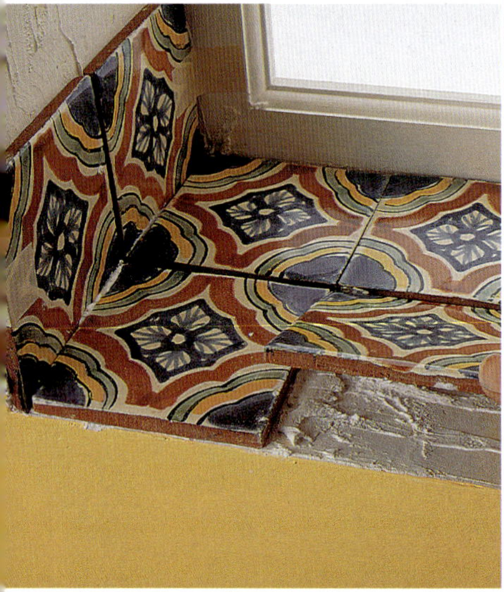
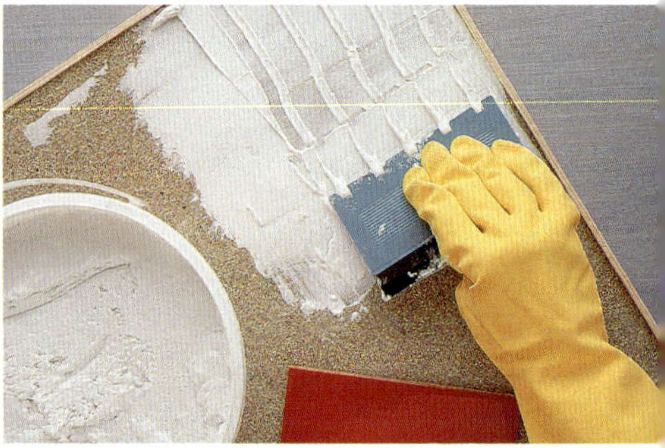
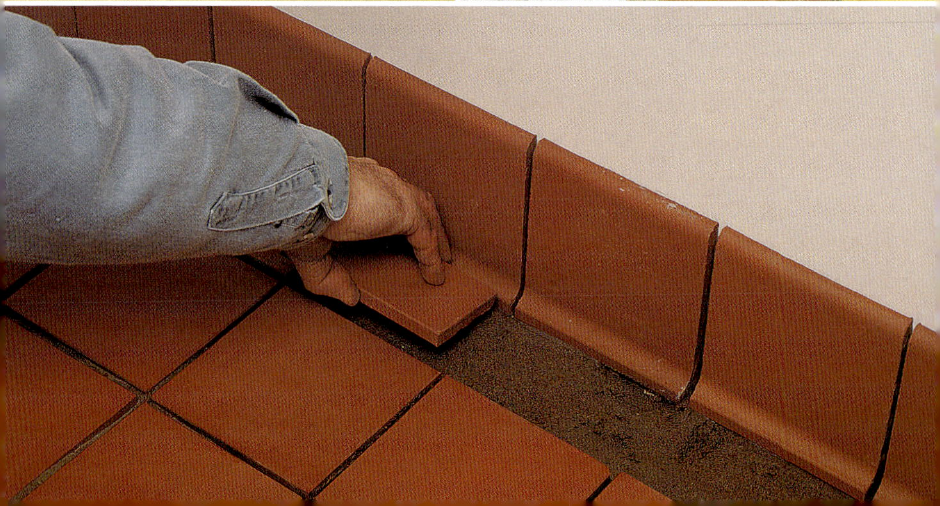

TILING TECHNIQUES

Tiling is relatively straightforward and does not require a lot of expensive equipment. It pays to plan each tiling project carefully and not to rush it. The more you practise, the more skilled you will become – tiling the walls or floor of a whole room is too large an undertaking for a beginner, but tiling a skirting (baseboard), window recess or splashback can be accomplished after only a little experience. Having thoroughly prepared the surface to be tiled, you will need to work quite quickly, as the adhesive and grout will begin to go off quite rapidly. Tackle small sections at a time, cleaning off any excess as you go before it has a chance to harden. This is particularly important with combined adhesives and grouts.

BEGINNING TO TILE

FITTING TILE SUPPORTS

Use masonry pins (tacks) to fix the support to the wall, aligned with the guideline. Drive the pins in only part of the way so that they can be pulled out to remove the batten (furring strip) later.

When tiling large areas or whole walls, pin a vertical guide batten to the wall as well to help keep the tile columns truly vertical.

FIXING TILES

Once all the necessary setting-out work has been done, the actual technique of fixing tiles to walls is quite simple: spread the adhesive and press the tiles into place. However, there must be an adhesive bed of even thickness to ensure that neighbouring tiles sit flush with one another. To obtain this, use a toothed spreader (usually supplied with the tile adhesive; buy one otherwise). Scoop some adhesive from the tub with the spreader, and draw it across the wall with the teeth pressed hard against the plaster to leave ridges of a standard height on the wall. Apply enough adhesive to fix about ten or twelve tiles at a time.

Bed the tiles into the adhesive with a pressing and twisting motion, aligning the first tile with the vertical guideline or batten. If using tile spacers, press one into the adhesive next to the top corner of the first tile, and place the second tile in the row.

MARKING OUT A SPLASHBACK

1 When tiling a small area with rows of whole tiles, use the tiling gauge to mark the extent of the tiled area on the wall. Here each row will have five tiles.

Carry on placing spacers and tiles until the end of the row is reached. Add subsequent rows in the same way until all the whole tiles are in place.

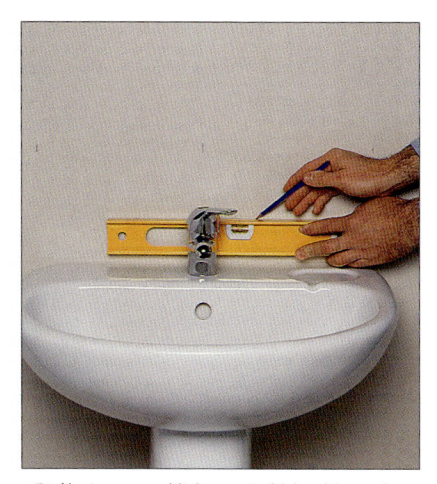

2 Next, use a spirit (carpenter's) level to mark a horizontal base line, above which the first row of whole tiles will be fixed. Cut tiles will fit below it.

3 Then use the spirit level again to complete a grid of horizontal and vertical guidelines on the wall surface, ready for a wooden tile support to be fixed.

FIXING TILES

1 Use a notched spreader to spread adhesive on the wall. Press the teeth against the wall to leave ridges of even height. Place the first tile on the tile support, with its side against the pencilled guideline or vertical guide batten (furring strip).

2 Insert a tile spacer at the tile corner and place the second tile. Add more tiles to complete the row, then build up succeeding rows in the same way.

CUTTING TILES

It is now time to tackle any cut tiles that are needed at the ends of the rows, and along the base of the tiled area beneath the horizontal tile support. Remove this, and the tile spacers, only when the adhesive has set; allow 24 hours.

When cutting border tiles, measure each cut tile individually at top and bottom or each side as necessary. The walls, floors and ceilings of houses are rarely true and you are likely to find that the gaps to be filled will vary from one tile to the next. Straight cuts can be made with a small cutter or cutting jig, while shapes will need to be nibbled out with nippers or cut with a tile saw.

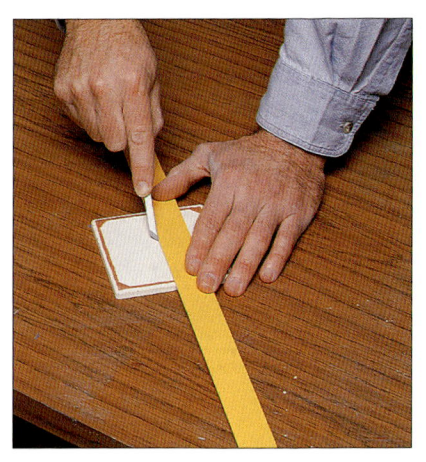

1 Use a pencil-type tile cutter and a straightedge to make straight cuts. Measure and mark the tile width needed, then score a line across the glaze.

4 The traditional way of making a cut-out in a tile is to score its outline on the tile, then gradually nibble away the waste material with pincers or tile nippers.

5 An alternative is to use a special abrasive-coated tile saw. This is indispensable for making cut-outs – to fit around pipes and similar obstructions.

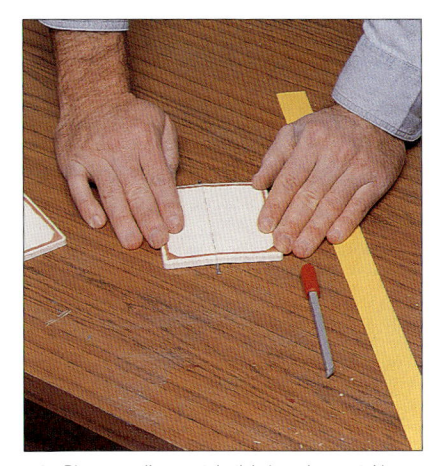

2 Place a nail or matchstick (wooden match) under the scored line at each side of the tile, and break it with downward hand pressure on each half of the tile.

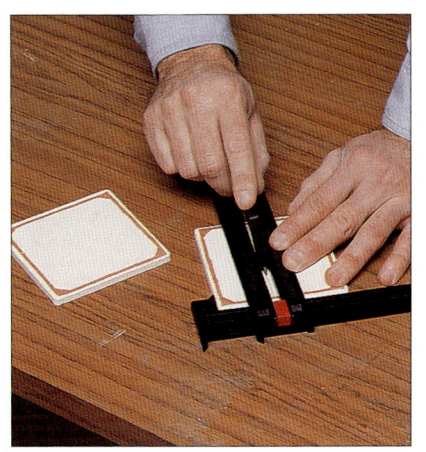

3 Use a cutting guide or tiling jig if preferred, especially for cutting narrow strips. This type holds the tile securely and also guides the tile cutter accurately.

USING A TILE-CUTTING JIG

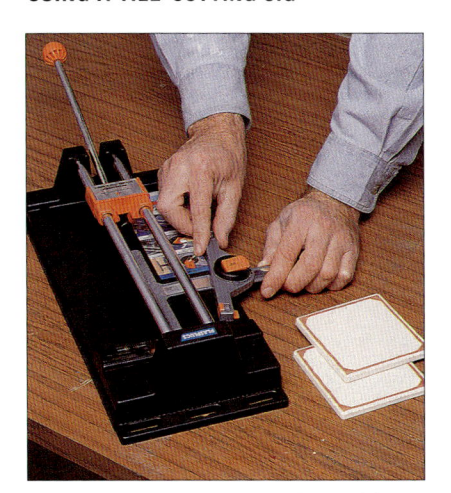

1 For making angled cuts as well as straight ones, a tile-cutting jig is invaluable. To set it up, first fix the side fence to the angle required.

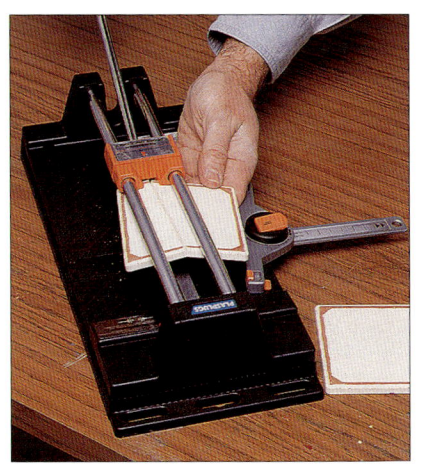

2 Draw the cutting point across the tile, scoring the tile only once. Snap the tile by holding it against the guide bars and lowering the cutter handle with its tip under the tile.

ADDING CUT TILES

When tiling a whole wall, cut tiles are likely to be needed at the corners at each end of the wall, and at the skirting (baseboard) and ceiling. If the tiling is to extend on to an adjacent wall, the horizontal rows must align, so extra care is needed when setting out.

At an internal corner, tile up to the angle completely on one wall so that its tiles overlap the edges of the tiles on the first wall. You can do the same thing at an external corner, using glazed-edge tiles on one wall to conceal the edges of the tiles on the other, provided the angle is truly vertical. If it is not, bed corner strip in the adhesive, set it vertical, then tile up to it.

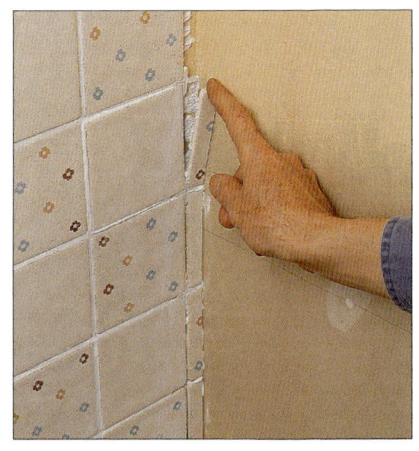

1 Measure, mark and cut the sections of tile needed to complete each row of tiling. Spread a little adhesive over their backs and press them into place.

2 When tiling adjacent walls, place all the cut pieces on the first wall. Repeat on the second, overlapping the original cut pieces. If cut tiles are only needed on one wall, make sure they are overlapped by the whole tiles on the adjacent wall.

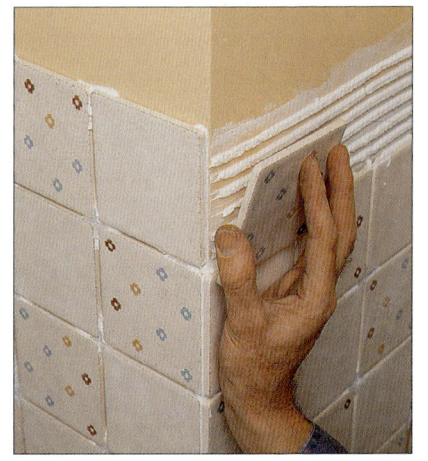

3 When tiling external corners, set out the tiles so that, if possible, whole tiles meet on the corner. Overlap the tiles as shown, or to fit plastic corner trim.

GROUTING

When all the tiles are in place, including any cut tiles that are required, it is time to tackle the final stage of the job – filling in the joint lines between the tiles with grout. You should leave adhesive to dry for at least 24 hours before grouting. Ready-mixed grout is a little more expensive than powdered, but more convenient to use. You need a flexible spreader (usually supplied with the grout) to force the grout into the gaps, a damp sponge or cloth to remove excess grout from the faces of the tiles, and a short length of wooden dowel or a proprietary grout shaper to smooth the grout lines. A clean, dry cloth will be needed to polish the tiles afterwards.

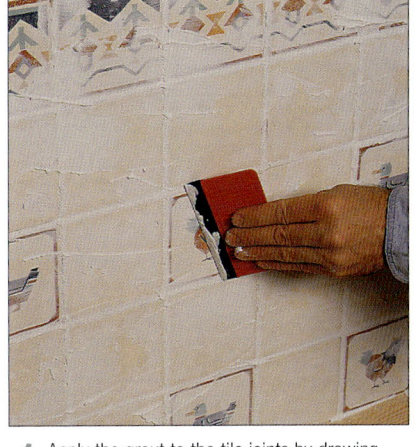

1 Apply the grout to the tile joints by drawing the loaded spreader across them at right angles to the joint lines. Scrape off excess grout and reuse it.

2 Use a damp sponge or cloth to wipe the surface of the tiles before the grout dries out. Rinse it in clean water from time to time.

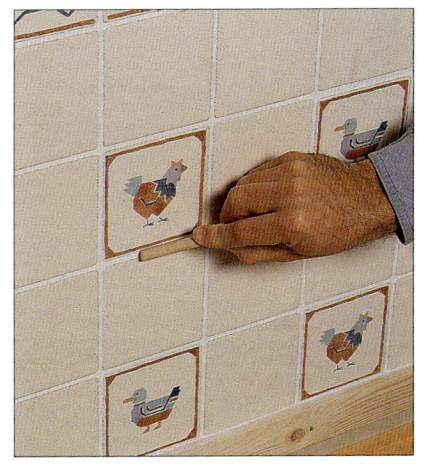

3 Then use a short length of wooden dowel or a similar tool to smooth the grout lines to a gentle concave cross-section. Allow the grout to harden completely, then polish the tiles with a dry cloth to remove any remaining bloom.

ALTERNATIVE EDGING TECHNIQUES

Most ceramic wall tiles have two glazed edges, making it possible to finish off an area of tiling or an external corner with a glazed edge exposed. However, there are alternative ways of finishing off tiling. It can be edged with wooden mouldings or plastic trim strips.

Wooden mouldings can be bedded into the tile adhesive on walls; to edge worktops they can be pinned (tacked) or screwed to the worktop edge.

Plastic edge and corner mouldings (nosings) have a perforated flange that is bedded in the tile adhesive before the tiles are placed. These mouldings come in a range of pastel and bright primary colours to complement or contrast with the tiling. Take care when fitting them to make sure they are vertical, checking with a spirit (carpenter's) level, otherwise they will cause problems when you come to add the tiles. Remember to allow a grouting gap between the moulding and the tiles.

Another method of finishing off the edge of a tiled area is to use proprietary border tiles. These are special narrow tiles that come in a variety of widths, normally coinciding with standard tile widths, and usually have a glazed edge that can be exposed. Border tiles offer a wide range of patterns to choose from, and some even have moulded relief patterns for added interest. They can be used horizontally or vertically.

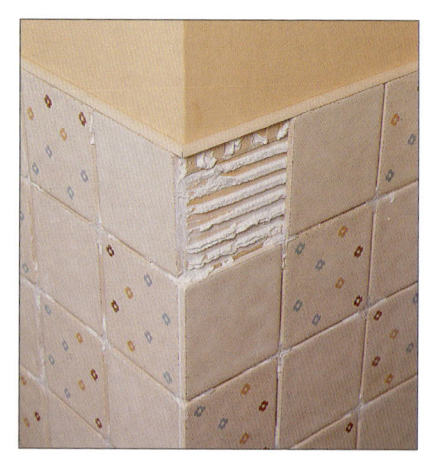

ABOVE: Bed plastic edge or corner trim into the adhesive, then position the tiles so that they fit flush against the curved edge of the trim strip.

EDGING A COUNTER TOP

1 Wood can be used to edge a tiled counter top. Start by attaching the moulding to the edge of the worktop so it will fit flush with the tiled surface. Mitre the ends of the lengths of moulding to produce neat internal and external corners.

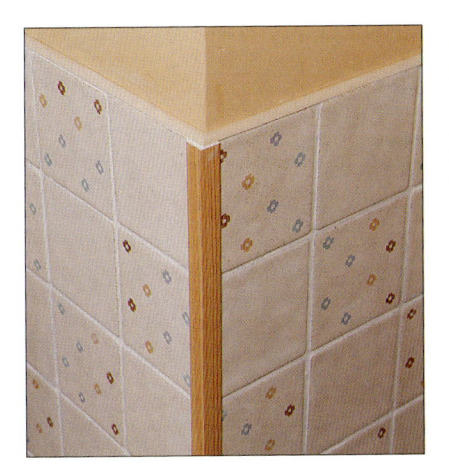

ABOVE: As an alternative to plastic, use wooden mouldings bedded in the tile adhesive. Here, an L-shaped moulding forms a neat external corner trim.

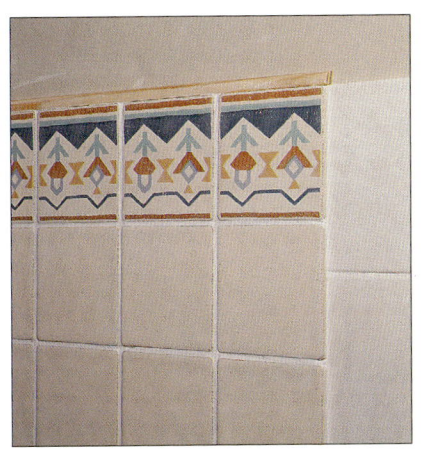

ABOVE: When tiling over existing tiles, some way of disguising the double thickness along exposed edges will be needed. A quadrant (quarter-round) moulding is ideal.

2 Spread the tile adhesive and bed the tiles in place, checking that they lie level with the top edge of the moulding and flush with each other.

3 Plug the counter-bored screw holes by gluing in short lengths of dowel and chiselling them off flush with the moulding. Sand them smooth. Finally, grout the tile joints for a neat finish and paint, stain or varnish the mouldings.

LAYING CERAMIC FLOOR TILES

Both glazed ceramic and quarry tiles can be laid directly over a concrete floor, as long as it is sound and dry. They can also be laid on a suspended timber floor if it is strong enough to support the not inconsiderable extra weight (check this with a building surveyor). In this case, cover the floorboards with exterior-grade plywood, screwed down or secured with annular nails (spiral flooring nails) to prevent it from lifting; this will provide a stable, level base for the tiles.

Glazed ceramic floor tiles are laid with specially formulated adhesive, which should be a waterproof type in bathrooms and a flexible type if tiling on a suspended floor. Quarry and terracotta tiles are laid on mortar over a solid concrete floor, and in thick-bed tile adhesive over plywood.

Old floor coverings should be lifted before laying ceramic or quarry tiles, but if a solid floor is covered with well-bonded vinyl or cork tiles, these can be left in place and tiled over, using tile adhesive. First remove any wax polish used on them.

Set out the floor as described previously, but transfer the starting point to the corner of the room farthest from the door once the setting-out has been completed.

1 Pin tiling guides to the floor in the corner of the room at right angles to each other, then spread some adhesive on the floor with a notched-edge trowel.

4 To cut border tiles to the correct size and shape, lay a whole tile over the last whole tile laid, butt another against the skirting (baseboard) and mark where its edge overlaps the tile underneath.

2 Place the first tile in the angle between the tiling guides, butting it tightly against them and pressing it down firmly into the adhesive bed.

3 As the tiles are laid, use the spacers to ensure an even gap between them. Use a straightedge and spirit (carpenter's) level to check that all the tiles are horizontal.

5 Cut the marked tile and use the cut-off piece to fill the border gap. Repeat step 4, using the same tile until it becomes too narrow to fill the border gap.

6 Spread grout over the tiles to fill all the joint lines. Wipe excess grout from the surface of the tiles with a damp cloth. Use a piece of dowel or similar rounded tool to smooth the grout. Polish the tile with a clean, dry cloth.

LAYING QUARRY TILES

Quarry tiles offer a hard-wearing floor surface, which is ideal for areas that will receive a lot of foot traffic such as hallways. However, they are quite thick, which makes them difficult to cut, so consider carefully where you want to use them; an area that requires a lot of cut tiles may be impractical. Some suppliers will offer to cut quarry tiles for you, which can solve the problem. However, make sure you measure them carefully and mark them clearly.

As with tiling a wall, guide battens (furring strips) will be needed and should be nailed to the floor in one corner, making sure they make a right angle. Their thickness should be about double the thickness of the tiles to allow for the mortar on which the tiles are bedded.

When laying the tiles, it is necessary to work in bays so that the mortar thickness can be kept uniform. This is achieved by nailing a third batten to the floor parallel with one of the other two and four tile widths away from it. Then a board is cut as a spreader for the mortar, with notched ends that fit over the parallel battens so that an even thickness of mortar is achieved as the board is drawn along them. This should be the thickness of a tile plus 3mm (⅛in).

Before laying the tiles, soak them in a bucket of water, as this will prevent them from sucking all the moisture out of the mortar and weakening it.

1 Add a third tiling guide to form a bay four tiles wide. Put down a thin mortar bed and place the first row of tiles, using a tiling gauge to space them.

4 Complete the second bay in the same way as the first. Continue in this fashion across the room until all the whole tiles are laid. Allow the mortar to harden so that you can walk on the tiles before finally removing the guide battens (furring strips).

2 Complete four rows of four tiles, then check that they are level. Tamp down any that are proud, and lift and re-bed any that are lying low.

3 Complete the first bay, then remove the third tiling guide and reposition it another four tile widths away. Fill the second bay with mortar and tamp it down.

5 If installing a tiled upstand, place this next, aligning individual units with the floor tiling. Then cut and fit the border tiles.

6 Mix up a fairly dry mortar mix and use a stiff-bristled brush to work it well into the joints between the tiles. Brush away excess mortar while working before it has a chance to harden, otherwise it will stain the faces of the tiles.

VINYL, LINO AND CORK FLOOR TILES

Vinyl, lino and cork floor tiles are available in both plain and self-adhesive types. Cork tiles may be unsealed or vinyl-coated. For plain vinyl tiles, an emulsion-type latex flooring adhesive is used, while plain cork tiles and lino tiles are best stuck with a water-based contact adhesive. For vinyl-coated cork tiles, use a special vinyl acrylic adhesive.

Since these tiles are comparatively thin, any unevenness in the sub-floor will show through the tiles. Cover timber floors with a hardboard underlay first. Concrete floors may need localized repairs or treatment with a self-smoothing compound.

If laying patterned tiles, set the floor out carefully. With plain tiles, setting out may not appear to be so important, but nevertheless the floor should still be set out carefully to ensure that the tile rows run out at right angles from the door.

1 If using self-adhesive tiles, simply peel the backing paper off and place the tile in position on the sub-floor against the marked guidelines.

2 Align self-adhesive tiles carefully before sticking them down; the adhesive grabs positively and repositioning may be difficult.

3 If using non-adhesive tiles, spread the appropriate type of adhesive on the sub-floor, using a notched spreader to ensure that an even thickness is applied.

4 After laying an area of tiles, use a smooth block of wood to work along the joints, pressing them down. This will ensure that they are all bedded firmly in the adhesive.

TILING TECHNIQUES • 185

5 At the border, lay a tile over the last tile laid, butt another against the skirting (baseboard) and mark its edge on the tile underneath.

6 Place the marked tile on a board and cut it with a sharp knife. The exposed part of the sandwiched tile in step 5 will fit the gap perfectly.

7 Fit the cut piece of border tile in place. Trim its edge slightly if it is a tight fit. Mark, cut and fit the other border tiles in exactly the same way.

8 At an external corner, lay a whole tile over the last whole tile in one adjacent row, butt another against the wall and draw along its edge.

9 Move the sandwiched tile to the other side of the corner, again butt the second whole tile against the wall and mark its edge on the sandwiched tile.

10 Use the utility knife to cut out the square waste section along the marked lines, and offer up the L-shaped border tile to check its fit before fixing it.

USING CORK WALL TILES

Cork wall tiles are usually sliced into squares – 300mm (12in) is the commonest size – or rectangles. They come in a range of natural shades, and may also be stained or printed with surface designs during manufacture. They are stuck to the wall surface with a special water-based contact adhesive, and since they are virtually impossible to remove once placed, they should be regarded as a long-term decorative option and their use carefully planned.

Cork tiles are not rigid like ceramic wall tiles and will follow the contours of the wall, so it is essential that this is prepared properly before the tiles are applied. The surface must be sound and as flat as possible, with all major cracks and holes filled and sanded down.

As with ceramic tiles, careful setting out will allow you to minimize the amount of cutting required, although this is not as difficult as cutting rigid tiles – a sharp knife is all that is required. To avoid problems of slight colour changes between batches of tiles, mix them all thoroughly before beginning.

1 To ensure that the tile rows and columns build up correctly, draw horizontal and vertical pencil guidelines on the wall. Place the first tile.

4 Fit the cut piece of border tile in place on the wall. Shave or sand its cut edge down a fraction if it is a tight fit. Cut and fit others in the same way until you have filled all the border areas completely.

> **TIP**
> If using cork tiles on walls, change the faceplate screws on light switches and socket outlets (receptacles) for longer ones; the originals may be too short to reach the lugs in the mounting box.

2 If border tiles are to be cut, hold a whole tile over the last whole tile fixed, butt another against the frame and mark where its edge overlaps the tile underneath it.

3 Place the marked tile on a board and cut it with a sharp utility knife. The exposed part of the sandwiched tile in step 2 should fit the border gap precisely.

5 To fit a tile around an obstacle such as a light switch, make a paper or card template and test its fit before cutting the actual tile.

6 Run a kitchen rolling pin or a length of broom handle over the completed cork surface to ensure that all the tiles are well bonded to the wall, paying particular attention to the joints between tiles.

USING MOSAIC TILES

Small mosaic tiles are an attractive alternative to square and rectangular tiles, especially for small areas of tiling where their size will look particularly appropriate. Modern mosaic tiles come in a range of shapes and sizes, from simple squares and roundels to interlocking shapes such as hexagons. They are generally sold in sheets backed with an open-mesh cloth that holds the individual mosaic pieces at the correct spacing and greatly speeds up the installation process, since the entire sheet is stuck to the wall in one go. If cut pieces are needed to fill in the perimeter of the tiled area, simply cut individual mosaic tiles from the sheet with scissors, trim them to size with a tile cutter and position them one by one. Mosaic tiles are fixed and grouted with ordinary tiling products.

1 Start by putting up a horizontal tile support and a vertical tiling guide, as for ordinary tiling. Then apply an area of tile adhesive to the wall.

CUTTING MOSAIC TILES

As well as using sheets of tiles, you can create mosaics with tesserae. Small pieces of tile can be shaped with mosaic nippers: wearing protective leather gloves and safety goggles, place the jaws of the nippers at right angles to the tile and press them together to make a clean cut. Clear away small, sharp shards of tile immediately and dispose of them safely. Alternatively, wrap each tile separately in heavy sacking and place on a wooden cutting board. Wearing protective leather gloves and safety goggles, tap the tile smartly several times with a hammer. Unwrap carefully and dispose immediately of small, unusable shards.

TILING TECHNIQUES • 189

2 Position the first sheet of mosaic tiles on the wall, in the angle between the tiling support and the tiling guide, and press it firmly into place.

3 After placing several sheets, use a mallet and a piece of plywood to tamp the mosaics down evenly. Use a towel or a thin carpet offcut as a cushion. Ensure the grouting spaces between each sheet are equal.

4 To fill in the perimeter of the area, snip individual mosaic tiles from the sheet, cut them to the size required and bed them firmly in the adhesive.

5 When the adhesive has dried, spread grout over the tiled area, working it well into the gaps between the individual mosaics. Wipe off excess grout with a damp sponge, and polish the surface with a cloth when dry.

TILING A WINDOW RECESS

Tiling a small area of a room will focus attention and add colour and pattern without being overpowering. Here, two different designs of hand-painted tiles have been used to accentuate a window recess, the colours complementing the bright-coloured wall.

For a completely different effect, plain terracotta tiles with curved edges would give a Mediterranean look to the window. Plain, matt-glazed tiles in rich shades of blue would create a very different note of Moorish magnificence.

Before you begin, measure the window recess carefully to determine how many tiles you will need. Allow a whole tile for each cut one to be on the safe side.

1 Wearing a face mask and gloves, sand the paintwork on the window sill and walls to remove any loose paint. Key (scuff) the surface to provide a base for the adhesive.

4 Place the first two tiles in position on the wall, butting them closely together and lining up the outside edge of the outer tile with the edge of the wall. Hold the tiles in place with masking tape until set. If the recess is less than two whole tiles deep, place the cut tiles next to the window frame.

TILING TECHNIQUES • 191

2 Wearing rubber gloves, spread a thick layer of tile adhesive in one corner of the window. Using a damp sponge, remove any adhesive that gets on to the wall.

3 Using the notched edge of the spreader, key the surface only halfway through, leaving a thick layer of adhesive.

5 Spread adhesive in the opposite corner of the window and key as before. Position two vertical tiles as in step 4. Lay tiles along the window sill, overlapping the edges of the vertical tiles at each end.

6 Spread adhesive up the sides of the window recess and key. Position the contrasting tiles, lining up the edges with the edges of the recess. Tape in place as before until set. Grout all the tiles, removing any excess with a damp sponge. Polish with a dry, lint-free cloth.

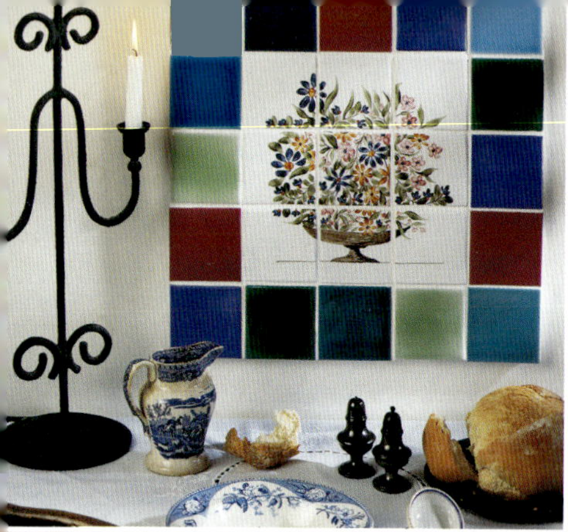
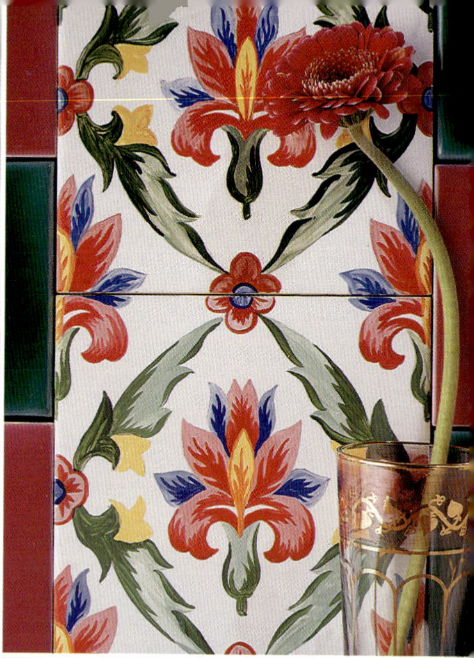
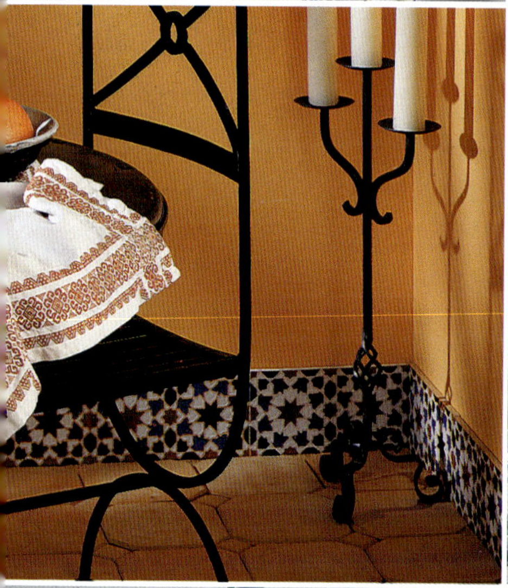
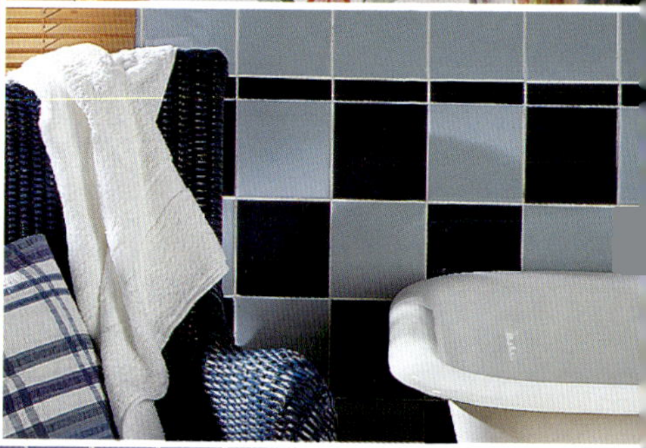
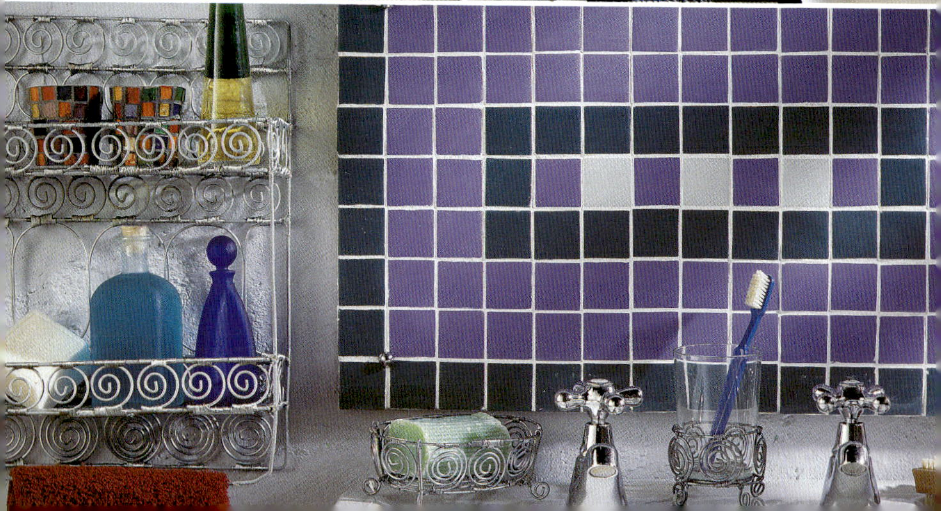

DECORATIVE TILING LAYOUTS

The preceding pages have dealt with tiling walls in the technical sense of planning the layout and fixing the tiles. However, tiles are more than just wallcovering units; they come in a range of sizes and designs that can also be used creatively in a variety of ways. Tile manufacturers offer a range of mass-produced designs you can choose from, which can be used to great effect with the application of a little imagination, or you can select from a variety of unique hand-painted tiles available from better tile suppliers, antique tiles from salvage companies, or even commission a motif panel from a specialist tile supplier. Plan the motif's position on the wall carefully, and build it in the usual way as tiling progresses.

CHECKED PATTERN

If you have your heart set on a particular tile, but find it is outside your budget, do not despair; you can create quite dramatic results with the cheapest of tiles as long as you use them imaginatively. Here, basic wall tiles in two shades of blue have been used to create a stunning chequerboard effect that is topped with a thin, decorative band of tile strips. The strips make a visual "dado rail" (chair rail) that divides the tiles' surface quite naturally into two distinct areas. The upper portion of the wall is then finished using lighter blue tiles. The strips can be cut from ordinary tiles, or use proper dado tiles.

1 Prepare the wall properly, then attach a pair of batten (furring strip) guides at right angles where the first row of tiles will start.

4 Lay the light coloured tiles in place above the border, using tile spacers as before. Cut any tiles you need to complete the edges and set them in place. Use a damp sponge to remove any excess adhesive and leave to dry.

DECORATIVE TILING LAYOUTS • 195

2 Wearing rubber gloves, apply tile adhesive using a notched spreader to key (scuff) the surface. Position the tiles, alternating light and dark.

3 When you have laid as many tiles as you want, cut 5cm (2in) strips of the darker tiles. Apply and key the tile adhesive as before, then set the strips in position using tile spacers.

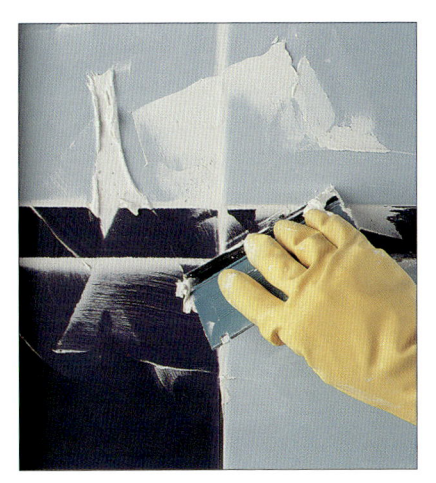

5 When the adhesive has set, grout the tiles thoroughly, wearing rubber gloves. Press the grout down into the gaps between the tiles.

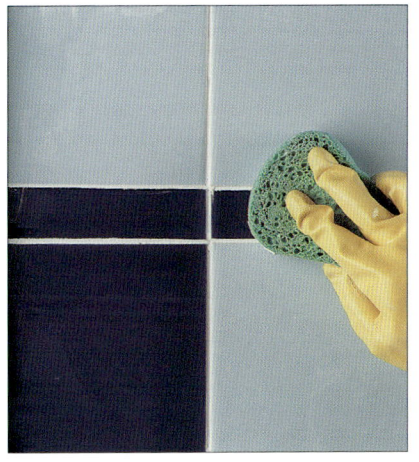

6 Remove any excess grout using a damp sponge and leave to dry. When the grout has set, polish the surface of the tiles with a dry, lint-free cloth.

GEOMETRIC CHEQUERBOARD

Shades of blue and ivory Venetian glass tiles make a lovely cool splashback for a bathroom basin. They are arranged here in a simple geometric design, but you can experiment with other patterns – position the tiles diagonally to make a diamond shape, or use alternate coloured squares like a chequerboard.

For a co-ordinated look, use one of the tile colours to make a thin border around the bath or repeat the design on the door of a bathroom cupboard. You could also continue the design around a window.

1 Using a craft knife, score the surface of a piece of waterproof chipboard to provide a key (scuffed surface) for the tiles.

4 Clamp the board firmly and drill the screw holes. Put a drinking straw in each hole to keep them open. Wearing rubber gloves, spread waterproof tile adhesive over about one-third of the board.

DECORATIVE TILING LAYOUTS • 197

2 Seal both sides with diluted PVA (white glue) to prevent it from warping.

3 Plan the design on the board. Mark a point in each corner for the screw holes, for hanging the splashback on the wall.

5 Position the tiles on the board, pressing them firmly into the adhesive. Repeat over the rest of the board, working on one-third of the board at a time. Remove excess adhesive with a damp sponge. Leave to dry.

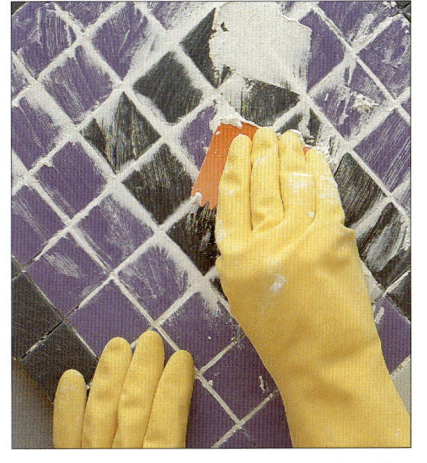

6 Spread waterproof grout over the surface of the tiles, taking care not to dislodge them. Remove excess with a damp sponge, then polish with a dry, lint-free cloth. Seal the back with two coats of yacht varnish. Mark the screw positions on the wall, and drill and plug them. Screw the board to the wall with chromed mirror screws.

PATTERNED WALL PANEL

Flowers have always been a popular theme for tiled wall panels, from the ornate vases of flowers produced at the Iznik potteries in Ottoman Turkey to the blue and white tulip panels made by Delft potters in Holland. Flowers are also a recurring theme in folk art in many countries.

These handmade and hand-painted tiles from the South of France are set directly on to the wall. A border of plain tiles in toning colours makes a perfect frame for the design. You could even edge the tiles with wooden moulding for a picture-frame effect.

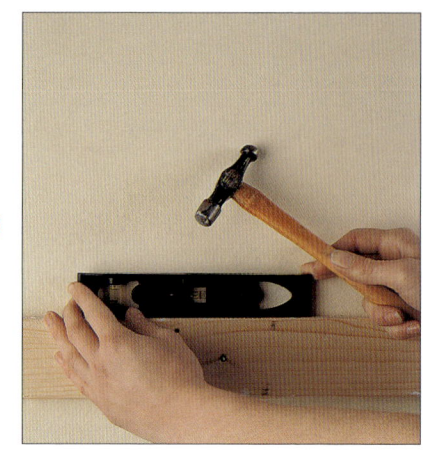

1 Prepare the surface of the wall thoroughly. Decide on the position of the panel, then fix two guide battens (furring strips) to the wall.

4 Start to build up the bottom and side of the border with plain tiles. Use tile spacers or space the tiles by eye.

2 Wearing rubber gloves, spread a layer of tile adhesive over the wall between the battens.

3 Using the notched edge of the spreader, key (scuff) the surface of the adhesive.

5 Begin to fill in the space between the bottom and side of the border with the floral tile panel. Continue to build up the panel and border gradually, moving diagonally from the starting point and making sure that the floral panel pieces are properly aligned. Remove excess adhesive with a damp sponge. Leave to dry overnight.

6 Wearing rubber gloves, grout the tiles, pushing the grout down well into the gaps between the tiles. When the grout has set slightly, remove the excess with a damp sponge. When completely dry, polish with a dry, lint-free cloth.

WALL BORDER

These long, star-studded Spanish tiles are a modern version of the tiles made by medieval Islamic potters. They were widely used in place of the more time-consuming tile mosaics that decorate buildings such as the Alhambra Palace in Granada.

Tiles with interconnecting patterns look wonderful as an all-over wall decoration. Here they are used to add a touch of Spanish style in a simple border along the base of a wall.

When using tiles in this manner, bear in mind that they are not designed to take knocks (unless you use thicker worktop or floor tiles), so consider carefully where you will put them.

1 Measure the length of one tile. Using a pencil, mark the wall into sections of this measurement.

4 Using the notched edge of the spreader, key (scuff) the surface only halfway through, leaving a thick layer of adhesive.

DECORATIVE TILING LAYOUTS • 201

2 Using a set square (T square), draw a vertical line at each mark to help position the tiles accurately.

3 Wearing rubber gloves, spread a thick layer of tile adhesive along the base of the wall. Cover enough wall to apply four or five tiles at a time.

5 Slide each tile into position. You may wish to use tile spacers or you could space them by eye. Wipe the surface of the tiles and the wall with a damp sponge to remove any excess adhesive. Leave to dry.

6 Grout the tiles thoroughly, pushing the grout down well into the gaps between the tiles. Using a damp sponge, remove any excess grout from the surface of the tiles. Use a length of dowel with a rounded end, or a grout shaper, to smooth the grout joint. Leave to dry. Polish the surface of the tiles with a dry, lint-free cloth.

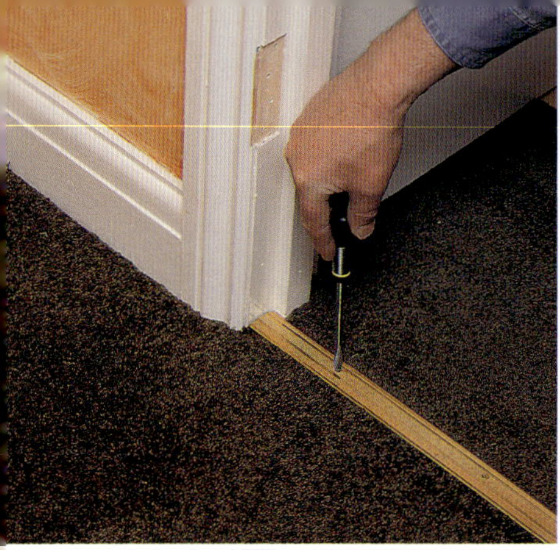
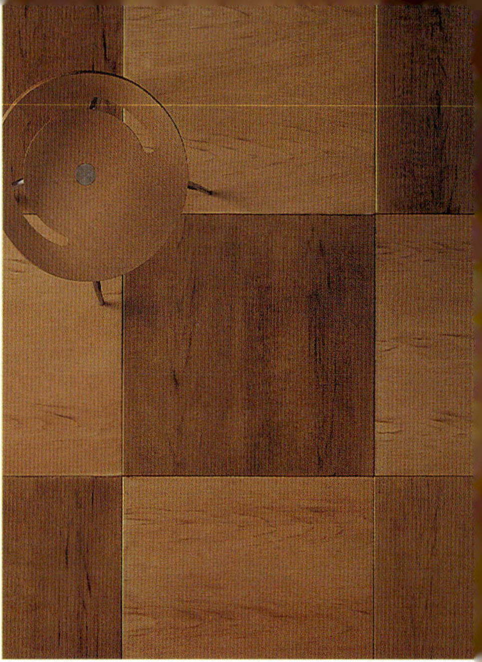
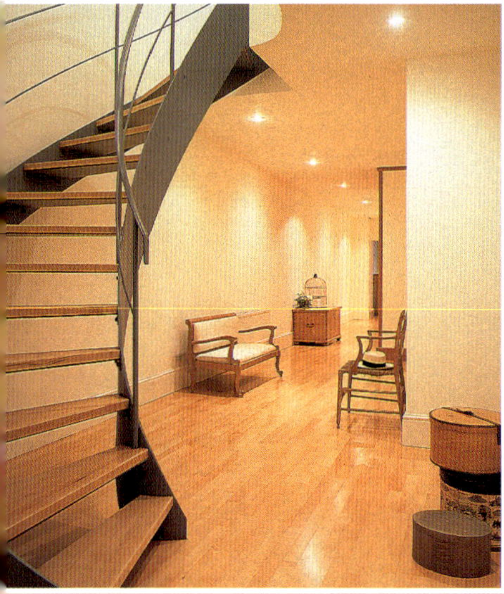
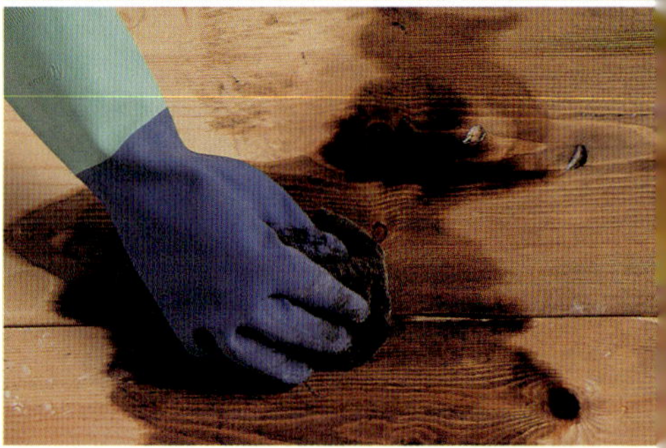
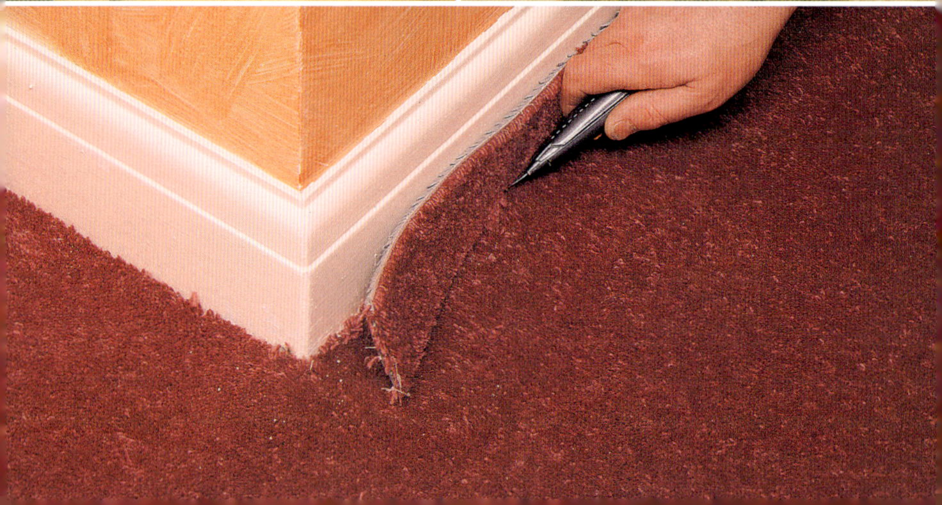

LAYING FLOORS

- Flooring materials
- Flooring preparation
- Flooring techniques
- Flooring variations

INTRODUCTION

The wide range of floor coverings available to choose from includes decorative wood panels and strips, sheet vinyl and carpets.

There are two main types of wooden floor covering: woodblock, sometimes called wood mosaic, and woodstrip. The former consists of small slivers of wood (usually a hardwood) laid in groups and stuck to strong cloth to form wooden "tiles", while the latter is just what its name implies: narrow tongued-and-grooved hardwood planks laid over an existing floor.

Sheet vinyl floor coverings come in a huge range of colours and patterns, and may also have a surface embossed along the lines of the design to give plausible imitations of other floor coverings such as tiles, marble, wood and cork. Some more expensive types have a cushioned underside formed by incorporating small air bubbles during manufacture, which makes them warmer and softer underfoot than their solid counterparts.

Carpets laid loose have been used on floors for millennia, but it was only a few decades ago that wall-to-wall fitted carpeting became popular. Traditional woven carpets made from natural fibres have been challenged by carpets made from synthetic fibres and by alternative methods of manufacture. There is now a huge choice of colours and patterns in types to suit all locations and wear conditions, available in a variety of widths.

While some floor coverings require more skill than others to lay,

LEFT: Subtle variations of colour make wooden floorboards particularly attractive. To make the most of the grain pattern of the boards, after sanding you could use a clear or tinted varnish, or a stain followed by a varnish.

INTRODUCTION • 205

with care and forethought all can be installed by the determined do-it-yourselfer. Moreover, with a little imagination, many floor coverings can be used to produce eye-catching and unusual effects to match or complement the décor of a room.

Remember that practicality is important when choosing a floor covering. Always consider whether the area to be covered will be exposed to water, as in a bathroom, or to heavy wear, as in a kitchen, and whether durability is paramount or a more whimsical surface would suffice. Above all, choose projects that appeal to you and that will produce floors you will enjoy creating and living with.

ABOVE: Sheet vinyl is durable and easy to clean, and is available in a range of colours and patterns.

BELOW: Carpeting provides luxury underfoot, and it is therefore ideal for bedrooms.

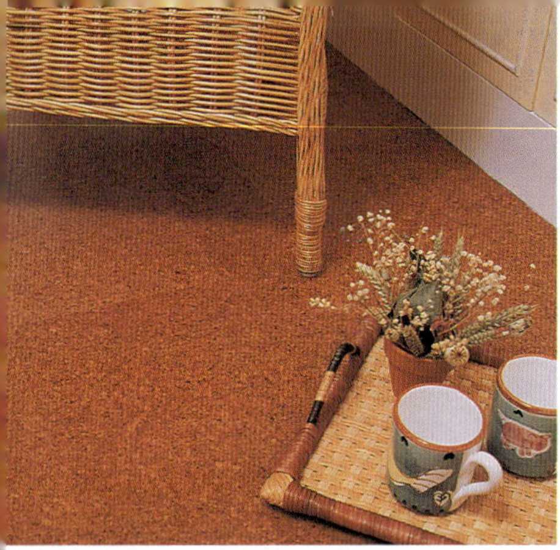
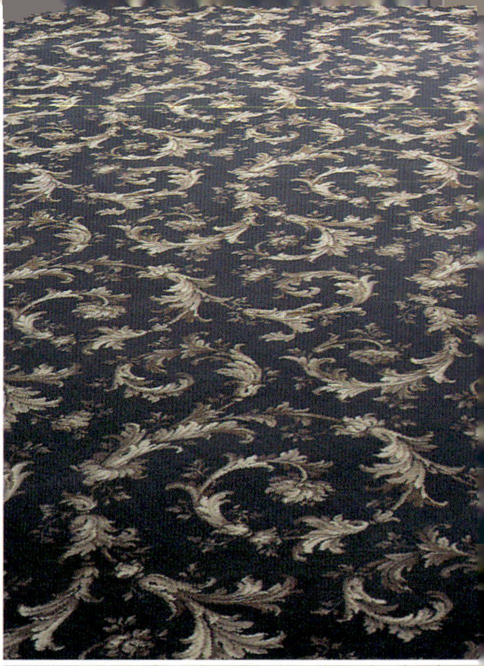
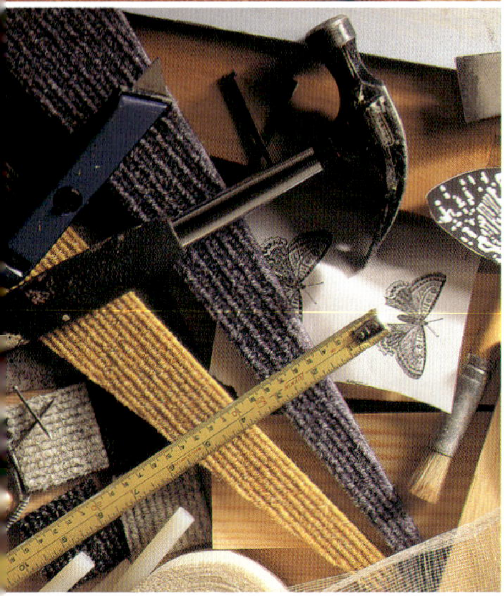
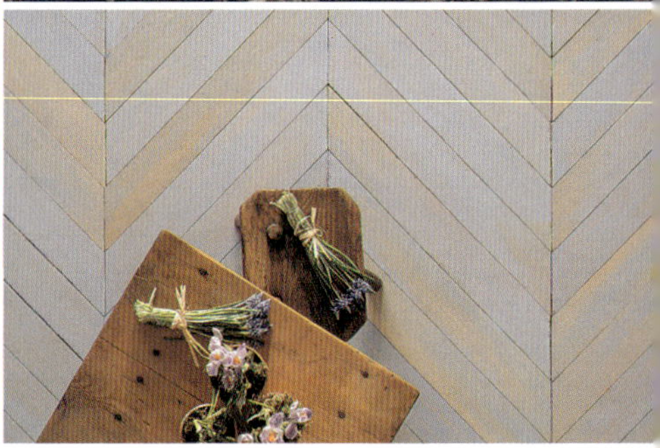
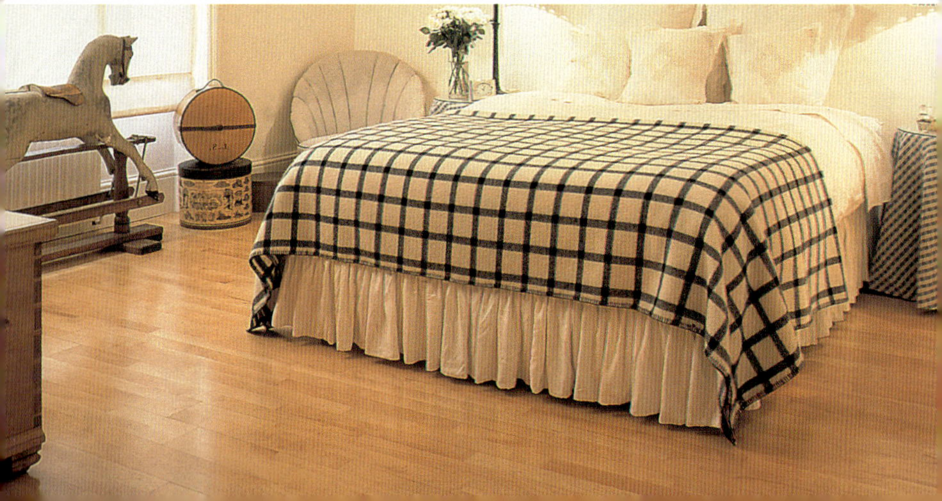

FLOORING MATERIALS

When choosing new floor coverings, remember that there is more to it than simply ordering wall-to-wall carpet throughout, and mistakes can be expensive. Floor coverings have to withstand a great deal of wear and tear in certain areas of the average home, especially if there are children or pets in the family, so choosing the right material is very important. Luckily, there is a wide choice of materials, and laying them is well within the capability of most people. Shopping for floor coverings has never been easier either. All the major do-it-yourself suppliers stock a huge range of materials – plus all the tools needed to lay them. If they do not stock what you need, try specialist flooring and carpet suppliers.

WOOD FLOOR COVERINGS

These come in two main forms: as square woodblock panels made up of individual fingers of wood stuck to a cloth or felt backing for ease of handling and laying; or as woodstrip flooring – interlocking planks, often of veneer on a plywood backing. They are laid over the existing floor surface. Most are tongued-and-grooved, so only occasional nailing or clipping is required to hold them in place.

Woodblock panels are usually 300 or 450mm (12 or 18in) square, while planks are generally 75 or 100mm (3 or 4in) wide and come in a range of lengths to allow the end joints to be staggered from one row to the next so that they all line up.

LEFT: Wooden flooring materials can be used like tiles, creating a combination of interlocking shapes and natural textures.

BELOW: Parquet is created by laying blocks of wood in a variety of geometric patterns.

ABOVE: Give a contemporary interpretation to traditional parquet flooring by colourwashing the blocks. This provides a subtle means of matching the floor to your decorative scheme.

RIGHT: Hard-wearing and elegant, woodstrip flooring is a practical choice for living rooms and hallways.

FAR RIGHT: Wood squares can be painted in alternate colours, creating a chequerboard design. It is also possible to combine different wood effects, such as walnut and maple.

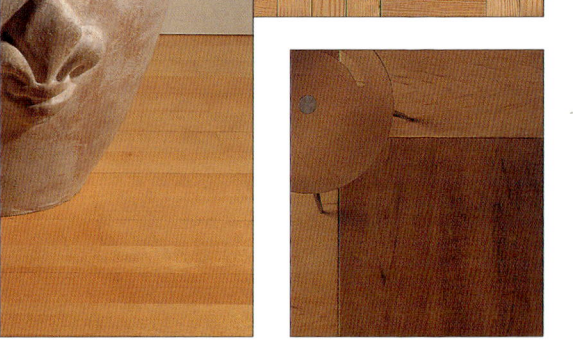

VINYL, LINOLEUM AND CORK

Vinyl is available as sheets and tiles. Sheet vinyl is a relatively thin material that provides a smooth, hygienic and easy-to-clean floor covering, which is widely used in rooms such as kitchens, bathrooms and hallways. It is made from layers of plastic resin, with a clear wear layer protecting the printed design and frequently an air-cushion layer between this and the backing for extra comfort and warmth underfoot. Vinyl tiles come in a wide range of plain and patterned types, and are laid with double-sided adhesive.

Linoleum (lino) is becoming popular again for domestic use, and is also available in sheet form and as tiles, in some stylish designs and colourways with optional contrasting border designs. Lino is more difficult for the amateur to lay, however, being heavier, less flexible and harder to cut than vinyl.

ABOVE: Vinyl flooring is available in a wide range of decorative designs, including realistic imitations of ceramic tiles, wood panels, cork tiles and stone. The covering shown here is imitating an intricate wooden pattern.

Cork is frequently used in work areas such as kitchens and bathrooms. It offers a unique combination of warmth and resilience underfoot, coupled with an easy-to-clean surface that looks attractive too.

ABOVE: Sheet vinyl can offer excellent imitations of a wide range of other floor coverings, including marble, terrazzo and, shown here, woodstrip.

ABOVE: Linoleum shapes can be cut and adhered to the floor to produce patterns. Lino is ideal for kitchens, with its hard-wearing, easy-to-clean surface.

CARPETS

Carpets consist of fibre tufts or loops woven or stuck to a durable backing. Woven carpets are generally the most expensive. Modern types are made by either the Axminster or the Wilton method, which differ in technical details, but both produce a durable product that can be either patterned or plain. Tufted carpets are made by stitching tufts of fibre into a woven backing, where they are secured by attaching a second backing under the first with adhesive. Some of the less expensive types have a foam underlay bonded directly to the backing; others require a separate underlay to be laid.

A wide range of fibre types is used in carpet construction, including wool, nylon, acrylic, polypropylene and viscose rayon, as well as modern natural materials such as coir, sisal and seagrass. Fibre blends can improve carpet performance; a mixture of 80 per cent wool and 20 per cent nylon is particularly popular for providing a combination of warmth, resilience, low flammability and resistance to soiling.

Pile length and density affect the carpet's performance as well as its looks, and most carpets are classified to indicate the sort of wear they can be expected to withstand. The pile can be cut, often to different lengths, giving a sculptured effect; looped (shag), that is, uncut and left long; corded, which means uncut and pulled tight to the backing; or twisted, which gives a tufty effect. A dense pile wears better than a loosely woven one, which can be parted to reveal the backing.

Carpet widths are described as broadloom, more than 1.8m (6ft) wide; or body (stair carpet), usually up to 900mm (3ft) wide. The former are intended for large areas, the latter for corridors and stairs. Broadloom carpet is available in various metric and imperial widths.

ABOVE AND LEFT: The range of colours and patterns of carpet available makes it possible to complement and enhance any style of interior. Carpets are made in qualities to match the requirements of every room in the house.

CARPET TILES

These are small squares of carpet of various types, designed to be loose-laid. Cheaper tiles resemble cord and felt carpets, while more expensive ones may have a short or long cut pile. Common sizes are 300, 450, 500 and 600mm (12, 18, 20 and 24in) square.

Along with lino tiles, carpet tiles are real winners in the practicality stakes. Almost unbeatable in areas that need to be hard-wearing and where children and their attendant wear and tear are concerned, carpet tiles have the single disadvantage that they never look like fitted carpet, no matter how well they are laid. Rather than fighting the fact that they come in non-fraying squares, make use of this very quality and create a fun floor-scape, such as a giant board game. Carpet tiles are very forgiving, allowing for slight discrepancies in cutting, and are very easy to replace if an area is damaged. A geometrical design is easiest; it is advisable to leave curves to the experts, but anything else – even the elegance of a painting by Mondrian – is possible.

ABOVE: Carpet tiles have a long commercial pedigree, and can be a clever choice in the home too, since they can be lifted for cleaning and rotated to even out the effects of wear.

LEFT: Small carpet tiles can be used to create intricate patterns, such as this large backgammon board game. Such patterns need working out carefully on paper first and can be fiddly to lay, but the finished effect is well worth the effort.

MATERIALS FOR DIFFERENT ROOMS

In principle, it is possible to lay any floor covering in any room of a home. However, custom and the practicalities of life tend to divide the home into three broad areas.

Access areas, such as halls, landings and stairs, need a floor covering that is able to cope with heavy traffic and muddy shoes. Ideal choices for hallways are materials with a water-repellent and easy-clean surface – for example, sheet vinyl, vinyl tiles, a woodstrip or woodblock floor, sanded and sealed floorboards, or glazed ceramic or quarry tiles. For stairs, where safety is paramount, the best material to choose is a heavy-duty carpet with a short pile, which can also be used on landings.

Work areas, such as kitchens and bathrooms, also need durable floor coverings that are easy to clean and, especially in the case of bathrooms,

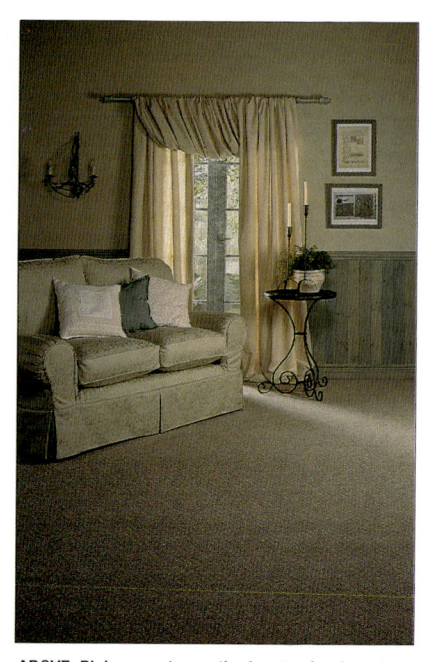

ABOVE: Plain carpets are the key to simple, yet sophisticated, colour schemes. Neutral tones can be offset with the subtlest of colour contrasts.

LEFT: Cork is the warmest of tiled floor coverings underfoot, and when sealed is good-looking and durable too.

water-resistant as well. Sheet vinyl is a popular choice for both rooms, but tiles of various types can also provide an excellent surface – sealed cork, with its warm feel underfoot, is particularly suitable in bathrooms. However, if carpet is preferred for these rooms, there are extremely hard-wearing kitchen carpets available, with a specially treated short nylon pile that is easy to keep clean, and also

RIGHT: Solid woodstrip flooring, shown here in beech, provides a luxury floor covering that looks stunning and will also last for a lifetime.

water-resistant bathroom carpets that give a touch of luxury underfoot without turning into a swamp at bath time.

Leisure areas – living rooms, dining rooms and bedrooms – are commonly carpeted wall to wall. Do not be tempted to skimp on quality in living rooms, which receive the most wear and tend to develop distinct traffic routes. However, it is reasonable to choose light-duty types for bedrooms.

Alternatives to carpets depend simply on taste in home décor. Options include sanded and sealed floorboards teamed with scatter rugs, or a parquet perimeter to a fine specimen carpet. Woodstrip, sheet vinyl or cork tiles may also be worth considering for children's rooms.

ABOVE: Wood is an excellent choice for entrance halls too, where a durable, yet good-looking, floor surface is essential.

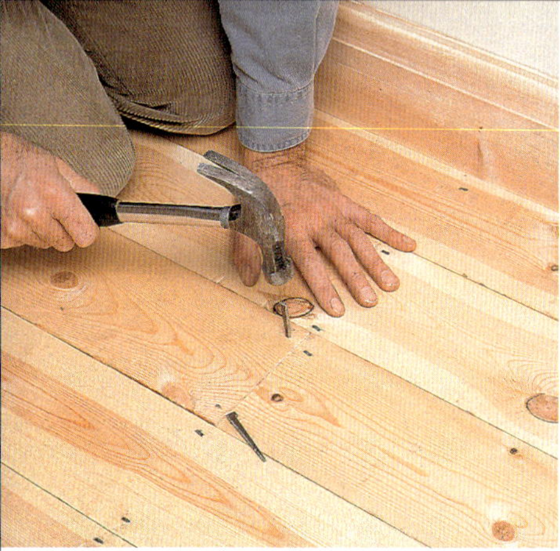
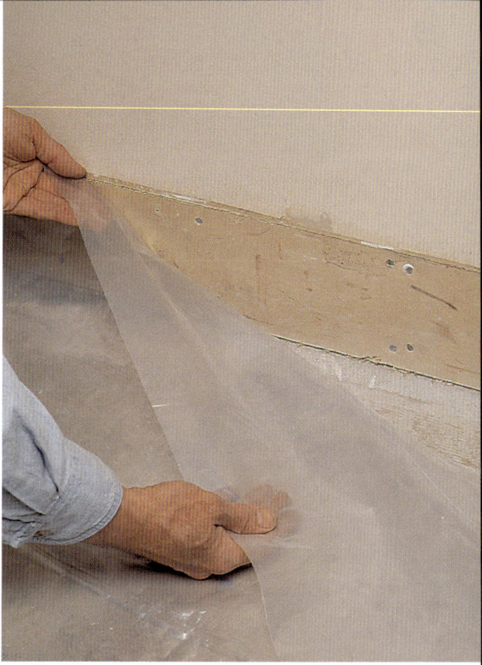
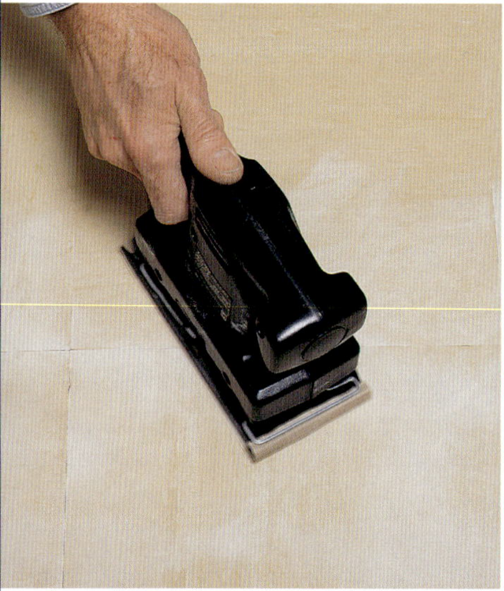
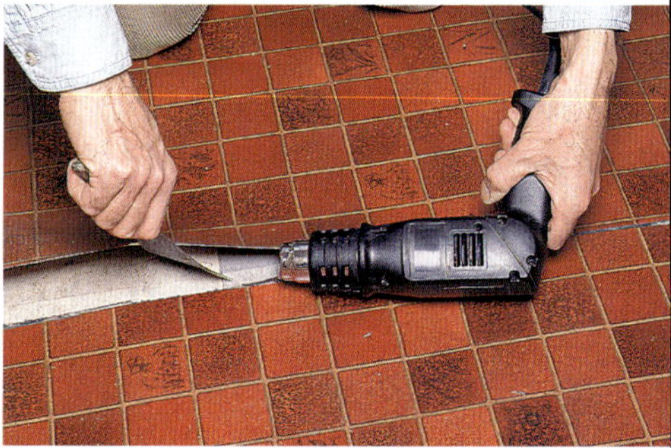
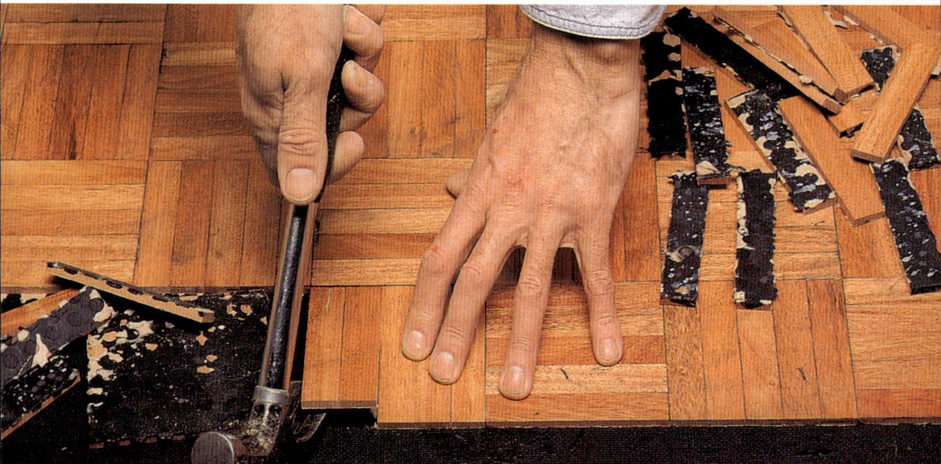

FLOORING PREPARATION

All floor coverings must be laid on a sound, flat surface. With a wooden structure, the older the floor, the more likely it is that there will be loose or damaged boards, or protruding nail heads. With a concrete floor there may be cracks, an uneven surface or, worse, damp patches. All of these conditions must be rectified before laying your new floor covering. If wooden boards are in reasonable condition, they may need only sanding to remove high spots; otherwise, they can be covered with sheets of hardboard, plywood or chipboard (particle board). Concrete can also be covered in this manner or finished with a self-levelling floor screed. If you are in any doubt about your ability in this respect, seek professional help.

REMOVING OLD FLOOR COVERINGS

Generally speaking, old floor coverings should always be lifted before laying new ones. This also provides an opportunity to inspect the floor itself and to carry out any repairs that may be necessary. However, there are some situations where it may not be practical or necessary to lift an existing floor covering – for example, where vinyl tiles have been laid over a concrete floor and they are firmly stuck to it. Stripping such a large area will be an extremely time-consuming job unless a professional floor tile stripping machine is hired.

Woodblock or woodstrip floors should be lifted if damaged or loose, otherwise cover them by pinning on hardboard sheets.

1 The backing of old foam-backed carpets may remain stuck to the floor surface after the carpet has lifted. Scrape and brush it up, and also remove any remaining staples and remnants of seaming tape.

2 To lift vinyl tiles or sheet vinyl that has been stuck along edges and seams, use a heat gun to soften the adhesive and quickly pull up the flooring. Work the blade of a scraper beneath the edges so that you can lift them.

3 If vinyl or cork tiles have been stuck on to a hardboard underlay, lift a few tiles to expose the board edges, then lever up the boards in one piece.

RENOVATING FLOORBOARDS

For suspended wood floors – boards laid over floor joists – start by lifting the old floor covering and checking that all the boards are securely fixed to their joists, and that they are reasonably flat and level. Loose boards will creak annoyingly when walked on, and raised edges or pronounced warping may show as distinct lines through the new floor covering.

Use either cut nails or large oval-headed nails to secure loose boards. When driving them near known pipe or cable runs, take care not to pierce them; it is best to drive the new nails as close to existing nail positions as possible for safety. If there are only one or two loose boards, secure them with screws rather than nails.

Another problem with floorboards, particularly if they are very old, is that gaps can open up between them. When laying a flexible floor covering over them, such as carpet or vinyl, the gaps may cause irregularities in the surface, leading to noticeable wear patterns. One solution is to glue strips of wood into the gaps, planing them flush with the boards when the glue has dried. If they are really bad, however, it may be worth lifting all the boards and relaying them, clamping them tightly together as you do so with hired flooring cramps. Any remaining gaps will need filling with a narrow board. Obviously, this is quite a drastic solution, and it may be simpler to clad the floor with hardboard sheets.

1 Drive in any nails that have lifted due to warping or twisting of the floorboards, then recess their heads slightly using a nail punch. If existing nails have pulled through a board, drive in new ones, slightly to one side.

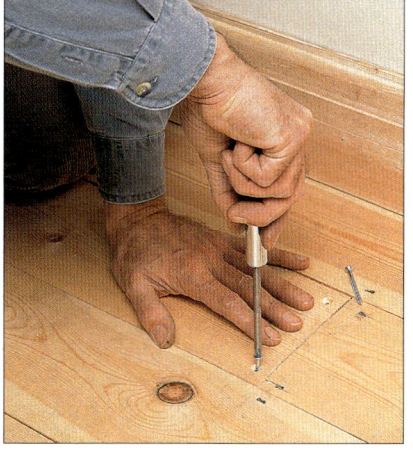

2 If nails will not hold the floorboard flat against the joist, drill pilot and clearance holes, and use wood screws to secure the board firmly in place. Countersink the holes so that the screw heads sit below the surface of the board.

LAYING HARDBOARD

Covering existing floorboards with a hardboard underlay is an alternative to floor sanding as a way of ensuring a smooth, flat surface ideal for thin sheet floor coverings. Lay the boards in rows with the joints staggered from row to row, and pin them down with hardboard pins (brads) driven in at 150mm (6in) spacings. Lay separate strips above known pipe runs so that you can get to them easily should the need arise.

Before you begin, condition the boards to the temperature and humidity conditions in the room so that they will not become warped after laying. Soak the textured sides of the boards with warm water, then stack them back to back in the room for at least 24 hours. It is best to lay the hardboard textured side uppermost to provide an additional key (scuffed surface) for the flooring adhesive. In addition, the indentations in the board will accommodate the nail heads, preventing them from damaging the floor covering.

Dry-lay the boards first, working out from the centre of the room and making sure that their edges do not coincide with the gaps between floorboards. Check also that you will not be left with impossibly narrow gaps to fill at the walls. If necessary, shift the position of the first board to one side or the other.

If preparing to lay glazed ceramic or quarry tiles on a suspended wood floor, put down exterior-grade plywood.

1 If hardboard sheets are used as an underlay for a new floor covering, start by punching in any raised nail heads all over the floor.

2 Nail the hardboard sheets to the floorboards at 150mm (6in) intervals along the edges and also 300mm (12in) apart across the face of each sheet. Lay the boards in rows, staggering the joints from one row to the next.

LAYING A CHIPBOARD FLOOR

To level and insulate a concrete floor, you can cover the concrete with a floating floor of chipboard (particle board), if raising the floor level will not cause problems at door thresholds. The chipboard can be laid directly on the concrete over heavy-duty plastic sheeting, which acts as a vapour barrier. If additional insulation is required, put down polystyrene (plastic foam) boards first, then lay the new flooring on top of them.

Treat damp floors with one or two coats of a proprietary damp-proofing liquid and allow to dry before laying the vapour barrier. Widespread rising damp may require more radical treatment, in which case, it is best to seek professional help.

1 Before you begin laying the chipboard (particle board) panels, prepare the floor surface. First, remove the skirtings (baseboards). Next, put down heavy-duty plastic sheets to prevent moisture rising through the floor.

2 Tape the sheets to the walls; they will be hidden behind the skirting later. Then butt-joint 25mm (1in) polystyrene (plastic foam) insulation boards over the floor, staggering the joints in adjacent rows.

3 Cover the insulation with tongued-and-grooved flooring-grade boards. Use cut pieces as necessary, and add a tapered threshold (saddle) strip at the door. When finished, replace the skirtings.

LAYING SELF-SMOOTHING COMPOUND

Ground floors of solid concrete are prone to two main problems: cracking or potholing of the surface, and rising damp caused by a failure in the damp-proof membrane within the floor structure. Cracks and depressions may show through new floor coverings, especially thinner types such as sheet vinyl, while dampness will encourage mould growth beneath the covering, so both these problems must be eradicated before laying a new floor.

Relatively narrow cracks can be patched with either a repair mortar of one part cement to three parts sand or with an exterior-quality masonry filler.

If the floor surface is uneven or pitted, it can be covered with a thin layer of self-smoothing compound. There are two types available; both are powders and are mixed with either water or with a special latex emulsion. The compound is mixed in a bucket and poured on to the floor surface, trowelling it out to a thickness of about 3mm (⅛in). The liquid finds its own level and dries to give a hard, smooth surface that can be walked on in about 1 hour. Leave it to dry for 24 hours before laying a floor covering over it.

At a door opening, it is necessary to nail a thin strip of wood across the threshold to contain the levelling compound and prevent it from spreading beyond the room. Use masonry nails to hold the wood in place, leaving their heads proud so that they can be prised out and the wood removed once the compound has dried.

1 Start by sweeping the floor clear of dust and debris. Then scrub away any patches of grease from the surface with strong detergent solution. Fill any cracks or holes deeper than 3mm (⅛in) with mortar or filler.

4 Mix up the self-smoothing compound in a bucket, following the manufacturer's instructions carefully to ensure that the mix is of the right consistency and free from lumps.

FLOORING PREPARATION • 221

2 Key the surface of vinyl floor tiles by sanding them before laying the compound. Wipe away the dust with a damp cloth.

3 If the concrete surface is very dusty or appears unduly porous, seal it by brushing on a generous coat of PVA building adhesive (white general-purpose adhesive) diluted with about five parts water.

5 Starting in the corner of the room that is farthest from the door, pour the self-smoothing compound on to the floor surface to cover an area of about 1 sq m (11 sq ft).

6 Use a plasterer's trowel to spread the compound out to a thickness of about 3mm (⅛in). Mix, pour and level further batches as required until the entire floor has been covered. Leave to dry for 24 hours.

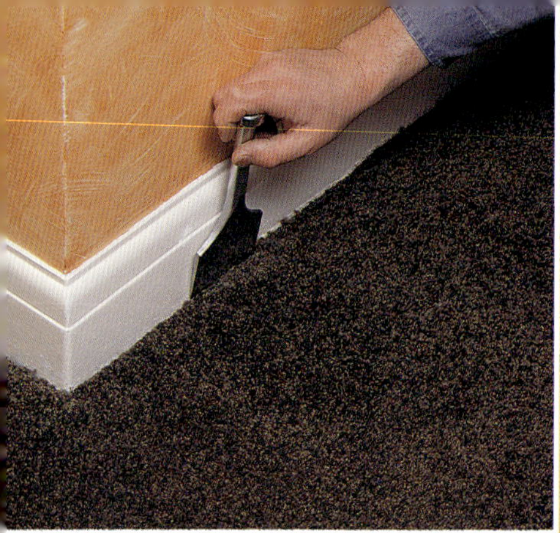

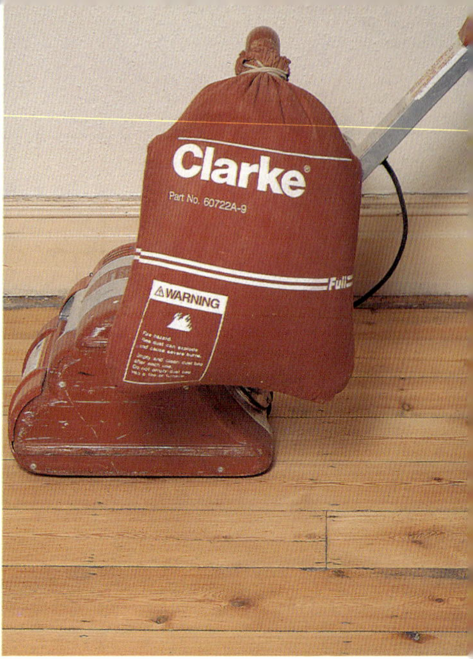
Clarke
Part No. 60722A-9
Full
WARNING

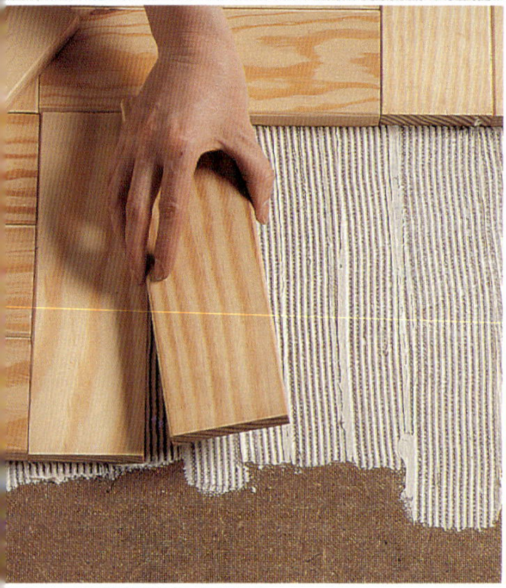

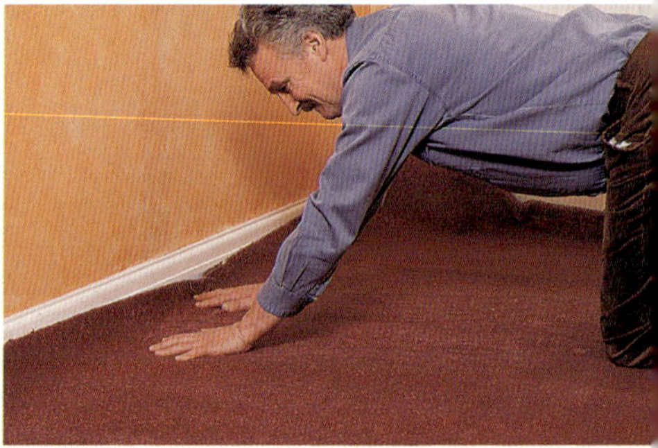

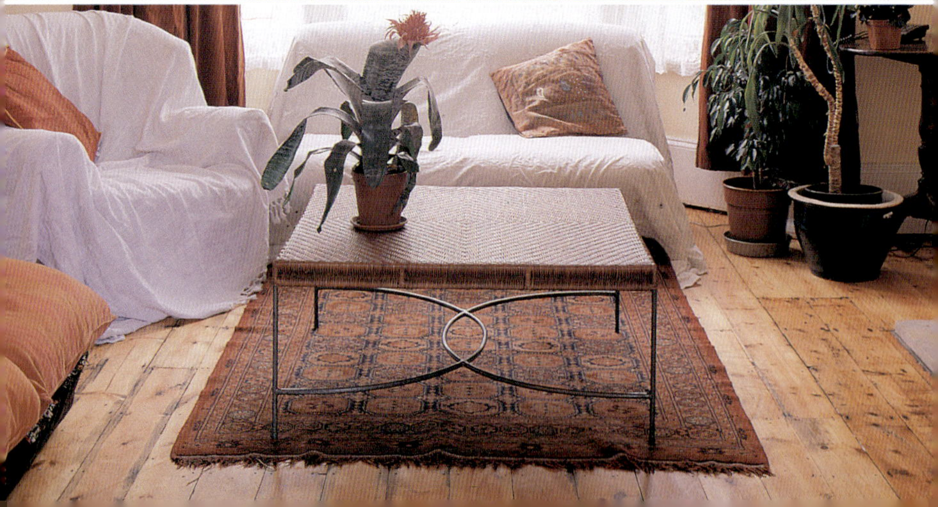

FLOORING TECHNIQUES

A variety of techniques can be used to give a floor a new lease of life, whether it is simply brightening up an existing boarded floor with a coat of varnish or paint, laying a practical, hard-wearing covering or putting down a thick carpet to provide some underfoot luxury. Always consider the type of wear and tear the flooring will be subjected to and choose appropriately. Take the time to work out the quantities of materials needed – your supplier will often be able to help you in this respect – and make sure that you have everything to hand before you begin work. Clear the room of all furnishings and keep children and pets out of the way until you have finished.

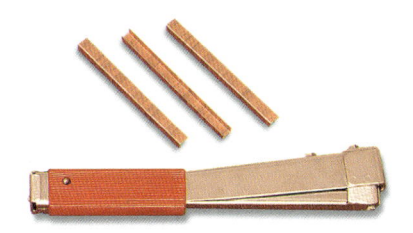

SANDING WOOD FLOORS

Where old floorboards are very uneven, or it is planned to leave them exposed but they are badly stained and marked, you will need to sand them. Hire a floor sanding machine to do this. It resembles a cylinder (reel) lawnmower, with a drum to which sheets of abrasive paper are fitted. A bag at the rear collects the sawdust; however, always wear a face mask and goggles when sanding floors. Also hire a smaller disc or belt sander for finishing off the room edges.

If necessary, drive any visible nail heads below the surface. Start sanding with coarse abrasive paper, running the machine at 45 degrees to the board direction, then use medium and fine paper in turn with the machine running parallel to the boards. Use the disc or belt sander to tackle the perimeter of the room where the large sander cannot reach. Even so, this will not sand right up to the skirtings (baseboards) or into the corners, and the only solution in these areas is to use a hand scraper.

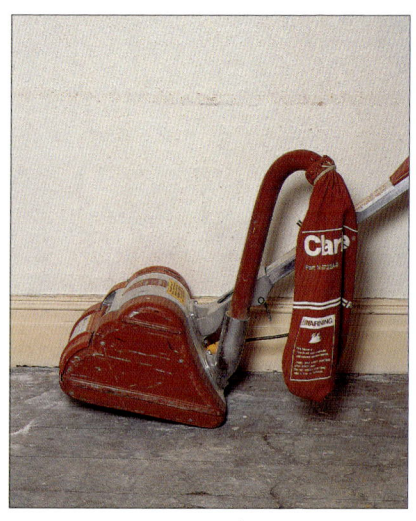

1 Use a floor sander to smooth and strip old floorboards. Drape the power cord over one shoulder and raise the drum before starting the machine up.

FINISHING

Once the floor has been sanded, sweep up the remaining dust and vacuum the floor. If you intend laying a floor covering, you need do no more. If you want to leave the boards exposed, wipe them with a cloth moistened with white spirit (paint thinner). This will remove any remaining dust.

If you want to make the most of the grain pattern of the boards, use a clear or tinted varnish, or a stain followed by a varnish. Brush stain on to two or three boards at a time, keeping a wet edge so that any differences in shade will be less noticeable. Brush on three coats of varnish, thinning the first with 10 per cent white spirit and allowing six hours between coats. Keep the room well ventilated.

TIPS

Sanding creates lots of dust, so wear a facemask and goggles. When sanding, raise the drum at the end of each pass to prevent damage to the boards while the machine is stationary. For safety, drape the power cord of the sander over one shoulder.

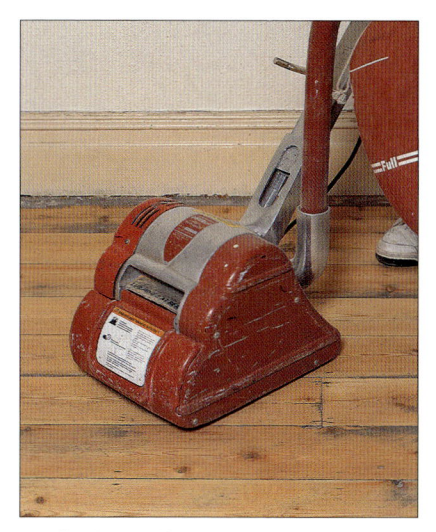

2 Run the machine at 45 degrees to the board direction to start with, first in one direction, then in the other, at right angles to the original passes made.

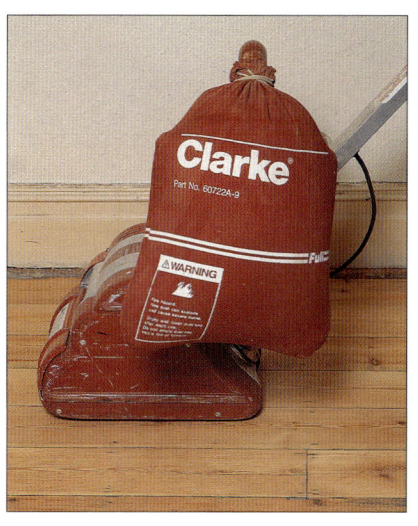

3 Then switch to a medium-grade abrasive and run the sander back and forth, parallel to the board direction. Finish off with fine-grade abrasive.

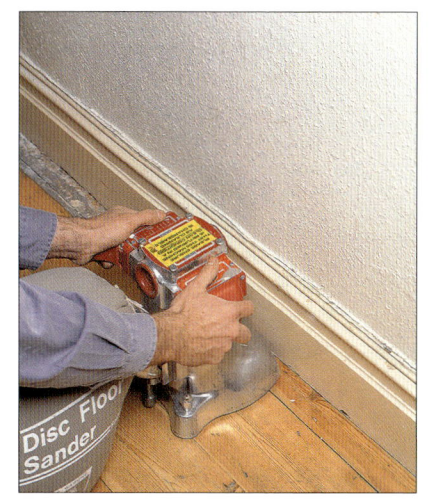

4 Use a smaller disc or belt sander to strip areas close to the skirtings (baseboards) and door thresholds.

5 Use a scraper to remove paint or varnish from inaccessible areas such as around pipework, then sand the stripped wood smooth by hand.

LAYING WOODSTRIP FLOORING

Woodstrip flooring is available in two main types: as solid planks, and as laminated strips (rather like plywood) with a decorative surface veneer. Lengths range from as little as 400mm (16in) up to 1.8m (6ft), and widths from 70mm (2¾in) up to around 200mm (8in). Solid planks are usually about 15mm (⅝in) thick; laminated types are a little thinner.

Both types are generally tongued-and-grooved on their long edges for easy fitting. Some are designed to be fixed to a wooden sub-floor by secret nailing; others are loose-laid, using clips to hold the strips together. Laminated strips are generally pre-finished; solid types may also be, but some need sealing once they have been laid.

All the hard work involved in putting down woodstrip flooring lies in the preparation; the actual laying, like so many decorating jobs, is simple.

Always unpack the strips and leave them in the room where they will be laid for at least seven days to acclimatize to the temperature and humidity levels in the home. This will help to avoid buckling due to expansion, or shrinkage due to contraction, when laid.

Should the manufacturer recommend the use of a special underlay – which may be plastic sheeting, glass fibre matting or foam – put this down first, taping or stapling the seams together for a smooth finish.

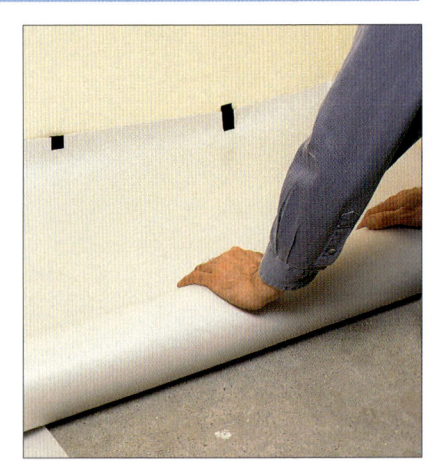

1 Remove the skirtings (baseboards) and make sure that the sub-floor is clean, dry and level. Unroll the special cushioned underlay across the floor, taping one end to keep it in place. Tape or staple the seams together to prevent them from rucking up.

4 The last board is fitted without clips. Cut it to width, allowing for the spacers as in step 2, and apply adhesive along its grooved edge.

FLOORING TECHNIQUES • 227

2 Prepare the boards by fitting the joint clips into their grooves. Lay the first length, clips outward, using spacers to create an expansion gap at the wall. Glue the ends of the boards together.

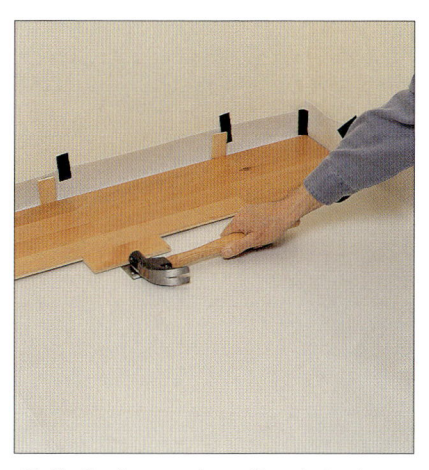

3 Position the second row of boards, tapping them together with a hammer and an offcut so that the clips on the first row engage in the groove of the second. Stagger the boards so that the joints don't coincide with those of adjacent rows.

5 Insert some protective packing against the wall before levering the strip into place. Tap it down level with a hammer and protect the floor with a board offcut. Replace the skirtings to hide the expansion gaps.

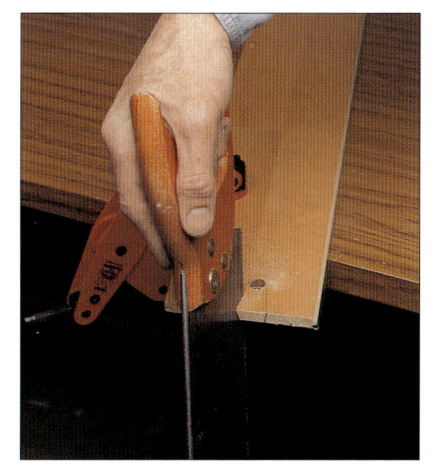

6 To fit a board around a pipe, mark its position and drill a suitably sized hole. Then cut out a tapered wedge, which can be glued back after fitting the board.

LAYING WOOD MOSAIC FLOORING

The least expensive way of creating a decorative timber floor finish is by laying mosaic floor tiles, which are square tiles made from a number of small fingers of decorative hardwood mounted on a cloth or felt backing sheet. This acts as an underlay as well as a means of bonding the fingers together; the result is a sheet that will bend along the joint lines, so it is easily cut to size if required. Alternatively, the fingers may be wired or stuck together to produce a rigid tile. In either case, tiles are generally 300mm (12in) or 450mm (18in) square.

The fingers themselves may be solid wood or veneer on a cheaper softwood backing, and are usually arranged in a basketweave pattern; however, other patterns are also available. A wide range of wood types is available. Some tiles are supplied sealed; others have to be sealed after being laid.

Laying woodblock floor tiles is a comparatively straightforward job, similar to any other floor tiling project in terms of preparation and setting-out. Store the panels unpacked in the room where they will be laid for at least seven days, to allow them to acclimatize to indoor temperature and humidity levels. This will help to reduce shrinkage or expansion after the tiles are laid. However, an expansion gap should always be left around the perimeter of the room.

1 Work from the centre of the floor outward, stretching strings between the centres of opposite walls to find the starting point. Mark out guidelines and spread some adhesive over a small area of the floor.

4 To cut edge pieces, lay a whole tile over the last whole tile laid and place another on top, butted against the skirting (baseboard). Draw along its edge on the middle tile. Over-cut to allow for the expansion gap.

2 Align the first tile carefully with the tiling guidelines and press it firmly down into the adhesive. Bed it down with a hammer, using a scrap of wood to protect the surface of the panel from the hammer head.

3 Lay the next panel in the same way, butting it up against its neighbour. Wipe off any adhesive from the tile faces immediately, otherwise it will spoil the finish.

5 The tile can be bent along the main joint lines between the fingers, then sections can be separated by cutting through the backing fabric with a sharp utility knife.

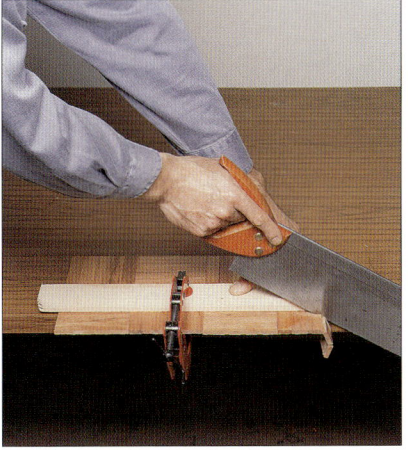

6 More complicated cuts running across the fingers of wood can be made with a tenon saw, using very light pressure to avoid splitting or tearing the thin strips. Sand the edges lightly to remove wood fibres. ▶

7 At door architraves (trims) and other similar obstacles, make a paper template or use a proprietary shape tracer to copy the required shape and mark the tile. Cut along the outline with a coping saw.

8 Cover the cut edges of the tiles by pinning (tacking) lengths of quadrant beading (base shoe) to the skirtings. Alternatively, fit expansion strips cut from cork tiles along the edges to finish.

9 On new work, do not fix the skirtings until the flooring has been laid. They will then hide the expansion gap.

10 Sweep and dust unsealed panels, then apply two or three coats of clear varnish or floor sealer, sanding the surface lightly between coats. Work from the corner farthest away from the door so that you do not become trapped.

FLOORING TECHNIQUES • 231

PARQUET

Good parquet is a very manageable kind of flooring. There are numerous patterns to be made by combining these wooden blocks. A good trick is to work out the pattern starting from the centre and making it as big a perfect square as you can; then lay a simple border to accommodate all the tricky outside edges. Parquet is often made in oak, but you could dye it with stain or varnish for a richer effect.

TOP RIGHT: You can make up lots of different patterns. The example here would be easy to do.

RIGHT: Classic herringbone presents problems at the edges if the room is not perfectly square, but it can be combined with a simpler pattern around the outside.

1 Make sure that your floor surface is clean, dry and level. Find your starting point as for laying wood mosaic flooring and draw guidelines on the floor. Using a ridged spreader, coat a manageable area of floor in the specified floor adhesive.

2 Apply wood blocks to the adhesive. Use a length of timber laid across the blocks to check that they all lie flush. Repeat until the floor is covered. Seal the floor with two or three coats of varnish, sanding between coats.

LAYING SHEET VINYL

Sheet vinyl flooring can be difficult to lay because it is wide and comparatively stiff, and edge cutting must be done accurately if gaps are not to be noticeable against skirtings (baseboards). Lengths of quadrant beading (base shoe) can be pinned (tacked) around the perimeter of the room to disguise any serious mistakes.

Most rooms contain at least one long straight wall, and it is often easiest to press the vinyl into the angle between wall and floor and cut along it with the knife held at a 45-degree angle. Then press the ends of the length neatly against the walls at right angles to the first wall, make small diagonal cuts at internal and external angles, and trim the edges to fit there.

1 Unless the wall is perfectly straight, make a cut at the corner and trim the adjacent edges of the sheet with a sharp knife along the angle of wall and floor.

4 To join sheet vinyl edge to edge, overlap the two sheets so that the pattern matches and cut through both layers against a steel straightedge. Discard the waste strips.

5 Place a strip of double-sided adhesive tape underneath the joint line, peel off the backing paper and press the two cut edges firmly down on to the tape.

2 At door architraves (trims), make cuts into the edge of the sheet down to floor level so the sheet will lie flat, and trim off the tongues of excess material.

3 Use a similar technique for trimming the sheet around larger obstacles, such as washbasin pedestals.

6 To fit the vinyl sheet around pipework, make a cut into it at the pipe position and then trim out a circle of the material to fit around the pipe.

7 At door openings, fit threshold (saddle) strips to anchor the edges of the sheet. Here, an existing strip has been prised up and is being hammered down again to grip the vinyl.

TEMPLATES FOR SHEET VINYL

Where sheet vinyl flooring is being laid around unusually shaped obstacles, such as washbasin pedestals and piping, the best way of obtaining an accurate fit is to make a template of the obstacle so that its shape can be transferred on to the vinyl. Tape together sheets of paper and cut them roughly to the outline of the room and the obstacle. Tape the template to the floor, and use a block of wood and a pencil (or a pair of compasses) to draw a line on the template parallel with the outline of the obstacle. Next, transfer the template to the vinyl, and use the same block of wood or compass setting to scribe lines back on to the vinyl itself. These lines will accurately represent the shape of the room and the obstacle. Cut along them and remove the waste, then stick down edges and seams as before.

A shape tracer, which incorporates a series of adjustable plastic or metal fingers, can also be used to transfer the shapes of obstacles to the vinyl.

1 Use a small block of wood and a pencil to scribe the wall outline on to the paper template laid on the floor.

4 Repeat step 2 to scribe the outline of the obstacle on to the vinyl. Fix the pencil to the block with tape or a rubber band if that makes it easier to use.

PREPARING THE TEMPLATE

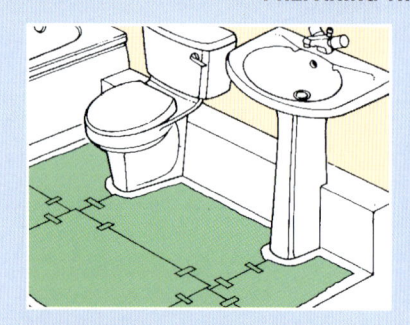

To make a cutting template for a room full of obstacles, such as a bathroom, tape sheets of paper together with their edges about 50mm (2in) from the room walls all around. Tear in from the edges to fit the template around the obstacles as shown, ready for the outline of the room and the obstacles to be scribed on to the template with a block of wood and a pencil.

FLOORING TECHNIQUES • 235

2 Tape the template over the sheet vinyl and use the same block with a pencil to scribe a copy of the room outline back on to the vinyl.

3 Use the same scribing technique to transfer the outline of obstacles such as washbasin pedestals on to the paper template.

5 Using a sharp utility knife, cut carefully around the outline of the obstacle. Make a cut into the waste area, test the cut-out for fit, and trim it slightly if necessary.

6 To make cut-outs around pipes, use a slim block and a pencil to scribe the pipe position on to the template as four lines at right angles to each other.

7 Place the template over the vinyl at the pipe position, and use the same block and pencil to mark the cut-out on the vinyl as a small square.

8 Use compasses or a pipe offcut to draw a circle inside the square, then cut around the circle and into the waste area from the edge.

LAYING FLEXIBLE FLOOR TILES

Flexible vinyl and lino floor tiles are available in plain and self-adhesive types. For plain vinyl tiles, an emulsion-type latex flooring adhesive is used, while lino tiles are best stuck with a water-based contact adhesive.

Because these tiles are thin, any unevenness in the sub-floor will show through the tiles. Cover wooden floors with a hardboard underlay first. Concrete floors may need repairs or treatment with a self-smoothing compound.

Set the floor out carefully. Find the centre-point of the floor by linking the midpoints of opposite pairs of walls with string lines. Dry-lay rows of tiles to see how many whole tiles will fit, move the rows if necessary, then chalk the string lines to mark the starting point.

1 At the border, lay a tile over the last tile laid, butt another against the skirting (baseboard) and mark its edge on the tile underneath.

4 At an external corner, lay a whole tile over the last whole tile in one adjacent row, butt another against the wall and draw along its edge.

5 Move the sandwiched tile to the other side of the corner, butt the second whole tile against the wall and mark its edge on the sandwiched tile.

FLOORING TECHNIQUES • 237

2 Place the marked tile on a board and cut it with a sharp knife. The exposed part of the sandwiched tile in step 1 will fit the gap perfectly.

3 Fit the cut piece of border tile in place. Trim its edge slightly if it is a tight fit. Mark, cut and fit the other border tiles in exactly the same way.

6 Use the utility knife to cut out the square waste section along the marked lines, and offer up the L-shaped border tile to check its fit before fixing it.

7 After laying an area of tiles, use a smooth block of wood to work along the joins, pressing them down. This will ensure that they are all bedded firmly in the adhesive.

LAYING FOAM-BACKED CARPET

Laying traditional woven carpet can be difficult for the amateur, because if it is to wear well it has to be correctly tensioned across the room by using gripper strips and a carpet stretcher. However, there is no reason why the do-it-yourselfer should not lay less expensive foam-backed carpet in, for example, a spare bedroom. It is possible to disguise any slight inaccuracies that creep into the cutting and fitting process more easily here than with a sheet vinyl floor covering.

Start by putting a paper or cloth underlay on the floor, taping the seams and stapling the underlay in place so that it cannot creep as work continues. Unroll the carpet across the room, with the excess lapping up the walls. Roughly trim the excess all around the room, leaving 50mm (2in) for final trimming. Make small cuts at external corners, such as around chimney breasts (fireplace projections), and let the tongues fall back into the alcoves, then trim off the waste across the face of the chimney breast. Next, press the carpet into internal corners and mark the corner point with a finger. Make cuts to remove the triangle of carpet from the internal angle. Finally, trim the perimeter with a knife drawn along the angle between skirting (baseboard) and wall, and secure the edges with double-sided adhesive tape. Fit threshold (saddle) strips across door openings.

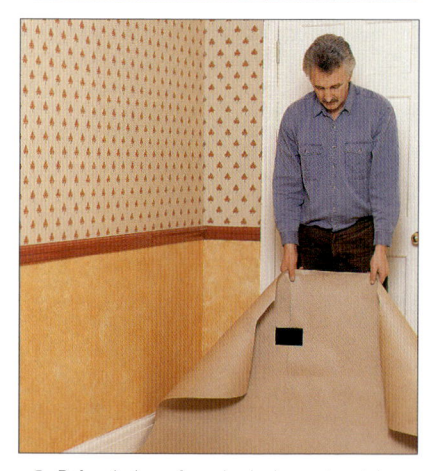

1 Before laying a foam-backed carpet, put down a paper or cloth underlay to keep the foam from sticking to the floor. Tape the seams and staple it in place to prevent it from creeping and rucking up as you work.

4 Work the carpet across the floor to the opposite wall to ensure that it is laying flat. Then trim that edge against the skirting (baseboard) and tape it down too.

FLOORING TECHNIQUES • 239

2 Put double-sided adhesive tape all around the perimeter of the room, then unroll the carpet and position it so that it laps up the room walls.

3 Butt the edge of the carpet against the longest straight wall in the room. Peel the backing paper off the adhesive tape and press the edge of the carpet into place, working along the wall from one end to the other.

5 Make cuts at internal and external corners to bed the carpet on to the tape. Trim excess carpet by drawing a knife along the angle. Take care not to over-trim.

6 Use adhesive seaming tape to join sections of carpet together where necessary in particularly large rooms. Pressure from a wallpaper seam roller ensures a good bond with the tape, preventing the edges from lifting.

LAYING WOVEN CARPET

The laying and trimming technique used for fitting woven carpets is broadly similar to that described for foam-backed carpets, with two main exceptions: the edges are secured on toothed gripper strips instead of by double-sided adhesive tape, and the carpet must be tensioned across the room to ensure that it wears evenly and cannot ruck up in use.

Start by nailing the gripper strips to the floor all around the room, using a hardboard or cardboard spacer to set them about 10mm (3/8in) away from the skirtings (baseboards). Then put down a good-quality foam underlay, paper side up, cutting it to fit just inside the gripper strips. Tape any seams and staple the underlay to the floor at regular intervals.

Now unroll the carpet, trim it roughly and make small diagonal cuts at internal and external corners. Use a carpet fitter's bolster or a clean brick bolster (stonecutter's chisel) to press one edge of the carpet down on to the gripper strips, then trim off excess carpet and use the bolster to tuck the carpet edge into the gap between the strips and the wall.

Use the carpet stretcher to tension the carpet along the adjacent walls and across the room, hooking it on to the gripper strips as each section is stretched. Trim along the other walls too, and fit the carpet neatly into the doorway, securing it with a threshold (saddle) strip.

1 Nail gripper strips around the perimeter of the room, using a spacer to set them slightly away from the skirting (baseboard). The edge of the carpet will be tucked into the gap.

4 Press one edge of the carpet on to the gripper strips with a carpet fitter's bolster (stonecutter's chisel) to ensure that the angled teeth are able to grip the carpet backing securely.

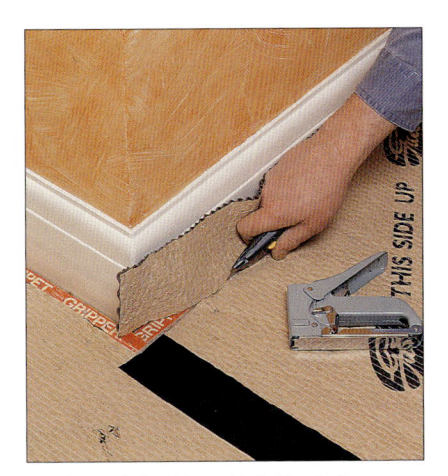

2 Lay underlay, trimmed to butt up to the gripper strips. Tape pieces together as necessary, then staple the underlay to the floor at regular intervals.

3 Unroll the carpet and trim it roughly all around. Then make cuts at external corners so that tongues of carpet will fit around them.

5 Cut off the excess carpet along this edge by running a sharp utility knife along the angle between the gripper strip and the skirting, as shown. Take care not to damage the skirting with the knife by holding the blade at an angle away from it.

6 Use the blade of the bolster to tuck the trimmed edge of the carpet into the angle between the gripper strip and the skirting. Then tension the carpet along adjacent walls with the carpet stretcher. Attach the carpet to the gripper strips in the same manner. ▶

7 Make release cuts at all the internal corners, then trim the waste carpet along the other walls of the room as before and tuck the cut edges into the perimeter gaps. This will provide a neat finish to the edges of the carpet.

8 At door frames and similar obstacles, trim the carpet to follow the contours of the obstacle as closely as possible, and press it on to the gripper strips.

9 Complete the installation by fitting a door threshold (saddle) strip. Different types are available for linking carpet to carpet, and carpet to smooth floor coverings.

STRETCHING CARPET

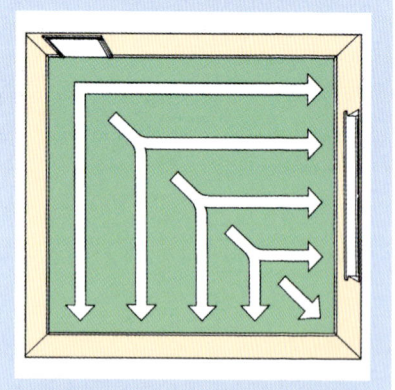

Stretch a carpet along two adjacent walls of the room, hooking it on to the gripper strips. Then stretch it across the room, first in one direction, then in the other.

LAYING STAIR CARPET

The technique of carpeting a flight of stairs is similar in principle to that used for carpeting a room, with gripper strips being used to hold the carpet securely to the treads. The job is easiest on a straight flight, but it is not too difficult to cope with winding flights or projecting bullnose steps because cuts can be made across the carpet at any point on the flight and the seams hidden neatly at the back of the tread.

Start by nailing on the gripper strips, just above the bottom edge of each riser and just in front of the rear edge of each tread. The space between them should be about the same as the thickness of a single fold of the carpet. Instead of two lengths of the normal plywood-based strip, special one-piece L-section metal grippers can be used here. Add short lengths of ordinary gripper strip to the sides of the treads, the thickness of the carpet away from the sides of the flight. Next, cut pieces of underlay to cover each tread and the face of the riser below, and fix them in position with the aid of a staple gun or carpet tacks.

Start laying the carpet at the top of the flight of stairs. If the same carpet is being used on the landing, this should be brought over the edge of the top step and down the face of the first riser. If you do this, the top edge of the stair carpet should be tucked into the gripper strips at the bottom of the first riser. Trim the edges of the carpet on the first tread, then on the next riser, and tuck them in before locking the fold of carpet into the gripper strips at the back of the next tread with a carpet fitter's bolster (stonecutter's chisel). Continue in this way to the bottom of the flight, where the stair carpet always finishes at the base of the last riser, whether or not the floor below is covered with the same carpet.

1 Cut lengths of carpet gripper strip to fit across the width of the flight, and nail them in position at the foot of each riser and also at the back of each tread.

2 Next, cut and fit a short length of gripper strip to the sides of each tread. Position them just less than the carpet thickness away from the sides of the flight. ▶

3 Cut underlay to fit adjacent treads and risers, and tack them in place so that they fit smoothly over the nosing at the front of the tread.

4 As an alternative to using two lengths of plywood gripper strip in the tread/riser angle, fit a one-piece L-section metal strip.

5 Begin fitting the carpet at the top of the flight, trimming each tread and riser in turn, then forcing a fold of carpet into the angled gripper strips.

6 On an open-string staircase, either trim the carpet to fit around each baluster or fold over the edge and tack it to fit against the baluster, as shown here.

7 On winder (curved) stairs, cut carpet to cover each tread and the riser below. Align the weave at right angles to the riser.

8 Secure each piece of carpet to the gripper strip at the rear of the tread first, then stretch it over the tread and down to the next gripper strip.

9 Trim off the waste from the bottom edge of the riser and tuck in the carpet at the sides. Repeat the cutting and fitting sequence for any other winder steps on the flight.

10 If the flight finishes with a projecting bullnose step, trim and tack the carpet to the riser, as shown, and cover the riser with a separate strip.

ALTERNATIVE FIXINGS

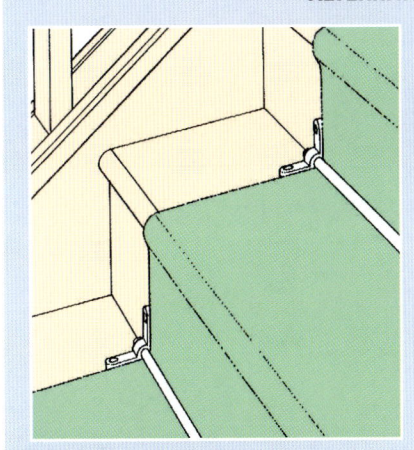

ABOVE: When laying a stair runner rather than a full-width carpet, paint or stain the stair treads and anchor the runner in place with stair rods.

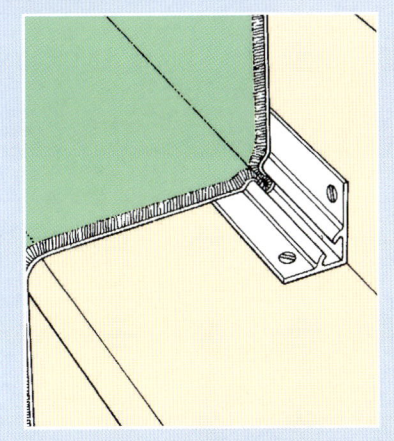

ABOVE: If you are using foam-backed carpet on your stairs, fit special gripper strips for foam-backed carpet into the angles between treads and risers.

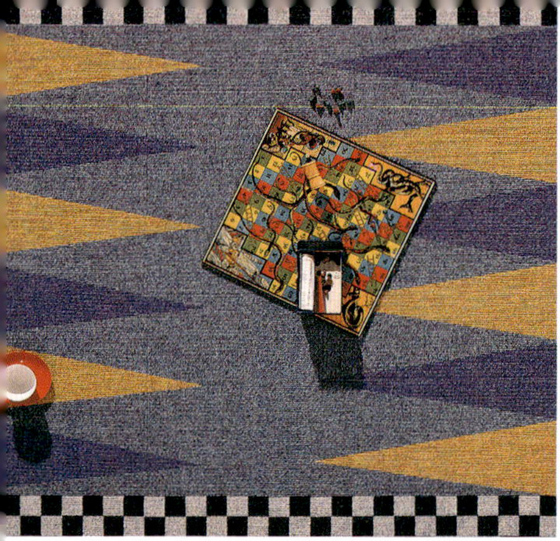
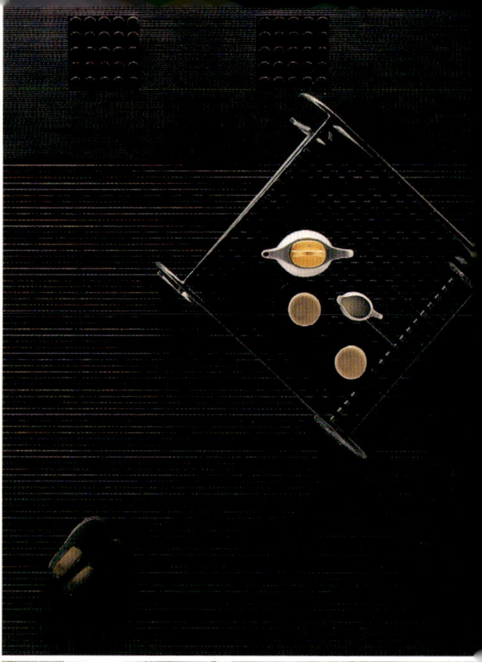
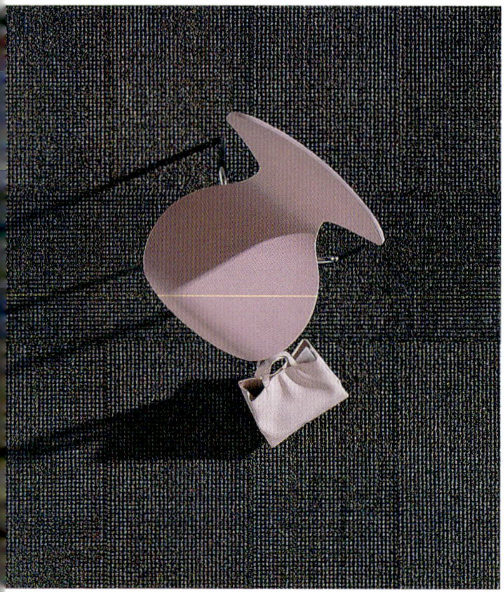
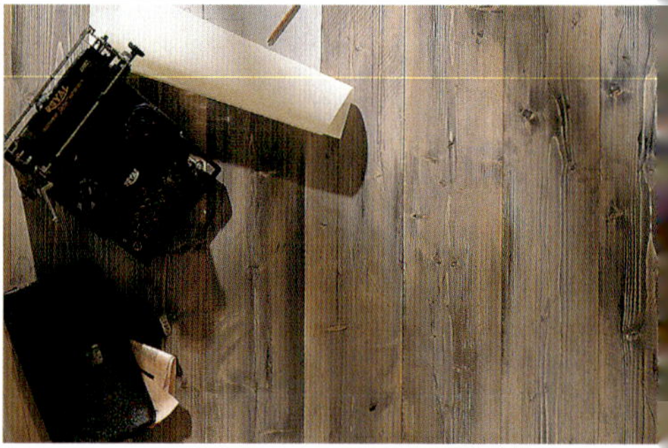
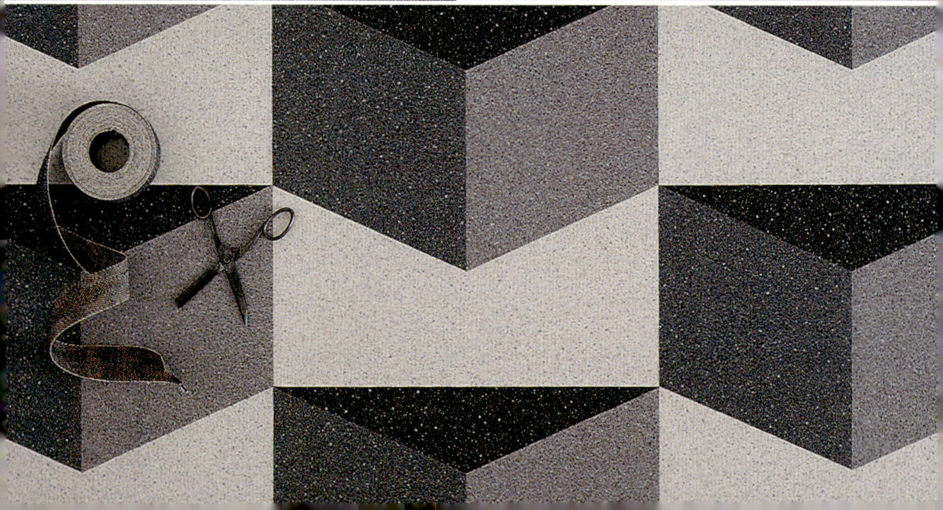

FLOORING VARIATIONS

In years gone by, people wanted floors to last a lifetime. Today we change our furnishings – and our homes – more often, so the need is for chic, inexpensive flooring with instant design impact. If in doubt about a room's final use or colour scheme, a beautiful neutral floor will allow you to alter either. The scale of a room is also important: large patterns are seen to best advantage only in large rooms with the minimum of furniture. However, floors are often the main feature of halls and passages, even more so when seen from an upper landing. In this situation, go for a really eye-catching treatment. The following pages will give you a taste of what is possible with the application of a little imagination.

DISTRESSED FLOORBOARDS

Wooden floors are often appealing because of their subtle variations of colour, which improve with age. Your wooden floors may not be in a great state to begin with, though, or may look uninteresting, and you don't really want to wait for the years to work their magic naturally. Wood stains can help to imitate that look in only a few hours. You can create the look of driftwood, weathered teak or other hardwood decking, as found in beach houses. All you need is three different dyes and a thin wash of white emulsion (latex) paint. This technique would give a bleached effect to any wood stain; for example, over a warm mahogany, a wash of cream or white instantly gives the faded look of maturity.

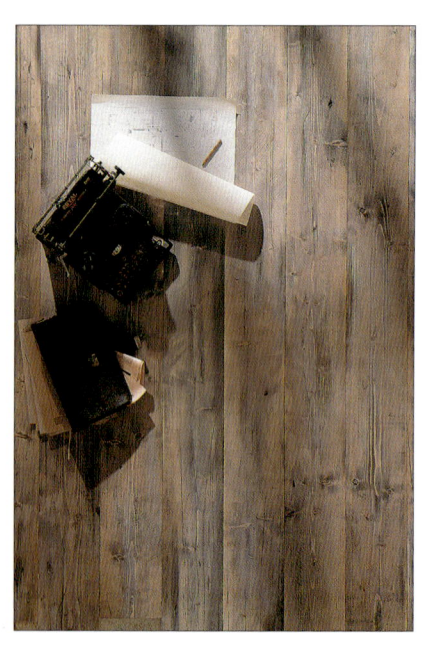

1 First prepare the surface by knocking in any protruding floorboard nails with a nail punch, and removing any old paint spills with a sander.

4 With either a lint-free cloth or a brush, apply the stain. This will colour anything porous, so protect your hands with rubber gloves and wear old clothes.

7 While the stain is still wet, brush on a wash of the diluted white or cream emulsion (latex) paint, about one part emulsion to four parts water.

FLOORING VARIATIONS • 249

2 Brush the boards with a wire brush, along the direction of the grain, with the occasional cross stroke to give a distressed effect.

3 Experiment with the stains, mixing colours together – a little should go a long way. Use scrap wood to test the effect.

5 Apply a generous quantity of stain, but rub off the surplus. For an even finish, complete in one session, keeping the joins between areas random and avoiding overlapping bands of stain.

6 It's better to apply one thin coat all over, then go back and add further coats, perhaps working the stain into knots or grooves with a brush, to give an uneven, weathered look.

8 Using a dry cloth, rub off surplus paint or apply more until you have achieved the effect you want.

9 Seal the finish by applying two coats of clear varnish, brushing along the grain and sanding very lightly between coats.

WOOD-GRAIN CHEQUERBOARD

Painted chequerboards are a recurrent theme for flooring, yet they are rarely seen in natural wood. If you are starting from a concrete or wooden floor, have the new floor covering cut into squares of the size you want, and either screw them in place or stick them down. If your floor is already covered in sheets of plywood or hardboard, mark out a chequerboard pattern, ignoring the natural joins. Wood-graining doesn't have to be done painstakingly carefully; you can alter the effect produced in oil paint until it starts to dry.

Obtain some reference for the wood effect; oak was the inspiration here. The grain effects resemble the wood treated in different ways, half "polished" and half "rough-sawn and sand-blasted". You could also use two different wood effects, such as walnut and maple.

1 Mark out the floor, edging alternate squares with masking tape. Paint them with two shades of cream.

4 After a few minutes, drag a dry graining brush over the finish, to give the grain effect.

7 Then repeat step 4, using a graining comb rather than a dry graining brush, so the grain looks wider.

2 Mix oil colours into an oil-based glaze, to match the wood reference. Thin the result with white spirit (paint thinner), if necessary.

3 For the "lighter" squares, brush the glaze in the direction of the "grain", leaving brush marks. Add cross-hatched strokes.

5 Using a darker oil paint and a fine artist's brush, gently draw in the chevrons of the wood grain.

6 Soften with a brush, adding white spirit if the paint has dried. Allow to dry. For the "darker" squares, repeat step 1.

8 Paint on more noticeable chevrons in the same way, following the grain.

9 Soften the effect, using the graining comb before the brush. Allow to dry. Apply two coats of satin varnish and allow to dry. If you like, burnish with a little non-slip polish.

LINOLEUM IN 3-D PATTERNS

Linoleum now comes in many thicknesses, colours and patterns, and by cutting it into *trompe l'oeil* patterns and playing with slight colour variations, you can create quite grand effects. Lino is hard-wearing, water-resistant and relatively inexpensive and, given this dramatic treatment, reminiscent of the optical effects in the drawings of Escher, it can become the centrepiece of any hall, kitchen or bathroom. Rolls of lino and floor adhesive were used in this project but you could also use self-glued tiles to make a floor reminiscent of a Venetian palazzo.

Before you begin, draw a plan of the design on squared paper and transfer this to the floor by laying out grid lines. To provide a means of cutting the linoleum to shape, make hardboard templates and cut around them with a sharp knife. Take great care to make your cuts accurate, otherwise you will be left with unsightly gaps between the pieces, which will collect dirt.

1 You need a smooth, flat surface on which to apply the lino. If necessary, lay a plywood or hardboard floor.

4 Draw grid lines on the floor to act as a guide when laying the lino shapes.

2 Having made sure no nail heads are exposed, lightly sand the floor, to make sure that it is perfectly flat.

3 Measure the floor. To ensure a good fit, it is very important to work out your pattern on paper first.

5 Draw each of the pattern shapes on to a sheet of hardboard and cut them out carefully with a saw.

6 Use the templates to cut out the lino shapes. Remember that lino isn't very forgiving and accuracy is all-important.

7 Try out your pattern in pieces of lino to see if any need trimming. If necessary, number them on the back to help you fit them together.

8 Apply contact adhesive to the floor and the backs of the tiles, then carefully fit them in place; you cannot adjust them once they are laid.

PATTERNS WITH CARPET TILES

Carpet tiles are among the simplest of floor coverings to lay, because they are highly tolerant of any slight inaccuracy in cutting to fit. The cheapest types are usually plain in colour and have a very short pile or a corded appearance, while more expensive tiles may have a longer pile and are available in patterns as well as plain colours. Most are designed to be loose-laid, with just the edges secured with bands of adhesive or double-sided tape. This makes it easy to lift individual tiles for cleaning or to even out wear.

Most carpet tiles are marked on the back with an arrow to indicate the pile direction. Align these for a plain effect, or lay them at right angles to create a chequerboard effect. When satisfied with the layout, lift perimeter tiles and put down double-sided tape all around the room. Peel the backing paper off the top of the tape and press the tiles into place. Finish doorways with threshold (saddle) strips.

Another possibility with carpet tiles is to make eye-catching patterns by choosing a selection of different coloured tiles and cutting them into a variety of shapes. Plan the design on paper first and do not start cutting the tiles until you are completely happy with it. If you need to cut very small pieces, make sure all of them are secured with double-sided tape.

1 Measure your room and make sure that the floor is level and all protruding floorboard nails have been driven in.

4 With a steel straightedge and a rigid-bladed knife, score along the marked lines. Don't attempt to cut the tile through in one action.

7 Stick the cut tiles in place, making sure not to pack them too tightly. In this case, the chequered border was laid first, followed by the central pattern. Tread the tiles down.

FLOORING VARIATIONS • 255

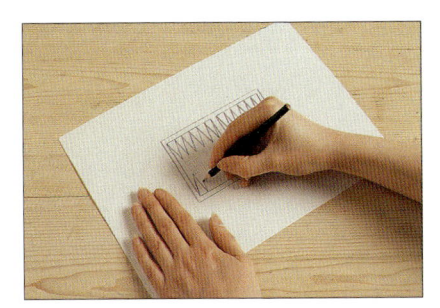

2 Plan your design on paper. Most rooms are not perfectly square or rectangular, so leave room for an area of plain tiles to edge the pattern.

3 Measure the tiles to work out how many will be needed. Draw the pattern on the backs of the tiles.

5 Starting at the top of the tile, cut down the scored lines. Do this on a solid surface and take great care in doing it.

6 Lay carpet tape and remove the backing. Cut all the tiles for one complete run and fit them, rather than laying little bits at a time.

HIGH-TECH RUBBER FLOORING

Available from specialist rubber manufacturers, rubber mats are valued for their non-slip and protective qualities, and, since they are waterproof, they are particularly useful in, say, a shower room. Rubber is sold from the roll in a broad spectrum of colours, widths and textures. In addition, it doesn't fray and will happily absorb any lumps or strange joins in a floor. To keep it looking good, clean and seal with a silicone spray polish.

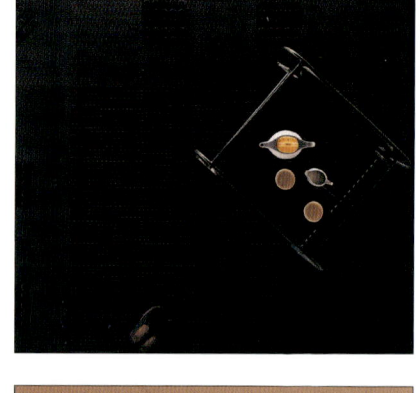

1 Rubber matting in two different designs and rubber tiles have been used here. Measure the floor and the rubber matting, then carefully trim the long runners for the border to size.

2 For each corner, cut a square from the same matting. Divide diagonally and fit them so that the grooves run at right angles to the grooves in the runners. Place the long runners between them.

3 Lay the second matting for the central area. Cut this second type into squares, then cut holes in the runners at regular intervals for them.

4 Secure all the pieces with rubber adhesive, applied to both surfaces. Spray with silicone polish and buff lightly.

CHEQUERBOARD CARPET TILES

Floor mats are easy and cheap to come by, and you can often cut them without the edges fraying. They come in many finishes, some even incorporating words or pictures, and all in manageable rectangles. When these very textured grey polypropylene mats are arranged with the pile running in different directions, a chequerboard effect is achieved. Alternatively, a variety of colours could be used to make an eye-catching pattern.

1 Use strings to find the room's centre and mark with a cross. Measure the floor and work out how many mats you will need. Mark the cuts with a white crayon or chalk on the reverse of the mats.

2 If the mats are of carpet quality, score along the lines with the craft knife, working from the back of the mat. Then cut the mats to size.

3 Using a notched spreader, apply floor adhesive to the floor, working on a small area at a time.

4 Starting at the centre, carefully lay the mats in position, remembering that, for the effect shown here, you need to alternate the weaves.

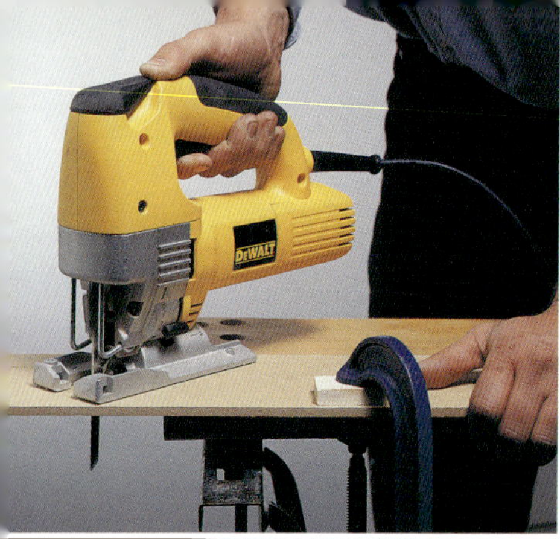
DEWALT

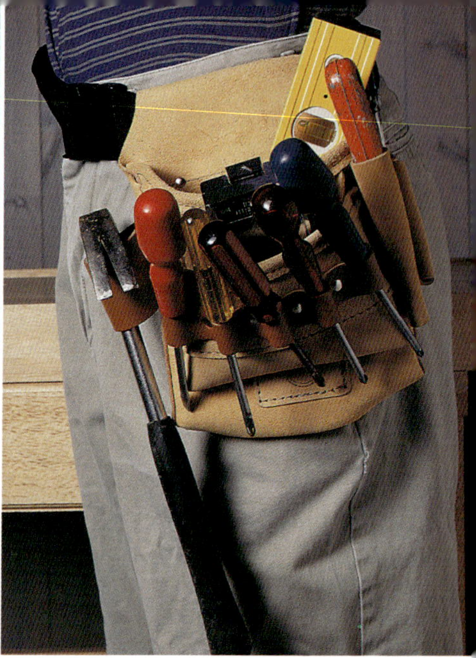

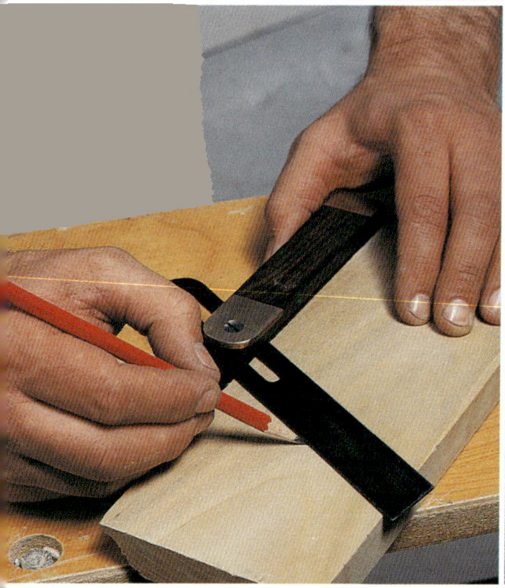

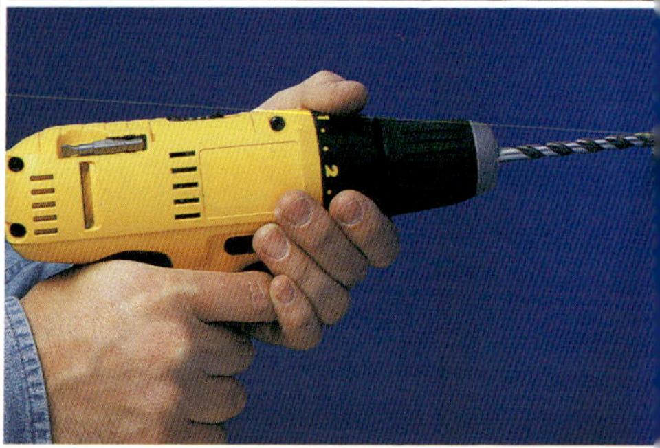

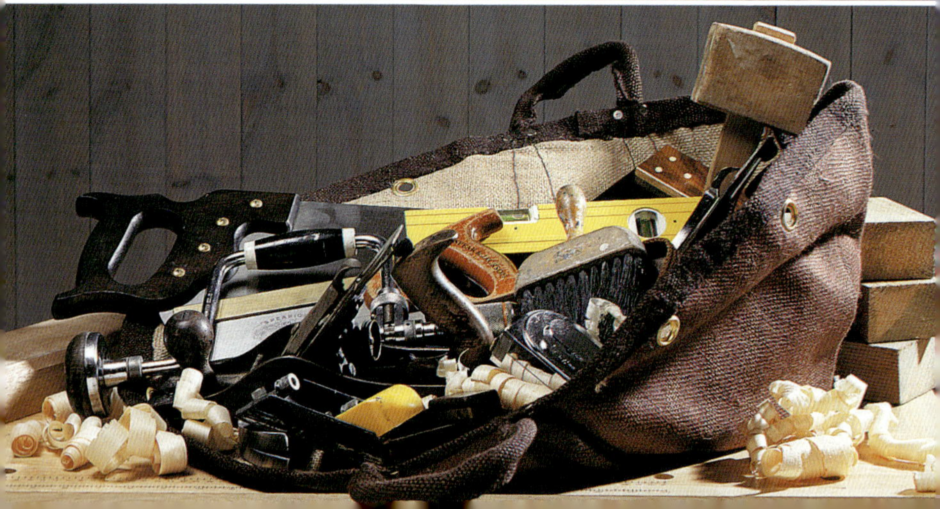

SAFETY & TOOLS

- Safety & preparation
- Measuring, shaping & cutting tools
- Assembling tools
- Finishing tools

INTRODUCTION

Most people have a few basic tools in their home: a hammer, a screwdriver or two, perhaps a saw of some sort and a couple of paintbrushes – just about enough to tackle the occasional simple job or essential temporary repair. The more competent are likely to have a more comprehensive basic toolkit containing such items as a retractable tape measure, a craft knife, adjustable spanner (wrench), hand and tenon saws, a spirit (carpenter's) level, screwdrivers for different types of screw head, perhaps a chisel or two, pliers, pincers, an electric drill and a variety of decorating tools.

ABOVE: A power drill makes drilling easy. Buy one that offers a choice of speeds, has a chuck capacity of at least 12mm (½in), and a hammer facility if you intend drilling masonry.

ABOVE: Mounting your tools on a perforated tool board is a good idea. You will be able to find what you need quickly, and it will be obvious when a tool is missing. Buy one or make your own.

Some people, of course, are determined do-it-yourselfers who gain much pleasure and satisfaction from doing as many jobs as they can around the home. Others may even have a practical hobby, such as woodwork or model-making, that requires a dedicated home workshop containing a variety of complex and versatile machinery together with a range of specialized hand tools.

Whatever your level of interest in do-it-yourself, choosing the right tools for each job you tackle is essential. Attempting any task without the proper tools is a recipe for disaster.

ABOVE: Of all the do-it-yourself tasks, decorating is probably the most common. Painting requires brushes and rollers; papering requires tools such as scissors, a pasting brush and a seam roller.

Most toolkits grow organically as specific tools are added when the need arises. The tools featured in this chapter show a useful selection for starting your own projects.

When buying tools, always go for the best you can afford; the adage, "You get what you pay for," is particularly appropriate. Cheap tools may bend or break and are unlikely to last long; good-quality tools will last you a lifetime. If your budget is tight, it is best to buy several hand tools rather than one power tool. This has the benefit of improving your manual skills at an early stage, which will give encouraging results as well as increase the range of jobs you can undertake.

LEFT: A belt sander is useful for heavy-duty shaping and sanding. As well as being hand-held, it can be inverted and secured in a woodworking vice.

USING PROFESSIONALS

As a do-it-yourself enthusiast, you have to be familiar with several trades, but it is often well worth employing a professional for structural work to save time and possibly money. There are many jobs, especially in plumbing and electrics, where professional help is welcome and indeed necessary. Professionals can also advise you in advance if your project is likely to fail for a reason you may not even have considered.

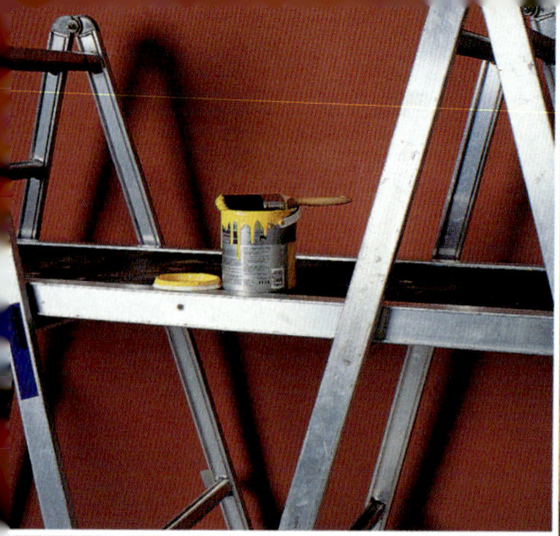
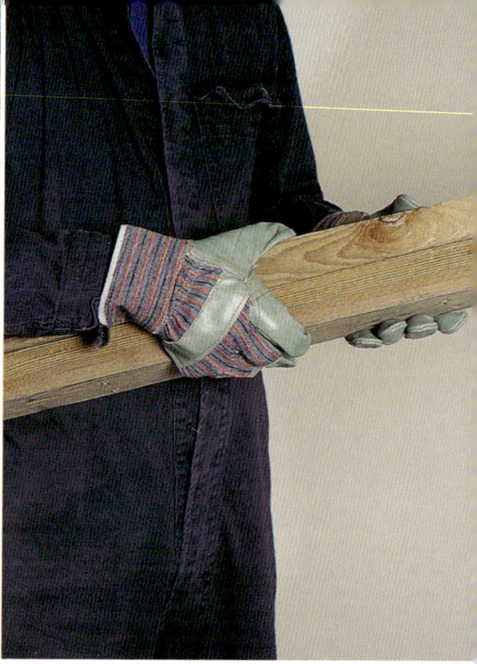
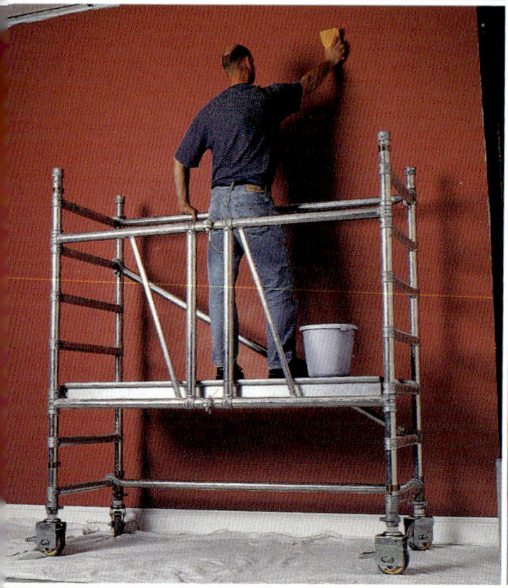
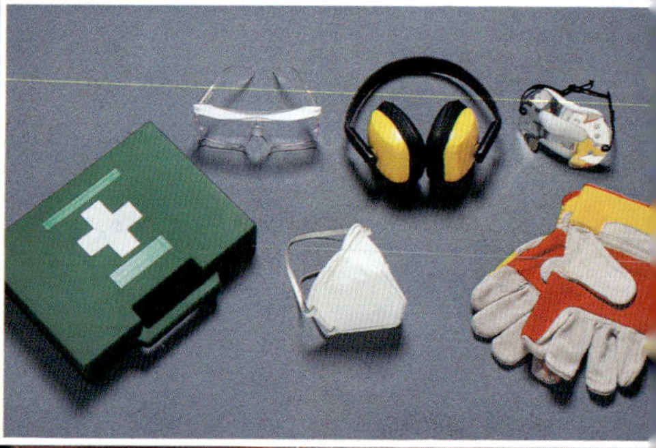
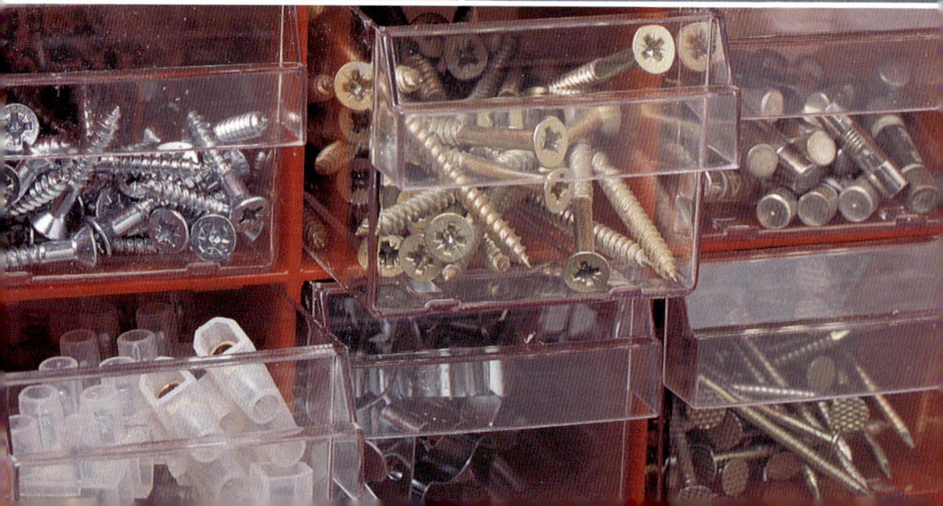

SAFETY & PREPARATION

Even the simplest of do-it-yourself jobs carries with it some degree of risk, if only from the danger of upsetting a can of paint. Some tasks, however, have the potential to cause serious injury, so safety should be uppermost in your mind at all times. You must use the proper tools in the correct manner, wear appropriate clothing, ensure you have safe access to the job and take steps to protect others who may be at risk. Storing your tools correctly is important, too. Not only will they be ready for use when you need them, but they will also be protected from damage and from damaging other tools. Completing any do-it-yourself task can be immensely satisfying; the following pages show you how to do so in complete safety.

AWARENESS AND CLOTHING

A complete book could be devoted to the subject of safety in the home, and there is a wide range of equipment designed to minimize our capacity for hurting ourselves. Nevertheless, there is one requirement that we cannot buy, without which all that equipment is virtually useless, namely concentration. This is particularly important when working alone.

ABOVE: Wear overalls to protect your clothes when painting, decorating or carrying out any dirty or dusty job. Disposable types are available for one-off jobs.

AWARENESS
Concentration is essential when using any form of power tool, especially a saw, where one slip can mean the loss of a finger, or worse. The dangers of accidents involving electricity are well documented, as are those involving falls from ladders, spillages of toxic materials, and burns and injuries caused by contact with fire or abrasive surfaces. In almost every case, there is a loss of concentration, coupled with poor work practices and inadequate protective clothing or equipment. So, although the items shown here are all useful, concentrating on what you are doing is the best advice to prevent accidents from occurring.

CLOTHING
Overalls are a good investment because they not only protect clothing, but are also designed to be close-fitting to prevent accidental contact with moving machinery. Industrial gloves provide protection against cuts and bruises when doing rough jobs, such as fencing and garden work. Safety boots should be worn when lifting heavy objects or when the use of machinery is involved.

Knee pads are necessary for comfort when carrying out any job that requires a lot of kneeling. They will also protect the wearer from injury if a nail or similar projection is knelt on accidentally. Finally, a bump cap will protect the head from minor injuries, but is not so cumbersome as the hard hat required on building sites.

SAFETY & PREPARATION • 265

ABOVE: A pair of thick gloves will be essential when handling rough materials such as sawn wood or sharp objects such as broken glass. Make sure they fit well.

ABOVE: If you have to do a job that involves a lot of kneeling, rubber knee pads will be invaluable. They provide comfort and protection from sharp projections such as nail heads.

ABOVE: Safety boots with steel toe caps will protect your feet from injury when working with heavy items such as large sections of wood, bricks and concrete blocks.

ABOVE: When working in situations where you may hit your head accidentally, the bump cap will provide protection without being as cumbersome as a conventional hard hat.

SAFETY EQUIPMENT

Make sure you have the appropriate safety equipment to hand when carrying out do-it-yourself tasks, and always use it. Doing so can prevent nasty accidents and serious injury.

AIRBORNE DANGERS

When you are working with wood, the most common airborne danger is dust, mainly from sawing and sanding. This can do long-term damage to the lungs. Many do-it-yourself enthusiasts do not do enough work to warrant a workshop dust extractor, but it would be worth considering if funds allowed. Such a

BELOW: Typical personal safety equipment – first aid kit, impact-resistant safety spectacles, ear protectors, two types of dust mask and sturdy industrial-type gloves.

KEEPING IN TOUCH

Perhaps the most basic advice is never to work alone with machinery and, if it is possible, always have a friend or colleague nearby to help. If there is no telephone, having a mobile (cell) phone in the workshop is useful.

device can be wall-mounted or portable. In the latter case, it can be moved around the house or workshop to suit any tool in use.

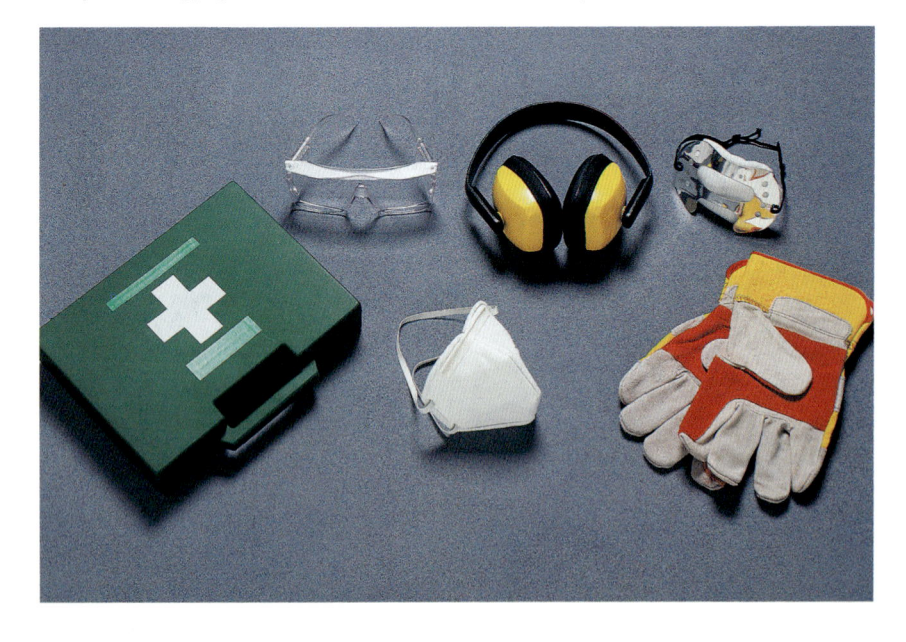

A simple face mask, however, will offer adequate protection for occasional jobs. These can also be purchased for protection against fumes, such as from solvents, which can be very harmful. Dust, of course, also affects the eyes, so it is worth investing in a pair of impact-resistant goggles, which will protect the wearer from both fine dust and flying debris. Full facial protection is available as a powered respirator for those working in dusty conditions over long periods.

Excessive noise is another airborne pollutant that can be dangerous over a long period. Power tools, particularly woodworking machinery such as planers and circular saws, are major culprits. Earplugs are the simplest solution and can be left in the ears over a long period. If you need to be able to hear between short bouts of working, ear protectors are the answer. These can be worn in conjunction with other facial protection quite easily.

FIRST AID

Keeping a basic first aid kit is a common and wise precaution even before any do-it-yourself work is envisaged. It should always be prominently displayed for people unfamiliar with your workshop.

You can buy a home first aid kit that will contain all the necessary items to cope with minor injuries, or you can assemble your own, keeping it in a plastic sandwich box with an airtight lid, which should be clearly marked. You should include items such as bandages, plasters, wound dressings, antiseptic cream, eye pads, scissors, tweezers and safety pins. If you have cause to use the kit, replace the items you have removed as soon as possible.

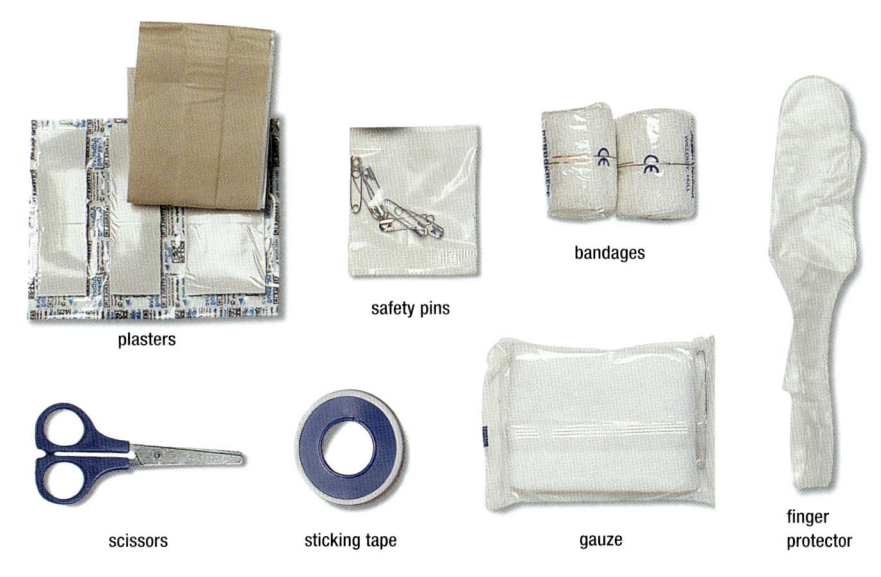

plasters

safety pins

bandages

scissors

sticking tape

gauze

finger protector

ABOVE: Some of the basic items found in a first aid kit.

ELECTRICAL AND FIRE SAFETY

If used incorrectly, the dangers of electrical equipment can be life threatening, and the dangers of fire are obvious. Always treat the former with respect, and take sensible precautions against the latter.

ELECTRICAL SAFETY

Some tools have removable switches that allow the user to immobilize them and prevent any unauthorized use. Provisions for the use of padlocks are also common on machinery, and it is wise to buy tools with such facilities.

To safeguard against electrocution, which can occur if the flex (power cord) is faulty or is cut accidentally, the ideal precaution is a residual current device (RCD). This is simply plugged into the main supply socket (electrical outlet) before the flex and will give complete protection to the user. Extension leads can be purchased with automatic safety cutouts and insulated sockets, and are ideal for outside and inside work.

The danger of electrocution or damage caused by accidentally drilling into an existing cable or pipe can be largely prevented by using an electronic pipe and cable detector, which will locate and differentiate between metal pipes, wooden studs and live wires through plaster and concrete to a depth of approximately 50mm (2in). These are not too expensive and will be very useful around the home.

FIRE SAFETY

The danger of fire is ever-present in both the home and workshop, so a fire extinguisher (possibly two or three) is necessary for every do-it-yourself enthusiast. It should be wall-mounted in plain view and serviced regularly.

LEFT: A simple circuit breaker can save a life by cutting off the power to faulty equipment.

ABOVE: A fire extinguisher is absolutely essential in the workshop or at home. Make sure the one you have is adequate for the size and type of your workshop, and the type of fire source.

LADDER SAFETY

Steps and ladders can be hazardous, so make sure they are in good condition. Accessories include a roof hook, which slips over the ridge for safety; a ladder stay, which spreads the weight of the ladder across a vertical surface, such as a wall, to prevent slippage; and a standing platform, which is used to provide a more comfortable and safer surface to stand on. The last often has a ribbed rubber surface and can be attached to the rungs of almost all ladders. Even more stable is a movable workstation or a board or staging slung between two pairs of steps or trestles. These can often be used with a safety rail, which prevents the operator from falling even if a slip occurs.

ABOVE: A ladder platform will provide a firm footing, especially if heavy footwear is worn.

ABOVE: A movable workstation simplifies the process of working at a height.

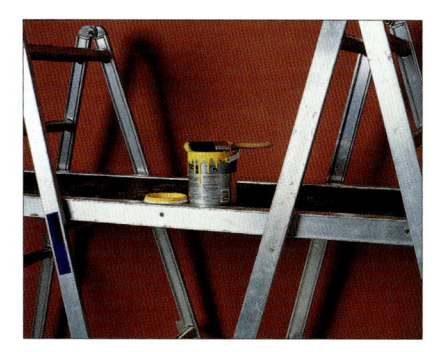

ABOVE: Platforms supported by trestles offer a safe means of painting from a height.

TIPS

• Never overreach when working on steps or a ladder; climb down and reposition it.
• Never allow children or pets into areas where power tools or strong solvents are being used.
• Do not work when you are overtired. This causes lapses in concentration, which can lead to silly and/or dangerous mistakes being made.
• Keep the work environment tidy. Flexes (power cords) should not be walked on or coiled up tightly, because it damages them internally. Moreover, trailing flexes can be a trip hazard, and long extension leads can be prone to overheating.

WORKBENCHES AND VICES

A solid and stable surface is essential for producing good work, and serious thought should be given to this by the enthusiast. A good bench need not be too expensive, nor too pretty; the prime requirements are sturdy construction, a flat-top surface and at least one good vice somewhere on the front of the bench. You can make your own or buy one, but beware of cheap benches that may not be up to the job. Suppliers and auctions of used industrial equipment are good sources.

PORTABLE WORKBENCHES

By far the most popular form of portable support is the foldaway workbench. This is really convenient to use, both in the workshop, in the home and outdoors. It has the ingenious feature of a bench top constructed in two halves, which is capable of acting as a vice. It is handy for holding awkward shapes, such as pipes and large dowels.

VICES

Your main workshop vice should be heavy and sturdy. It is normally screwed to the bench, close to one of the legs. If you intend doing a lot of woodworking, buy one with a quick-release action that allows you to open and close the jaws quickly, using the handle for final adjustments. You should certainly be able to fit false wooden jaws to prevent damage to the material you are working with.

ABOVE: Lightweight plastic sawhorses can be useful if you are undertaking small jobs.

ABOVE: A portable foldaway workbench with adjustable bench top.

ABOVE: Wooden sawhorses come in pairs and are often home-made.

Additional ways of protecting the work in the vice take the form of magnetic vice jaws faced with cork, rubber or aluminium, which fit inside the main jaws of the steel bench vice.

Another useful and portable addition to the bench is the swivelling bench-top vice. This can be fitted easily and removed very quickly, usually by means of a screw clamp. It is particularly handy for holding small pieces of work in awkward positions, when carving, for example. However, it is too light in construction to support work that is to be struck with any force.

The mitre clamp can also be considered as a bench vice of sorts and is useful for holding any assemblies that require clamping at 45 degrees, such as picture and mirror frames. Good quality examples are made from metal, since plastic will tend to flex when pressure is applied.

carpenter's vice

vice jaws faced with rubber

swivelling bench-top vice

mitre clamp

TIPS

- Spend time adjusting your workbench to the exact height that suits you. An incorrect height can prove to be very tiring and is not good for your back. Never shorten the legs of a bench if it is too high; work off a duckboard if necessary.
- Always buy the best-quality vice you can afford; second-hand ones can be particularly good value.

TOOL STORAGE

Tidy and effective storage of your tools pays off in many ways. Properly stored tools will be protected from the atmosphere and will not rust or discolour. The sharp cutting edges of saws and chisels will be protected from damage, as will the potential user's fingers. Moreover, tools will always be easily found near at hand when they are needed.

STORAGE
Efficient storage saves bench and floor space for other uses, and tools will be more easily located, saving time and frustration. It is well worth taking the trouble to devise and even make your own storage facilities. There are plenty of benches, cabinets, racks, clips and tool rolls on the market so that you can equip your workshop with exactly what you need. Remember, too, that storage for tools often needs to be portable, so tool pouches and carrying bags also need to be part of the overall picture.

metal toolbox

drill bit roll

ABOVE: A tool pouch worn around the waist is ideal for carrying tools when working in different parts of the home.

PORTABLE STORAGE
The traditional carpenter's tool bag can still be obtained. Made from heavy canvas, it has two carrying handles and brass eyelets for closing.

Compact, compartmentalized plastic or metal toolboxes with drawers, carrying handles and safety locks are another option for carrying tools from one job to another.

A leather tool pouch can be worn around the waist and has loops and pockets for tools as well as screws and nails. Various sizes and styles are available. They are ideal for use on projects that require you to keep moving about.

Drill bits and chisels should always be carried in a tool roll with their tips covered for protection. Some chisels are provided with individual plastic blade caps, and many saws are sold with a plastic blade guard to protect the teeth when not in use. Always make sure that these are fitted correctly.

STATIC STORAGE

The most important static storage space is that below the workbench top, and often this takes the form of cabinets or drawers. A useful device is a large tilting drawer, which can easily be made and is ideal for storing tools that are in frequent use.

Wall-mounted cabinets with sliding doors are really practical in the workshop. The sliding doors allow them to be sited in confined areas and make it impossible to hit your head on them when they are open, which is especially important above the bench.

Shelving units come in a variety of materials, shapes and sizes, and most can be added to as the need arises.

The tool board has the advantage of not only displaying the tools, but also making it obvious when a tool has not been replaced. To make one, arrange the tools on a flat board and draw around them with a marker pen. Then fit hooks, pegs or clips as necessary.

ABOVE: Specifically made in transparent plastics for easy identification of the contents, storage drawers for screws, nails, clips and a host of other small items are a must.

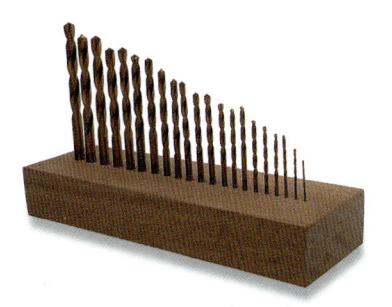

ABOVE: Use a length of wood to make your own storage block to keep your drill bits tidy.

MAKING A TOOL BOARD

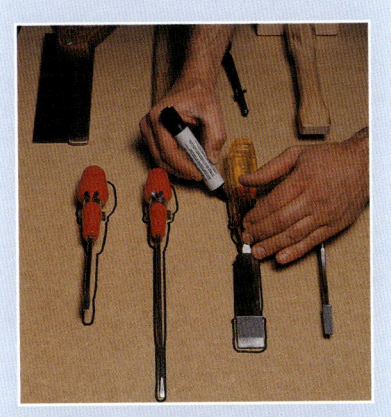

When making a tool board, remember to leave space around each tool so that it can be lifted clear when the board is on the wall. Draw around the tools with a felt-tipped pen to indicate their positions. Hammer in nails or hooks that will hold them in place. Wall hooks will hold larger items, such as saws. Alternatively, you can buy a tool board made from perforated plywood from a local builder's merchant.

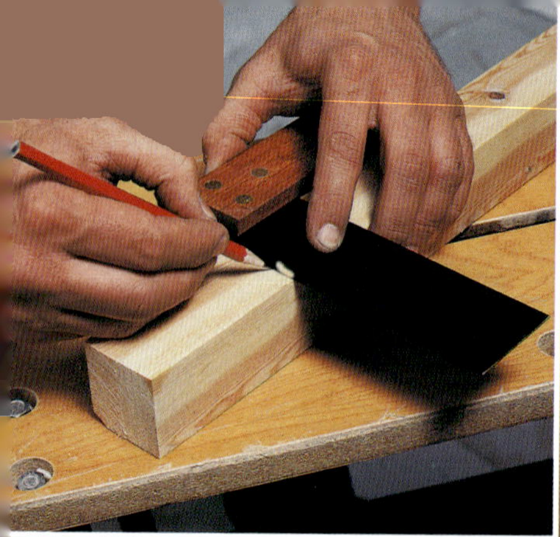
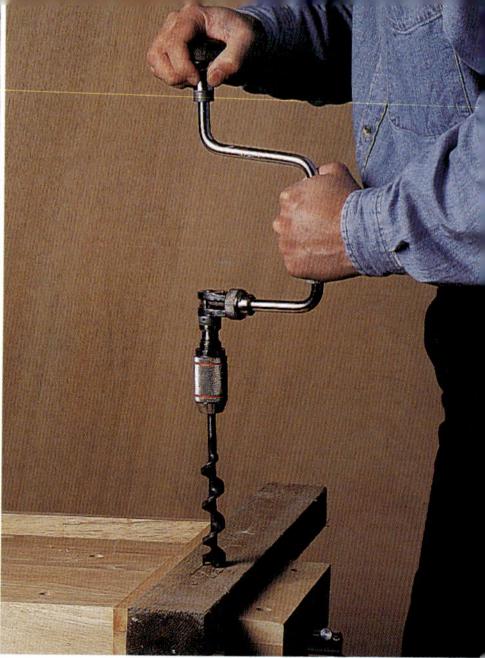
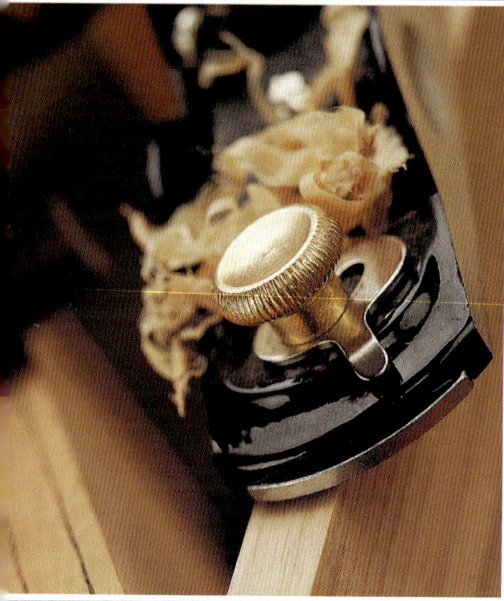
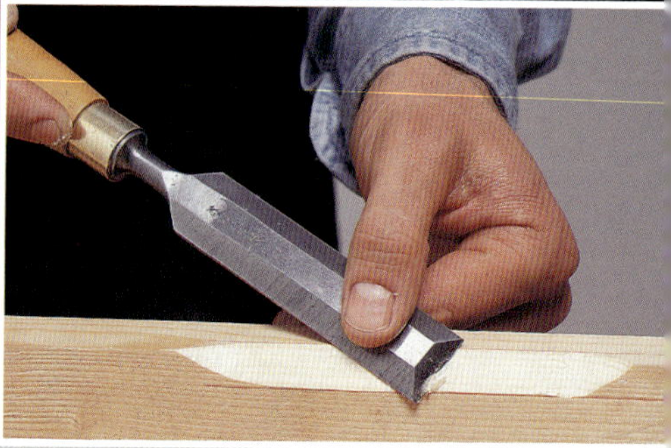
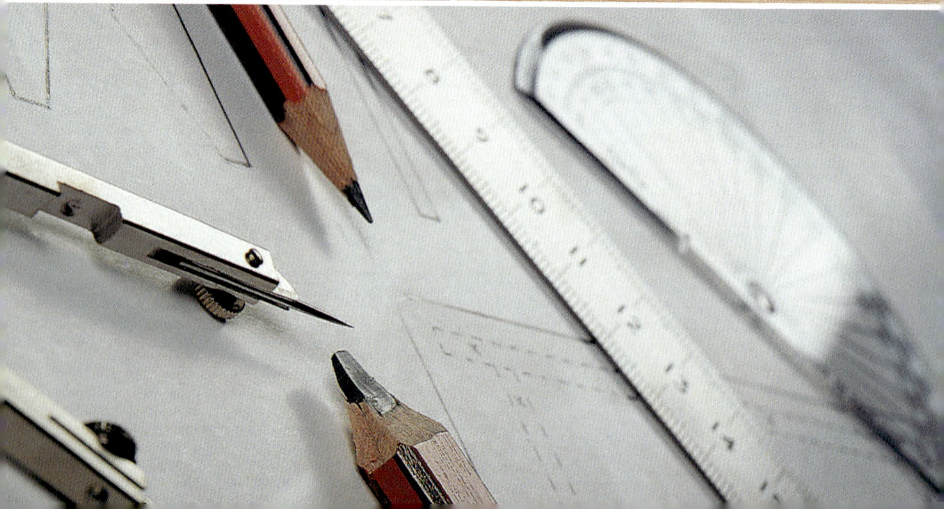

MEASURING, SHAPING & CUTTING TOOLS

One of the most crucial skills for do-it-yourself work is the ability to measure accurately. The quality of much of the work you undertake will rely on that skill, so it is worth taking time and care when measuring and marking out. Shaping wood is a task required for many projects, and knowing how to use a plane will pay dividends. Chisels are also used for this purpose, as well as making cut-outs. To be effective, both tools must be kept sharp. A good toolkit will also include a variety of saws and knives; make sure you know which to use and when. Drilling holes is something you will need to do on a regular basis, and there are many types of drill and drill bit to choose from.

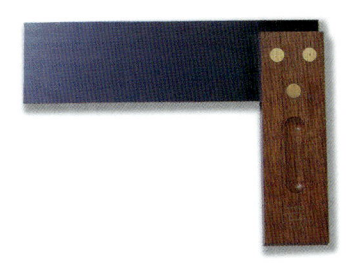

MEASURING TOOLS

Accurate measuring is a very basic, but essential, skill for the do-it-yourself enthusiast to master. Time spent on perfecting measuring is never wasted. The golden rule is to measure twice and cut once. Buy good-quality tools – poor measuring and marking devices can lose their accuracy very quickly and spoil your work.

HOW TO MEASURE

There are dozens of types of flat, rigid rule for marking out, most of which are calibrated in both metric and imperial units. They may be wood or steel, although some cheaper varieties are plastic. Where curves are involved, greater accuracy will be achieved with a flexible steel rule or even a retractable steel tape, which can be bent around the work.

The T-square is useful for marking out large sheets of manufactured board such as plywood, MDF (medium-density fiberboard) and blockboard. Remember, however, that it must be used on a perfectly straight edge to produce a 90-degree line across the sheet. Any small discrepancy in the edge will be greatly magnified across the sheet width and even more so along the length.

The combination square incorporates a number of functions in one tool, and is used for both measuring and marking out. It comprises a graduated steel rule that slides within a shaped body. A clamping screw permits the rule to be secured at any point along its length, while the body itself has flat edges that allow guidelines to be marked at 90 and 45 degrees to a straight surface. Many combination squares also feature a spirit bubble, allowing the tool to be used for checking horizontals.

FITTING PRE-MADE STRUCTURES

When fitting previously assembled cabinets or shelving to a wall, the most accurate method is to mark out the wall using a spirit (carpenter's) level. These are available in long and short lengths. Do not rely on existing lines, such as architraves (trims) around doors, picture rails or skirtings (baseboards), as these may not be truly horizontal.

Transferring measurements from one point to another can also be done with a straightedge, and although this is very similar to a heavy steel rule, the bevelled edge gives it the added advantage of being very easy to cut or mark against. Straightedges often have handles, making them easy to hold in place.

CONVERTING MEASUREMENTS

On small work in particular, never be tempted to convert from metric to imperial or vice versa. Some quite large errors can occur with standard conversions. Always work in the unit specified.

MEASURING, SHAPING & CUTTING TOOLS • 277

retractable steel tape

T-square

combination square

short spirit (carpenter's) level

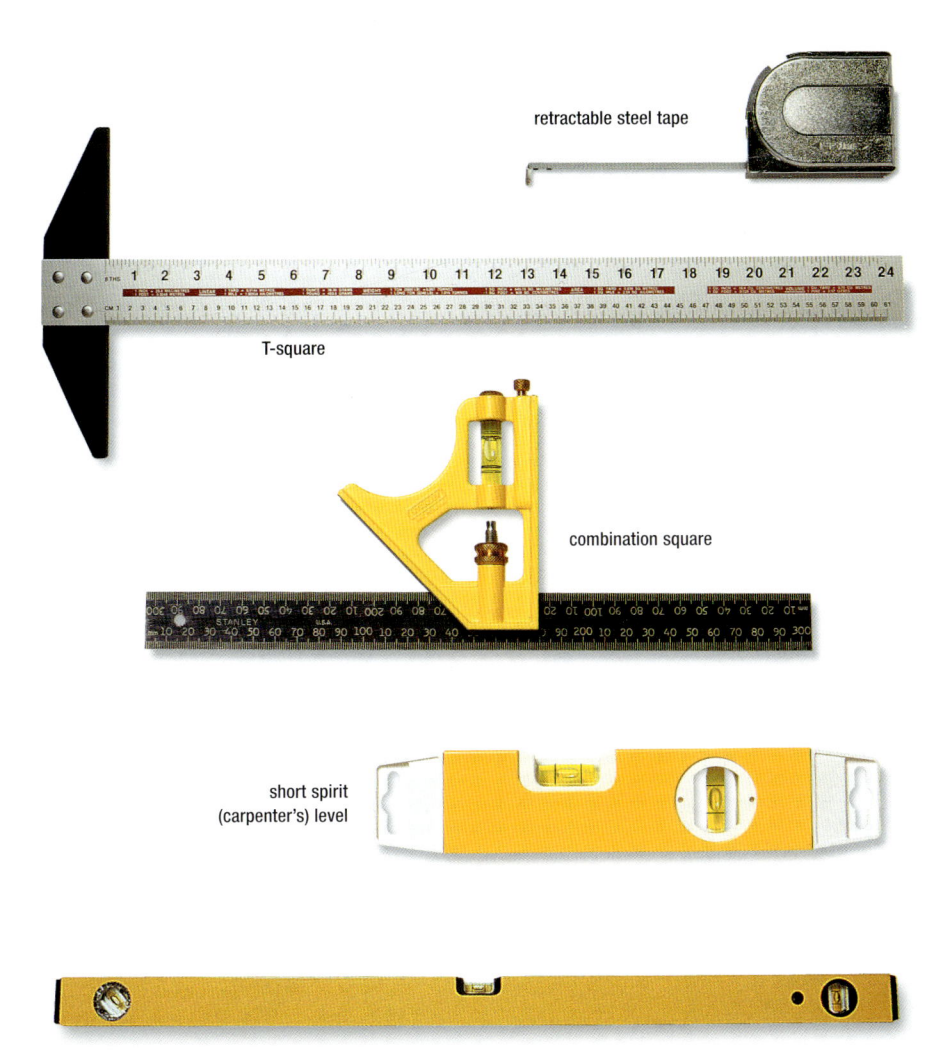

long spirit (carpenter's) level

straightedge

MARKING-OUT TOOLS

Another essential do-it-yourself skill is marking out, which can make or mar many projects.

Where you need to mark off a series of equal spacings, simply set a pair of dividers or callipers to the correct distance, using a flat wooden or steel rule, and step off the divisions.

You can mark out your workpiece for cutting and/or shaping with a pencil or a marking knife. The latter is particularly useful for fine work. An ordinary pencil is quite acceptable, but a flat carpenter's pencil will have a chisel-shaped tip when sharpened, making for more accurate marking.

MARKING JOINTS

Marking joints needs a fair degree of accuracy, so the first thing to ascertain is that your prepared wood is flat and square, which is done with a combination square or a try square. Either of these tools should be slid down the length of the wood to be cut, thus ensuring its uniformity and squareness.

For marking out a mortise, use a mortise gauge and set the points to the width of the chisel you intend to use to cut the mortise, not from a rule. This is far more accurate, as well as being much more convenient.

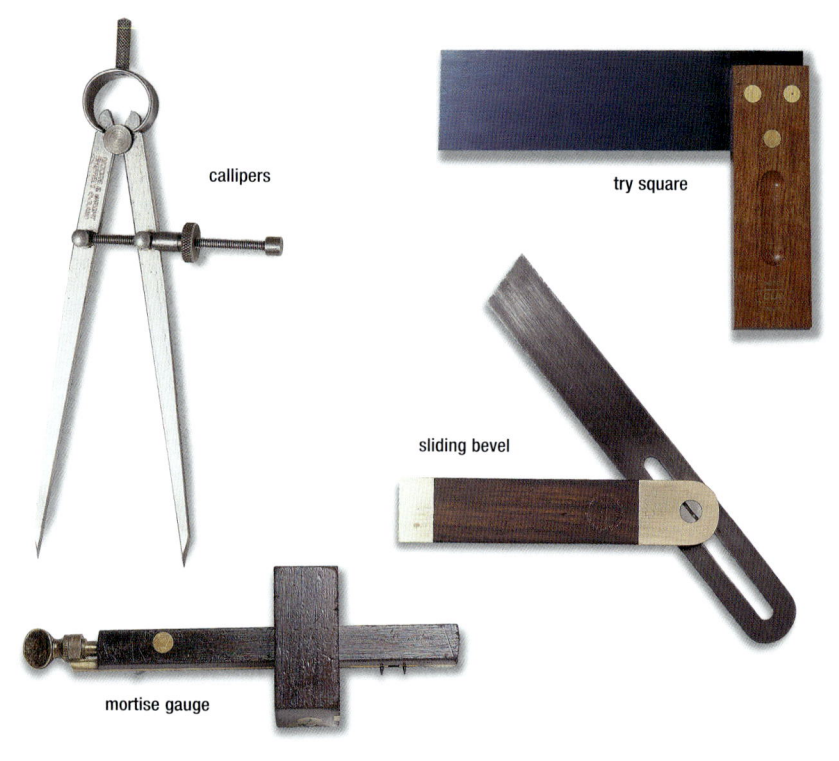

callipers

try square

sliding bevel

mortise gauge

A sliding bevel is a tool used for marking angles on to a square piece of wood. It can be adjusted to any angle, and is especially useful if the angles are to be repeated, such as when setting out treads for a staircase.

A good alternative for marking frequently repeated angles, such as on a staircase, is to make up a jig or template that can be laid on to the stringer (the long diagonal part of the staircase) and mark the treads accordingly. You should be able to buy such templates from most professional workshops. They are available in hardboard and Perspex.

ABOVE: Use a try square for marking right angles. Keep it clean and make sure the blade is not loose. It can be used with a pencil or a marking knife as required.

THE RIGHT MARKER

Use a carpenter's pencil, ordinary pencil or chinagraph for setting out measurements. Never use a magic marker or a ballpoint pen, since the marks are virtually impossible to remove and will spoil your work. Whichever marking tool you choose, keep it sharp to ensure accuracy.

ABOVE: Use a mortise gauge to scribe directly on to the wood. The two steel pins of the tool are independently adjustable on accurate brass slides, while the sliding stock runs against the face of the work. There may be a single pin on the opposite side for marking a scribed line, used to gauge thickness.

PLANES

The most commonly used varieties of plane are the jack plane for flattening the faces and edges of boards, and the smoothing plane for fine finishing. Good-quality examples are sufficiently weighty to avoid "chatter", which occurs when the plane skips over the surface of the wood without cutting properly. A block plane is often used for planing end grain because its blade is set at a low angle that severs the wood fibres cleanly.

block plane

smoothing plane

jack plane

PLANING TECHNIQUE

Body weight plays a large part in planing technique. Position your body with your hips and shoulders in line with the plane, and your feet spaced apart.

At the beginning of the stroke, apply pressure to the front handle of the plane, switching to a general downward pressure during the middle of the stroke, and finish off by applying most of the pressure to the back of the plane at the end of the board.

PLANING END GRAIN AND BOARDS

Plane end grain and boards using a block plane. To avoid splitting the ends of the wood, work from each side toward the middle. A useful technique for planing wide boards is to work diagonally, or even at right angles, across the grain. This method will remove material efficiently. To finish, it will be necessary to make fine cuts with the grain to obtain a smooth surface. Run your fingers lightly over the surface to identify any unevenness that needs removing.

TIPS

- Cheap planes often serve to blunt enthusiasm by poor performance. Always buy the best you can afford and keep them sharp.
- Check for sharpness and adjustment each time a plane is used – and make sure the wood to be planed is held firmly.

STARTING TO PLANE

1 The correct body position helps to achieve the desired result. Keep your hips and shoulders parallel to the direction in which you are planing, with your weight balanced on both feet.

2 Apply pressure to the front of the plane as you begin the stroke, equal pressure to front and back in the middle of the stroke, and pressure on the back of the plane at the end of the stroke.

3 When planing a narrow edge, make sure you keep the plane centralized to ensure an even cut. To do this, you can tuck your fingers under the sole plate as a guide.

4 If you have identical edges to plane, clamp them together and work on both at once. Check from time to time that you are planing them square with the aid of a try square.

CHISELS

Each with its own specific use, chisels come in a variety of shapes and sizes. For jobs around the home, only three basic types are required. Most commonly used is the firmer chisel, which is a compromise between a mortise chisel and a bevel-edged chisel. It can be regarded as a general-purpose tool, having a strong blade of rectangular section designed for medium/heavy work. Most home woodworkers will find blade widths of 6mm (¼in), 12mm (½in), 19mm (¾in) and 25mm (1in) sufficient for their needs.

SPECIAL-PURPOSE CHISELS

Bevel-edged chisels have thinner blades than firmer chisels. The tops of the blades are bevelled along their length to allow better access into small recesses and corners, and to permit fine slicing cuts to be made in the wood.

The mortise chisel is a sturdy tool with a lot of steel just below the handle. It is used for chopping deep mortises across the grain, so it has to be able to withstand blows from a heavy mallet. For this reason, a wooden-handled mortise chisel may have a metal band around the top of the handle to prevent it from splitting. The thickness of the steel blade also allows it to be used as a lever for cleaning the waste from the mortise.

Many new chisels have shatter-resistant polypropylene handles that can be struck with a mallet, or even a hammer, without damage since the material is virtually unbreakable.

> **TIPS**
> • Always make sure your chisels are sharp. A blunt tool needs more pressure to force it through the work and is more likely to slip, possibly causing an accident.
> • Do not leave chisels lying where the blades can touch metal objects. Fit them with blade guards or keep them in a cloth.

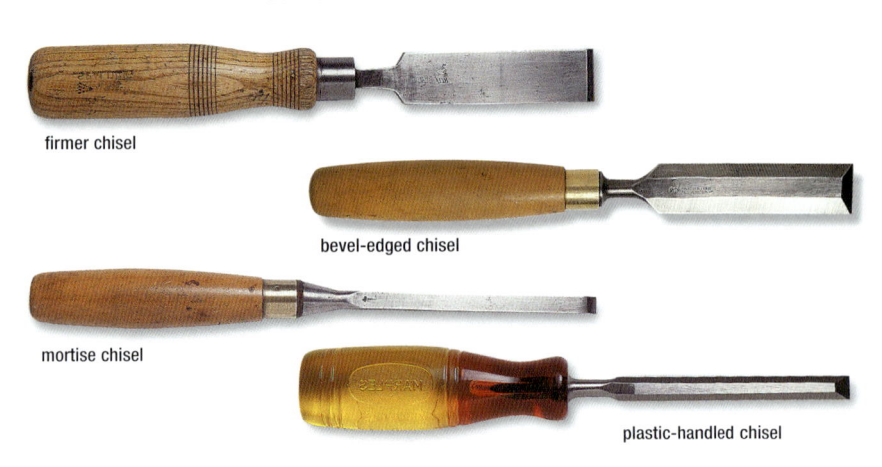

firmer chisel

bevel-edged chisel

mortise chisel

plastic-handled chisel

CHISELLING TECHNIQUES

Always aim to remove as much waste wood as possible from the cut before using the chisel. For example, remove the waste with a saw before cleaning up with a chisel or, when cutting a mortise, drill out the waste and use the chisel to clean and square-up the sides.

When using a router to cut slots and rebates (rabbets), square the ends by hand with a chisel.

Remember to cut away from the marked line when chiselling so that any splitting will occur in the waste wood, and always cut away from yourself to avoid injury. Work patiently and never be tempted to make cuts that are too large. The chisel should be pushed or struck with one hand while being guided with the other.

HORIZONTAL PARING

1 Horizontal paring, working from both sides to the middle, prevents "break out" and results in clean work using less pressure.

2 Chamfer an edge, first using the chisel with the bevel down to remove most of the waste. Then make the finishing cuts with the blade held bevel up, taking fine parings.

3 When making the finished cuts, use your thumb to control the cutting edge of the chisel, holding it close to the end of the blade. Make sure the chisel is sharp.

VERTICAL PARING

ABOVE: When paring vertically by hand, guide the chisel blade with one hand while pushing down firmly on the handle with the other.

REMOVING LARGE AMOUNTS

ABOVE: To remove larger amounts of waste wood, hold the chisel vertically and strike the handle firmly with a wooden mallet.

MORTISING

ABOVE: You can form a mortise completely with a chisel, but it is much quicker to remove most of the waste by drilling it out, then use a chisel to clean up the sides and ends of the cutout.

DOVETAILS

ABOVE: Dovetail joints are common in cabinet work. Begin by removing the bulk of the waste with a coping saw before using a narrow, bevel-edged chisel to finish off.

SHARPENING EQUIPMENT

A good sharpening stone is a vital part of the toolkit. Without a sharp edge, a chisel will be not only difficult to work with, but also dangerous. The chisel will follow where the wood directs it, rather than where you want it to go, and can easily slip.

Chisels should be sharpened at the beginning and end of every session. If they are attended to regularly, just a few minutes' work will keep the honed edges in prime condition. Once in a while, a longer honing session might be necessary – if the bevel loses its original angle or if the edge is chipped.

Natural sharpening stones are quite expensive, and synthetic versions are commonly used. Japanese water stones are of natural stone and need water as a lubricant. They can produce a finely ground edge on the best-quality steel. For more general use, however, oilstones are sufficient.

A combination stone is the best buy, two stones of different grades being bonded together back to back.

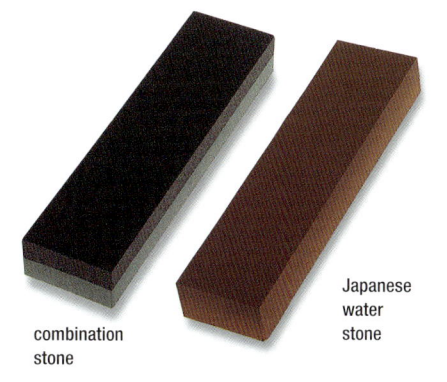

combination stone

Japanese water stone

SHARPENING PLANE IRONS

To sharpen a plane iron, apply a coat of thin oil to the oilstone, hold the blade at 35 degrees to the stone and maintain this angle while working it backward and forward. Honing jigs, which set the angle exactly, are readily available. Lay the back of the iron flat on the oilstone and rub off the burr formed by the sharpening process. Clean out the inside of the plane before reassembly, and apply a drop of oil to the adjustment mechanism.

1 Hold the iron at a steady angle while rubbing it on the oilstone.

2 Remove the burr from a sharpened blade by rubbing the back flat on the stone.

SAWS

The most common saw used by the do-it-yourselfer is the hand saw. This is used for cross-cutting (across the grain) and ripping (along the grain), and the teeth of the saw are set accordingly, so you will need to ask your tool supplier for the correct one. There are also general-purpose hand saws that are reasonably suited to both tasks. These are quite often hardpoint saws, which cannot be sharpened, but their specially hardened teeth give them a long life.

The tenon saw, sometimes called a backsaw because of the solid strengthening bar along its top edge, is made specifically for cutting the tenons of mortise-and-tenon joints and other fine work. Really fine work is done with a dovetail saw, which is similar to a tenon saw, but has more teeth to the inch to give a finer cut.

The tenon saw is often used with a bench hook for making cross-cuts in small pieces, and one can be made quite easily as a do-it-yourself project. They usually measure about 300 x 150mm (12 x 6in). The mitre box is another handy aid for use with a tenon saw, allowing 90- and 45-degree angles to be cut accurately, but the beginner is best advised to buy one rather than attempt to make one.

A mitre saw makes short work of cutting accurate angles and offers fine adjustment. It is well worth the investment if working with delicate mouldings or making picture frames.

cross-cut hand saw

hardpoint saw

tenon saw

dovetail saw

bench hook

mitre box

mitre saw

SAWING TECHNIQUES

When beginning a cut with a hand saw, draw the saw back toward your body to sever the wood fibres and produce a small kerf – the groove in which the saw blade will run. Always cut on the waste side of the marked line for perfect results.

When using a mitre box to make an angled cut, begin with the back of the saw raised slightly. This will make the cut easier to start.

> **TIP**
> Always find a comfortable position in which to saw. It will produce better results and reduce the risks of back strain or other injury.

ABOVE: Draw the saw back a few times to start the cut, using your thumb to support the blade until a kerf has formed.

ABOVE: Use a tenon saw for cutting small components or sawing tenons and the like. A bench hook aids the cross-cutting.

ABOVE: A standard mitre box permits 90- and 45-degree angled cuts to be made with a tenon saw for a variety of applications.

KNIVES

The do-it-yourself enthusiast will need a variety of knives, some of which have very specific functions. Some do not actually conform to the conventional idea of a knife at all, but all have metal blades and are essentially cutting tools.

MARKING KNIVES

The purpose of a marking knife is to mark a sawing line, by lightly cutting the surface wood fibres, and assist in the beginning of a saw cut. Not only does this provide a permanent guide line, but it also prevents the fibres from splintering as the saw cuts through. These tools are usually about 200mm (8in) long and make a much finer line than a pencil.

They are normally used in conjunction with a steel rule, straightedge or try square and are bevelled on one side only so that they can be used tightly against the steel edge for accuracy. They are available in both left- and right-handed versions.

Marking knives without pointed ends are also frequently used, and these are bevelled on either the left- or right-hand side, depending on the needs of the user.

Twin-bladed knives are available and are adjusted by a set screw and locking knob. Typically, the blades can be set to a spacing of 3–19mm ($1/8$–$3/4$in). This type of knife is used for marking parallel lines, gauging mortises and cutting thin strips from veneers for decorative inlay work.

GENERAL-PURPOSE KNIVES

By far the most common and useful general-purpose knife is the craft knife, which has a store of replacement blades in the handle. This is an indispensable tool which can be used for many purposes.

Another very handy tool is the scalpel. More delicate and invasive than the craft knife, a scalpel is ideal for cutting out templates and particularly useful for cleaning up deeply indented

marking knife with bevel on one side

scalpel

twin-bladed adjustable marking knife

putty knife

craft knife

filling knife

MARKING OUT

ABOVE: Mark a line across the grain with the knife held firmly against the steel edge of a try square. This gives a very fine line of severed wood fibres, which is ideal to work to with either a saw or a chisel.

ABOVE: A typical example of a knife being used with a steel rule. Note how the fingers are spread to keep a firm and even downward pressure on the rule, allowing the knife to be used hard against the rule's edge.

cuts in carvings and routed work. Scalpels are made with a variety of handles and have replaceable blades.

MISCELLANEOUS KNIVES

Putty knives often find their way into the do-it-yourselfer's toolkit. They have specially shaped ends to their blades to make "cutting off" easier. This means withdrawing the knife from the work without damaging the soft putty that is being applied to a window pane or moulding, for example.

The filling knife is a familiar decorator's tool with a flexible spring-tempered blade that is ideal for forcing soft material, such as wood filler, into knot holes, cracks and blemishes in wood, and plaster filler into cracks in walls. These come in a variety of shapes and sizes and are often confused with stripping knives, which have thicker and less flexible blades.

TIPS

- Never use a scalpel or craft knife with excessive pressure. The blade may shatter and sharp pieces fly up into your unprotected eyes.
- Always place the hand not holding the knife behind the blade. This prevents injury if the blade slips.

DRILLS AND BITS

Accurate drilling is an important do-it-yourself technique. It is much easier with a hand-held power drill, and even more so with a bench-mounted pillar drill.

CARPENTER'S BRACE

Drilling by hand with a carpenter's brace still has a place, and a hand drill is useful for smaller jobs, especially in sites far removed from electric power. However, even in these circumstances, the cordless power drill has largely overcome the difficulty of finding a source of electric power.

CORDLESS DRILL/DRIVER

This tool is worth its weight in gold in situations without power, and it is particularly safe near water. It is rechargeable and usually comes with a spare battery. The variable torque and speed settings make it ideal for doubling as a screwdriver. Although generally not as powerful as a mains-powered drill, it is more than adequate for most jobs. Use it for drilling clearance holes for screws, fitting and removing screws, and drilling holes for dowels.

Heavier work, especially that which involves using flat bits or Forstner bits to remove very large areas of wood, is best undertaken with a mains-powered electric drill to save time and avoid the need for constant recharging of the battery.

VARIETIES OF BIT

Great advances have also been made in the pattern of drill bits. For example, there are bits designed for setting dowels. Dowel jointing is often used in projects built with manufactured boards, such as chipboard (particle board) and plywood, and the bits produce flat-bottomed holes.

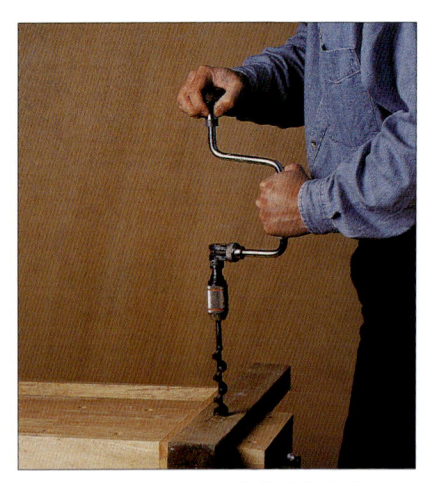

cordless drill

ABOVE: A carpenter's brace is ideal for boring large holes. Its design provides plenty of leverage to turn flat and auger bits.

dowel bit   flat bit

Forstner bit

plug cutter   countersink bit

from a piece of scrap wood. Then the plugs are glued into holes in the workpiece to conceal fixing screws. Most cutters come with a special matching bit that bores a screw clearance hole and plug countersink in one operation.

Another common drilling accessory is the countersink bit. This allows the head of a screw to be set flush with the surface of the wood. Again, this is best used in a pillar drill with a depth stop to ensure accuracy.

Forstner bits are designed to drill large, flat-bottomed holes that do not pass through the wood, such as holes that might be needed to accommodate kitchen cabinet hinges. The bits will drill deep holes accurately, even in the end grain of the wood, which is usually very difficult.

There are also flat bits that work with a scraping action, cutting large holes very rapidly, although these are not as accurate as conventional twist bits. The latter are used for making small holes in wood, metal and other rigid materials, but specially hardened types are needed for steel. For the do-it-yourselfer on a limited budget, an adjustable bit is a good investment, but these can only be used in a hand brace.

DRILLING ACCESSORIES

Plug cutters are useful additions to any workshop, especially when quality work is undertaken. The cutter is fitted in a pillar drill and used to remove plugs

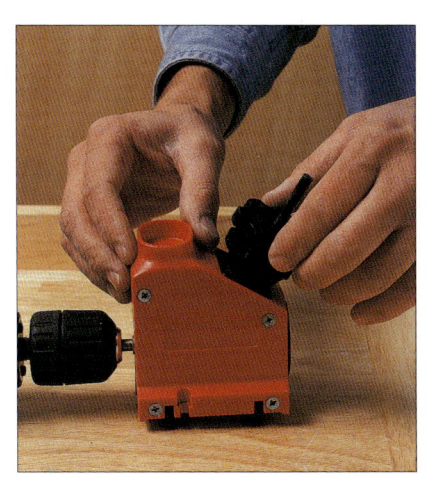

ABOVE: Many drill bits can be sharpened with a specialized grinding attachment designed to be run off a hand-held power drill.

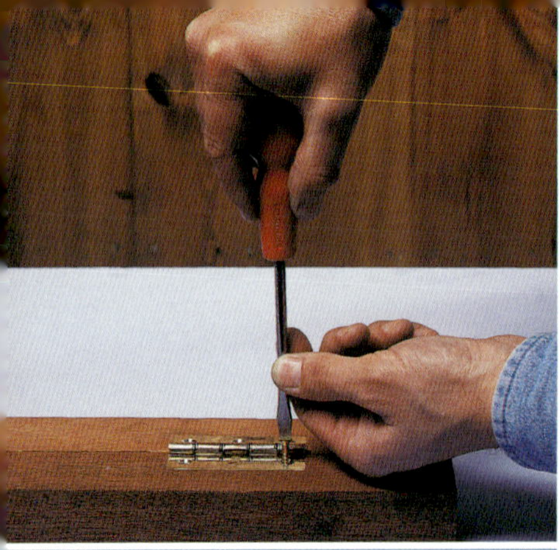

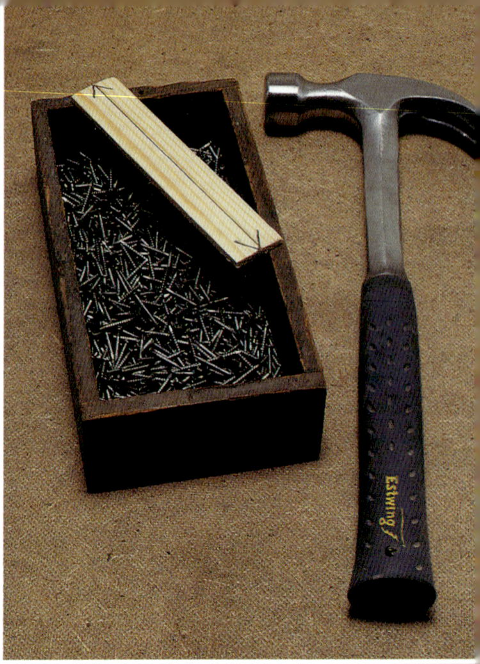
Estwing

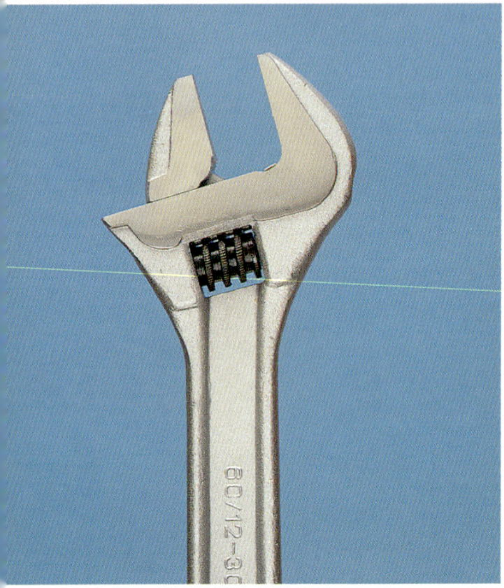

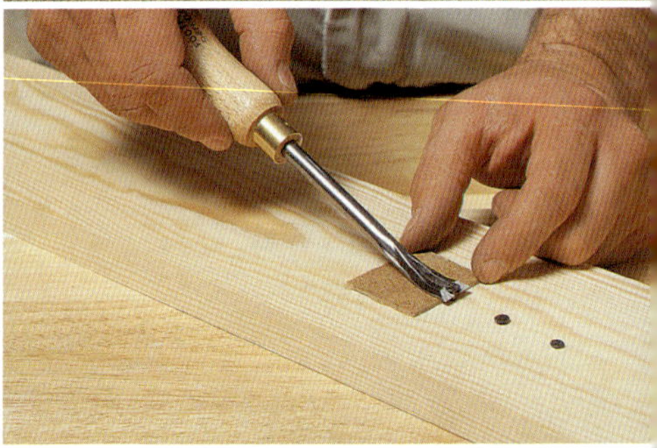

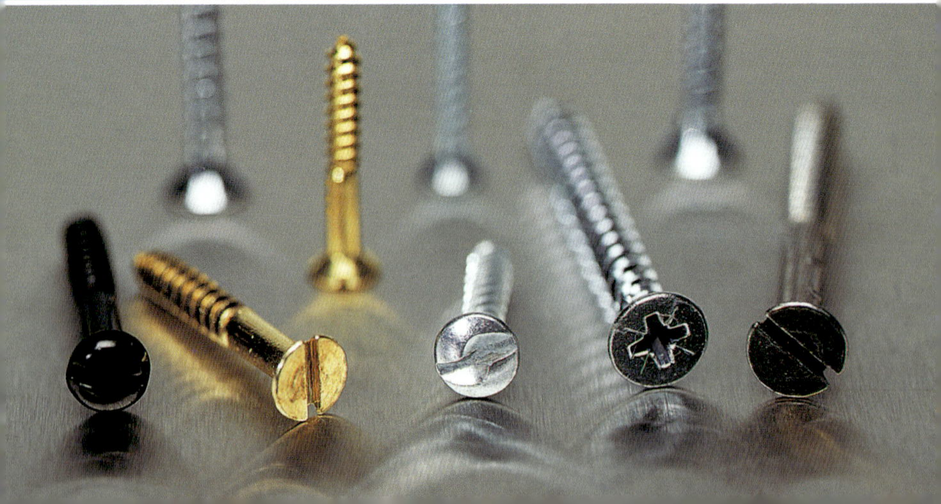

ASSEMBLING TOOLS

Sooner or later, the do-it-yourselfer is likely to be faced with the need to join two or more pieces of a workpiece together. In some cases, this can be done by forming joints and using glue, although some means of clamping the pieces together while the glue dries must be found. Often, however, some form of mechanical fixing is called for. The most commonly used fixings are nails and screws, although occasionally nuts and bolts may be required. There are many types of nail, some of which require special hammers to drive them, while screws have different head designs and need the correct type of screwdriver. Nuts and bolts can be assembled and dismantled with spanners and/or sockets.

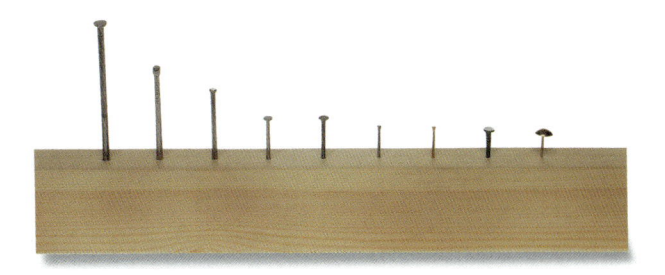

CLAMPS

Many do-it-yourself tasks require two or more sections of a workpiece to be held together temporarily while a more permanent fixing is made, often with glue. A variety of clamps is available for this purpose, many of them with specific uses. Keen woodworkers may make their own clamps (or cramps as they are often called) from scrap wood or other materials.

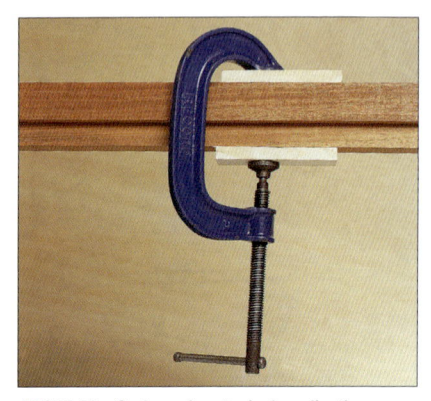

ABOVE: The G-clamp in a typical application. Note the packing pieces beneath the jaws to prevent bruising of the wood.

COMMONLY USED CLAMPS

The most common clamp in the workshop is the G-clamp. This is a general-purpose tool that is available with a variety of throat sizes. It may be used on its own or in conjunction with others when, for example, working on the surface of a wide board or holding boards together for gluing.

The sash clamp was designed specifically for assembling window frames, or sashes, but it is also often used when edge-jointing boards to form large panels for table tops and similar items.

Sometimes, it is useful to be able to apply a clamp with one hand while holding the workpiece in the other, which is when the single-handed clamp comes into its own. It works on a simple ratchet system, rather like a mastic (caulking) gun.

For picture frames and heavier items with 45-degree mitred joints at the corners, there is the mitre clamp. This can be quite a complex affair with screw handles for tightening or a very simple "clothes-peg" (pin) type arrangement, that can be applied to the work very quickly.

SPECIAL-PURPOSE CLAMPS

There are many of these, but one that the do-it-yourself enthusiast may find useful is the cam clamp, which is wooden with cork faces. This is a quickly operated clamp often used by musical instrument makers. Its advantages are its speed in use, its lightness and its simplicity. The cam clamp is ideal for small holding jobs, although it cannot exert a great deal of pressure.

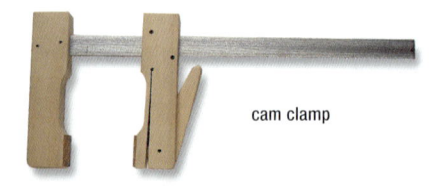

cam clamp

ASSEMBLING TOOLS • 295

ABOVE: Small wooden picture and mirror frames can be easily assembled with the aid of inexpensive mitre clamps.

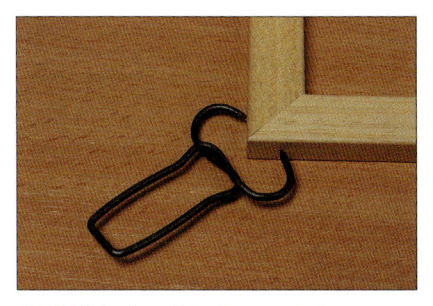

ABOVE: This clever little clamp works by means of spring pressure. It can be applied quickly and easily to small assemblies.

ABOVE: Use sash clamps to edge-joint boards to form a panel such as a table top. Reverse the central clamp to even out the pressure.

ABOVE: Home-made clamps used for the same purpose, but this time the pressure is exerted by means of wedges.

CLAMPS IN USE

Apply pressure to a joint or the assembly you are working on as soon as possible after gluing – make a habit of preparing everything you need in advance. Keep a box of small scraps of wood handy and use them to protect the surface of the work. It is often said that you can never have too many clamps, and you will soon start collecting a selection of different types and sizes to suit all kinds of assembly technique. Many can be home-made.

TIPS

• Do not be tempted to release clamps too quickly. Be patient, allowing plenty of drying time for the glue – overnight at least, or as specified by the maker.
• Think through the sequence for the clamping process and make sure you have enough clamps to hand before you apply any glue. With a complex or large structure, you may decide you need another person to help.

NAILS AND HAMMERS

There is no such thing as an "ordinary" nail. All nails have been derived for specific purposes, although some can be put to several uses. Similarly, various types of hammer are available – always use the correct tool for the job. Wooden-handled hammers have a natural spring in the handles, which makes them easier to control than steel-handled types.

NAILS

The wire nail can be used for many simple tasks, such as box-making, fencing and general carpentry. Lost-head and oval nails are useful where there is no need for a flat head, or when it is desirable for the nails to be concealed, such as when fixing cladding or boards.

Oval nails can be driven below the surface of the work with less likelihood of them splitting the wood. They should be inserted with their heads in line with the grain.

The cut nail is stamped from metal sheet and has a tapering, rectangular section, which gives it excellent holding properties. It is largely used for fixing flooring.

Panel pins (brads), as their name suggests, are used for fixing thin panels and cladding. They are nearly always punched out of sight below the surface, as are veneer pins.

When there is a need to secure thin or fragile sheet material, such as roofing felt or plasterboard (gypsum board), large-headed nails are used. These are commonly called clout nails, but may also be found under specific names, such as roofing nails and plasterboard nails. Their large heads spread the pressure and prevent the materials from tearing or crumbling. They are usually galvanized to protect them against rust when used outdoors. Zinc nails are used for roofing because they are rustproof and easy to cut through when renewing slates.

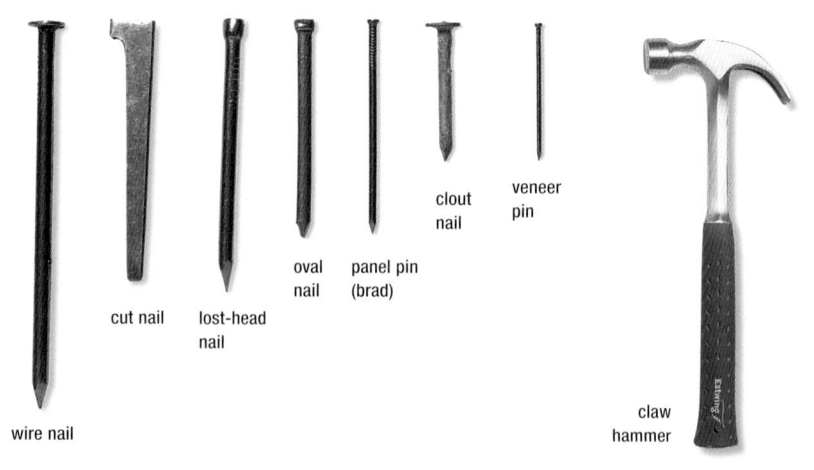

wire nail

cut nail

lost-head nail

oval nail

panel pin (brad)

clout nail

veneer pin

claw hammer

HAMMERS

The essential hammer for the do-it-yourselfer is the claw hammer, the claw being used to extract nails. About 365–450g (13–16oz) is a good weight to aim for, since the hammer should be heavy enough to drive large nails. It is a mistake to use a hammer that is too light, as this tends to bend the nails rather than drive them.

For lighter nails, a cross-pein or Warrington hammer is useful, since the flat head can be used to start the nail or pin without risk of hitting your fingers. For even smaller panel pins, the pin hammer is used.

CARPENTER'S MALLET

It should be remembered that the carpenter's mallet, often made from solid beech, is a form of hammer, but it should never be used for striking anything other than wood or similar soft materials, otherwise serious damage will result.

cross-pein hammer

carpenter's mallet

DOVETAIL NAILING

Cross, or dovetail, nailing is a simple and useful method of holding a butt joint strongly in end grain. When several nails are being driven into one piece of wood, avoid putting them in straight; slanting them will help prevent splitting.

ABOVE: The claw hammer's ability to extract as well as drive nails makes it a useful tool for do-it-yourself projects.

SCREWS AND SCREWDRIVERS

The holding power of screws is much greater than that of nails, and screwed work can easily be taken apart again without damage to any of the components, unless of course it is also glued. Driving screws does take longer than nailing and they are more expensive, but they will give the appearance of quality and craftsmanship to most work.

TYPES OF SCREW

The most common woodscrews may be made of mild steel or brass, often with countersunk heads that may be flat or raised. There are many different plated finishes available, ranging from chrome, used for internal fixings such as mirrors, to zinc, which will resist rust.

Brass screws will not rust at all and are often used in woods such as oak, where steel would cause blue staining due to the tannic acid in the sap.

HEAD PATTERNS AND SCREW SIZES

There are various types of screw head used for both hand and power driving. The most common is the slot-head screw, followed by the Phillips head and the Pozidriv, both of which have a cruciform pattern in the head to take the screwdriver blade.

Screw sizes are complex, combining the length and the diameter (gauge): for example, "inch-and-a-half eight" describes a screw that is $1\frac{1}{2}$in (40mm) long and gauge 8.

TYPES OF SCREWDRIVER

For woodworking, the traditional hand screwdriver has an oval wooden handle and is used to drive slot-head screws only. It is available in a variety of sizes. A range of plastic-handled tools of

flat and raised countersunk screws

slot-head screwdriver

stubby screwdriver

slotted screw head

Phillips screwdriver

Phillips screw head

Pozidriv screwdriver

Pozidriv screw head

various sizes is also available, designed to drive Phillips and Pozidriv screws, as well as slot-heads.

A recent innovation is the screwdriver bit set, containing a handle and a number of interchangeable tips to fit various screw types and sizes.

Power screwdrivers and drill/drivers vastly increase the rate of work. They can offer various torque settings that allow the screw heads to be set just flush with the work surface. Power drivers are also very useful for dismantling screwed joints and furniture because they will run in reverse.

Keeping the head of a slot-head screwdriver correctly ground to prevent it from slipping is very important. Remember also that the blade width must equal the length of the screw slot for the greatest efficiency and to prevent both slipping and damage to the screw head. Always use the correct size of screwdriver with Phillips and Pozidriv screws, otherwise both the screw head and the screwdriver are likely to be damaged.

cordless electric drill/driver

USING SCREWS

Driving a screw is a more skilled task than nailing. It is usually advisable to drill pilot holes first to ease the screws' passage through the wood and to ensure that they go in straight. In hardwoods, pre-drilling is vital, otherwise the screws will shear off when pressure is exerted by the screwdriver. Brass screws are particularly soft, so steel screws of the same size should be inserted to pre-cut the threads.

ABOVE: Screw holes should be marked very carefully when fitting hinges.

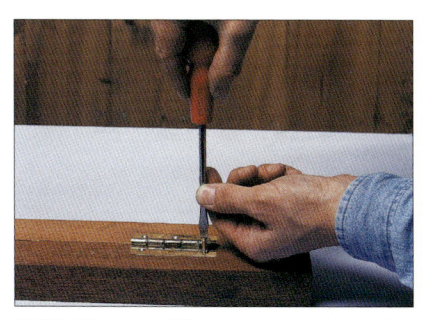

ABOVE: Where possible, use the screwdriver with both hands to prevent slipping.

PINCERS AND PLIERS

Every do-it-yourself enthusiast's toolkit should include a range of hand tools for gripping small items. Chief among these are pincers, used for removing nails and similar fixings, and general-purpose combination pliers, which offer a variety of gripping and cutting features.

PINCERS

A good pair of pincers will remove nails and tacks with little trouble. The rolling action required to remove a nail with pincers is very similar to that used with a claw hammer. An ideal length is about 175mm (7in) to ensure good leverage, which is essential. The jaws should touch along their entire width and be properly aligned to provide maximum grip.

It is important that pincers do not damage the work, and for this reason, broad jaws – about 25mm (1in) wide – that will spread the load are best.

Some pincers come with a handy tack lifter at the end of one of the handles. Purpose-made tack lifters are very useful for upholstery work, and if you intend doing any furniture making or restoration, it is well worth investing in such a tool.

Another special tack and nail remover is the nail puller, or "cat's-paw", as it is sometimes known. This tool has a standard tack remover at one end and a large, right-angled claw at the other for getting under the heads of stubborn nails. The claw can be tapped under the head of an embedded nail with a small hammer.

pincers

pincers with a tack lifter

tack lifter

nail puller

combination pliers

heavy-duty pliers

long-nosed (needlenose) pliers

PLIERS

These come in a bewildering range of types and sizes, many of which have very specific uses.

Combination pliers and heavy-duty pliers are used for gripping, twisting and cutting. They come in various sizes, but a good pair would be about 200mm (8in) long and probably have plastic or rubber handle grips for comfort and to provide insulation against electric shock.

Long-nosed (needlenose) pliers are rather more specialized and are used for gripping small objects in confined spaces. Some have cranked jaws at various angles for access to awkward places. They come in many sizes.

ABOVE: When using pincers to remove a nail, protect the wood by slipping a piece of hardboard or plywood below the pincer head.

ABOVE: Remove tacks from wood with a tack lifter. Protect the surface with hardboard or a piece of plywood.

ABOVE: The flat behind the claw of this Japanese nail puller can be tapped with a hammer to drive the claw under the nail head.

ABOVE: When using pliers, hold them firmly, keeping your palm away from the pivot, which can pinch your skin as the jaws close.

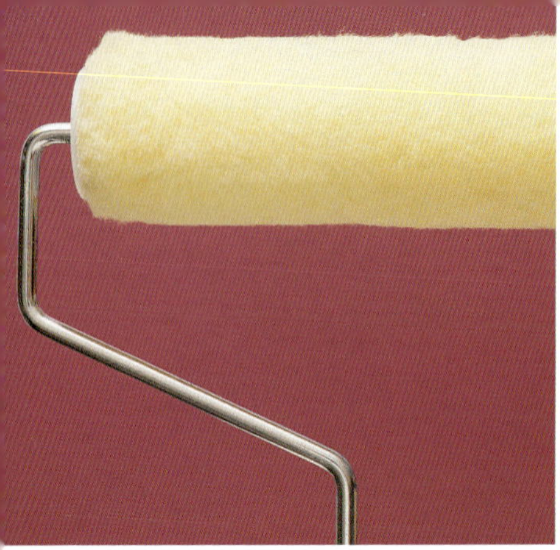

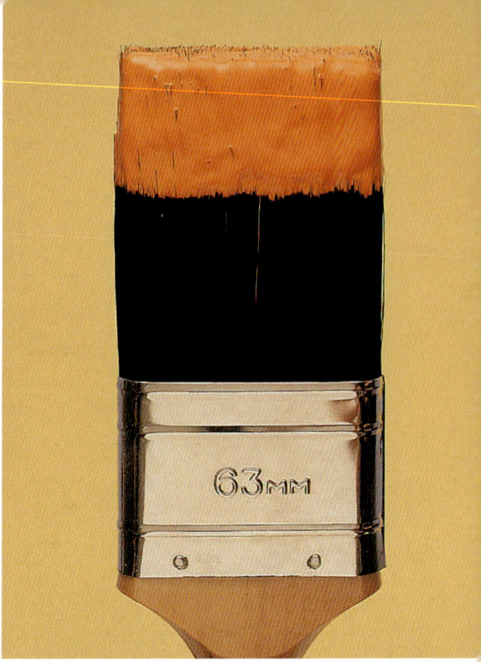
63MM

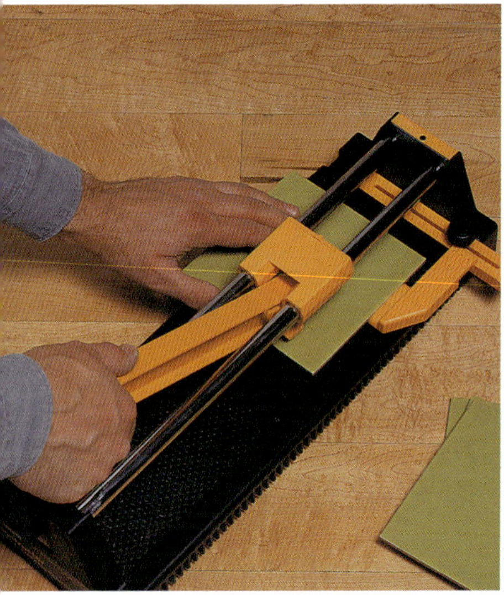

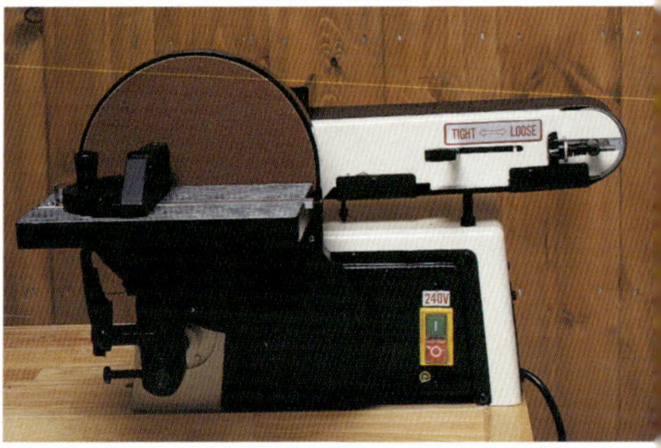
TIGHT LOOSE
240V

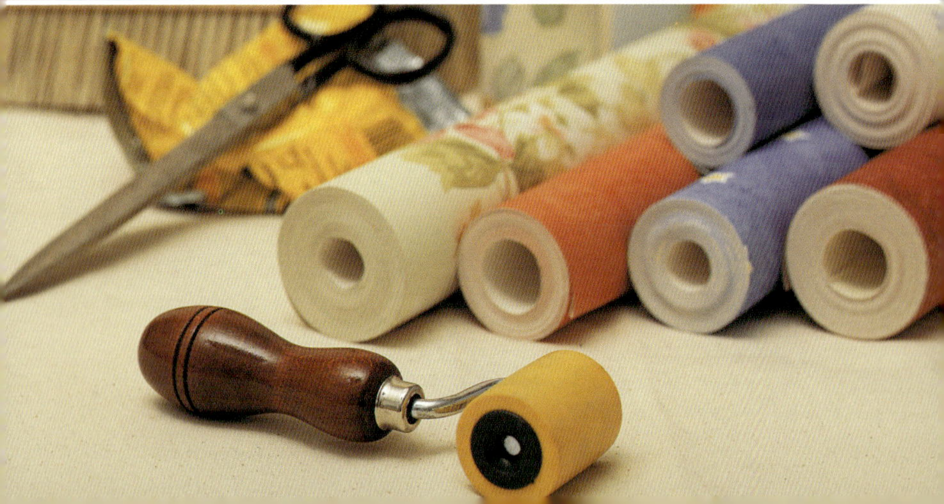

FINISHING TOOLS

No matter what type of finish you apply to a surface, in practically all cases, the smoother the surface, the better the finish. A primary method of achieving smoothness is by sanding with abrasive paper, which can be done by hand or by machine. Paint is the most common finish for a variety of surfaces in the home, and you will need a selection of brushes and rollers to apply it. An alternative to paint is wallpaper – there is no limit to the versatility of modern wallpapers, which can be used for decorating both walls and ceilings. A few specialized tools are needed to do the job. Tiles are a good means of providing a durable, waterproof surface to walls and floors, and again, having the right tools makes the task of laying them a lot easier.

SANDERS

Although the term "sanding" is generally used for do-it-yourself projects, it is something of a misnomer. A truer description would be "abrading", because what we call "sandpaper" is, in fact, "glasspaper". In addition, we also use garnet paper, and silicon-carbide and aluminium-oxide abrasive papers, all of which shape wood very efficiently.

GRIT SIZE

One thing abrasive papers all have in common is classification by grit size, and the golden rule is to work progressively down through the grit sizes, from coarse to fine, when smoothing a piece of work. For example, 400 grit is finer than 200 grit and should be employed later in the finishing process. Abrasives can be used by hand or with a variety of machines, both hand-held and stationary. Sanders are also suitable for shaping work, using coarse abrasives for rapid material removal.

TYPES OF SANDER

A tool commonly used for heavy-duty shaping and sanding is the belt sander. This normally has a 75mm (3in) wide belt, running continuously over two rollers, and a dust collection facility.

A belt and disc sander is an inexpensive alternative. It is used for shaping and trimming rather than smoothing, as the piece of work is taken to them.

Many do-it-yourselfers are likely to own an orbital sander, which is useful for general light sanding work such as finishing boards. These sanders are designed to accept either half or a third of a standard-size abrasive sheet and quite often have dedicated sheets made for them. Random orbital sanders are similar, but may employ self-adhesive abrasive sheets that are easy to fit. They can be small enough to be used with one hand in tight spots, but still give a good finish.

HAND SANDING

Always wrap abrasive paper around a cork or rubber block when sanding flat surfaces. Clear the dust away as you work to avoid clogging the paper, particularly on resinous and oily wood. To finish off a rounded edge, wrap a square of paper around a section of moulded wood with the correct profile for the job.

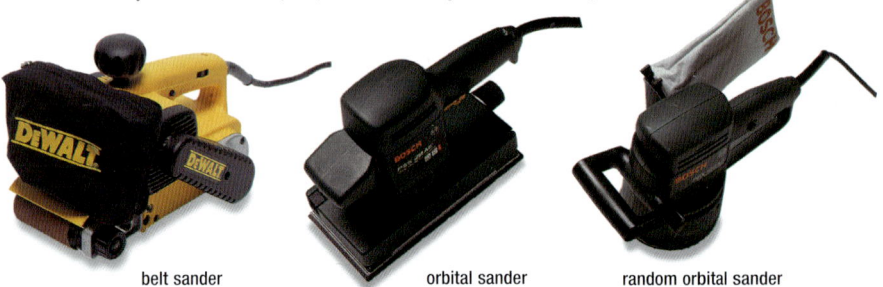

belt sander   orbital sander   random orbital sander

FINISHING TOOLS • 305

ABOVE: You should hold a belt sander with both hands to prevent it from running away.

ABOVE: The belt sander can be inverted and secured in a woodworking vice.

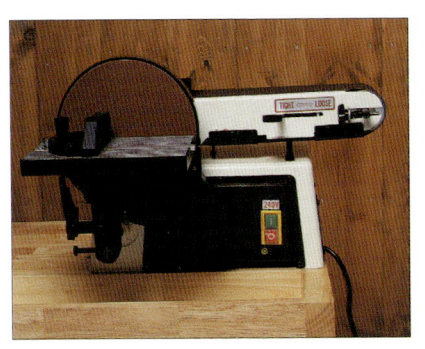

ABOVE: Belt and disc sanders are used for shaping and trimming, and can be aggressive.

ABOVE: The orbital sander is less ferocious than the belt sander and is easy to control.

MAKING A SANDING BLOCK

1 Fold your sheet of abrasive paper to size and tear it along a sharp edge.

2 Wrap the paper around a cork or rubber block before starting to sand.

PAINTING TOOLS

This is one aspect of do-it-yourself work where you cannot afford to skimp on materials. You will not achieve professional results by using cheap brushes that shed their bristles as you work, or cut-price rollers that disintegrate before the job is finished. Invest in the best quality equipment your budget allows.

CHOOSING BRUSHES

Paintbrushes come in pure bristle, synthetic fibre and even foam versions. The last guarantees that you will not be left with brush strokes, and they are inexpensive enough to discard when you have finished. All natural brushes shed a few bristles in use, but cheap brushes are the worst offenders. Usually, these have fewer bristles to start with and they are often poorly secured. Regard pure bristle brushes as an investment; you can use them repeatedly, and many painters claim that they improve with age.

Synthetic brushes, usually with nylon bristles, have the advantage of being moult-free, and they perform well with water-based paints. A more expensive version, made of polyester and nylon, is particularly easy to handle and said to give a superior finish.

paintbrushes ranging from 100–25mm (4–1in)

cutting-in (sash) brush

special-effects brushes

foam brush

paint pads

roller sleeves

roller handle

radiator brush

TOOLBOX ESSENTIALS

Serious painters will need a range of brushes: slimline, 12 and 25mm (½ and 1in), for fiddly areas such as window frames; medium-sized versions, 50 and 75mm (2 and 3in), for doors, floors and skirtings (baseboards); and large types, 100mm (4in), for quick coverage of walls and ceilings. You might like to add a few extras to this basic kit:

• A cutting-in (sash) brush, specially angled to cope with hard-to-reach areas, is particularly useful if you are painting around window frames.

• Special-effects brushes allow you to create distinctive looks such as woodgrain and marbling.

• A radiator brush is designed to reach the wall behind a radiator.

PAINT PADS

If you are new to decorating, you may find that a paint pad is easier to handle than a brush. Paint pads can be useful for clean, flat painting and precise edges. They give a speedy and even finish, are light to handle and work well with acrylic paints.

Each pad consists of a layer of fibre on top of a layer of foam, attached to a plastic handle. Use paint pads with a paint tray. If you purchase a kit, a tray will usually be provided.

THE RIGHT ROLLER

If speed is of the essence, a paint roller will be an indispensable part of your decorating toolkit. Once you have a roller, you can simply buy replacement sleeves that fit its existing handle. Many types of specialist roller are used in decorating. Specific covers are suitable for different surfaces and you can buy rollers designed for creating particular patterns.

ABOVE: Load paint on to a paint pad using the tray supplied with it.

ABOVE: A power roller will make painting large areas easier, but watch for drips.

A radiator roller has a long handle for reaching into tight spots. Use small craft and mini-rollers for applying paint in techniques such as stamping.

Power rollers are mains- or battery-operated and, in theory, they can simplify the whole process, with the paint contained in a portable reservoir. Their disadvantage, however, is that they can result in drips and streaks.

Mini-rollers have a cover made from dense foam or pile. Available in several widths, they are used for painting narrow stripes or coating stamps.

Masonry rollers are generally 23cm (9in) wide and have a long pile. Use them for covering rough-textured surfaces and for roller fidgeting.

Sheepskin rollers are used for basic quick coverage of flat paint. They are usually available in 18cm (7in) and 23cm (9in) widths.

Use a sponge roller as a cheaper alternative to a sheepskin one. Sponge rollers are also available in 18cm (7in) and 23cm (9in) widths.

SPONGES AND CLOTHS

A selection of natural and synthetic sponges is essential for numerous overall decorating techniques, as are lint-free cloths and rags. Each makes its own individual marks.

Natural sponges are mostly used for sponging. Synthetic sponges make a more obvious mark than natural sponges, so use natural examples for producing tight, fine marks and to create special marbled effects.

A chamois, made from real leather, can be scrunched into a ball for ragging. Or use a special ragging chamois, made from strips bound together.

LEFT (clockwise from top left): natural sponge, cloth, pinched-out synthetic sponge, two paint pads, mini-roller, small cellulose sponges, gloss roller, masonry roller, ragging chamois.

SPECIALIST PAINTING TOOLS

There are many items that will make it easier to plan your decoration. For careful measuring and marking before you start, you may need a spirit (carpenter's) level, long rule, tape measure and pencil. A plumbline, which consists of a small weight suspended on a fine string, is helpful for marking vertical drops. Masking tape is useful for keeping edges straight and covering light switches and sockets.

For certain techniques, special tools are needed. Different shapes of rubber combs will give a variety of woodgrain effects. A heart grainer (graining roller) with its moulded surface will enable you to reproduce the characteristics of a particular wood more accurately. For gilding, a gilder's pad is a useful investment and consists of a soft pad surrounded by a screen of parchment to shield gold leaf from draughts. Craft knives can be bought with double-ended blades that are screwed into the handle and turned or replaced when blunt. Others have a long retractable strip blade that allows you to break off and dispose of the blunt portion. For safety, keep your fingers behind the cutting edge. Never leave the knife within reach of children or where it will be a danger to animals; a piece of cork makes a good protective cap to put on the end of the blade. Craft knives are ideal for cutting out stencils and stamps.

Keep a supply of different grades of abrasive paper, and a sanding block to use with them. A power sander can also save time when tackling larger jobs. If you need to sand an area of floorboards, the best solution is to hire a purpose-built industrial-quality sander.

RIGHT (clockwise from top left): spirit (carpenter's) level, long rule, sanding block, two combs, plumbline, tape measure, heart grainer (graining roller), sanding sponge, craft knife, pencil, selection of abrasive papers (far right).

WALLPAPERING TOOLS

Using the correct tools will make the job of hanging wallpaper much easier, allowing you to achieve a more professional finish. Some are needed specifically for wallpapering; others are likely to be part of your standard do-it-yourself toolkit. When buying decorating tools, opt for quality rather than quantity.

MEASURING AND MARKING

A retractable steel tape is essential for taking measurements, while a long metal straightedge, a spirit (carpenter's) level or plumbline and a pencil will be needed for marking levels, vertical guidelines on walls and the positions of fixtures.

CUTTING AND TRIMMING

For cutting wallpaper to length and trimming edges, you will need a pair of paperhanger's scissors, which have long blades and curved tips used for creasing paper into angles. Choose scissors that are at least 250mm (10in) long and made from stainless steel, or which have been specially coated so that they will not rust.

A sharp craft knife can also be used for trimming and will be easier to use with vinyl wallcoverings. Various trimming tools are also available, including the roller cutter, which enables you to crease and cut into edges with a single movement, and is accurate and simple to use.

PASTING

For mixing and applying paste, you will need a plastic bucket and a paste brush. Proper paste brushes have synthetic bristles and will be easier to clean than ordinary paintbrushes. A pasting table is not essential, but

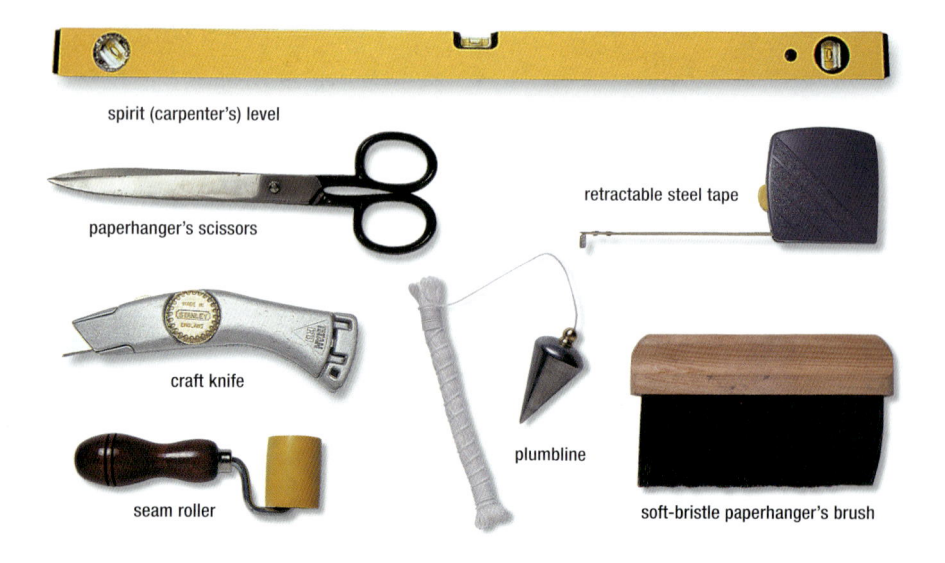

spirit (carpenter's) level

paperhanger's scissors

retractable steel tape

craft knife

plumbline

seam roller

soft-bristle paperhanger's brush

is extremely useful. They are also inexpensive and fold for easy storage. For ready-pasted wallcoverings, a polystyrene soaking trough is required.

SAFE ACCESS

Hanging wallpaper may also involve working at heights, so safe access equipment will be required. A set of sturdy steps will be suitable for papering walls, but a safe platform will be needed for access to ceilings and stairwells.

FINISHING

A paperhanger's brush is the best tool for smoothing down wallpaper, although a sponge can be used for vinyl wallcoverings. For the best results, choose a brush with soft, flexible bristles and buy the largest size that you can manage comfortably. Do not use wallpaper brushes with a metal ferrule or collar on them for this job, as you might inadvertently tear or mark delicate wallcoverings.

Use a cellulose decorator's sponge rather than an ordinary household sponge. This type of sponge is made of a higher-density material, which is firmer and will hold water better.

A seam roller will give a neat finish to joints and the edges of borders, but should not be used on wallpaper with an embossed pattern. Types made from wood and plastic are available. A soft plastic seam roller is the best option as it is less likely to leave marks on thin or overpasted wallpapers.

ABOVE: For smooth wall coverings, a seam roller can be used to make sure that the seams are well bonded to the wall. Do not use a seam roller on textured or embossed wall coverings, though, as it will flatten the embossing.

AVOIDING PASTE DRIPS

A length of string tied tightly across the top of a wallpaper paste bucket makes a handy brush rest. Use the string rather than the side of the bucket for removing excess adhesive from the pasting brush.

TILING TOOLS

Even the simplest of ceramic tiling jobs will require a small selection of specialized tools, while a major project requires quite a few. In addition, you will have to call on tools from your normal do-it-yourself toolkit, such as a retractable steel tape, a straightedge, spirit (carpenter's) level, a saw and a hammer. You will also need to make a tiling gauge, for setting out the rows of tiles. This should be a wooden batten, 1.2m (4ft) long, marked off in tile widths (with an allowance for the joints between).

ADHESIVE AND GROUTING TOOLS

Apply adhesive to the wall with a small pointing trowel, then create a series of ridges in it with a notched spreader. This allows the adhesive to spread when the tile is pressed home, ensuring an even thickness.

Tile spacers are required when using standard field tiles to provide a uniform grouting gap between them. Other types of tile have bevelled edges that create a grouting gap automatically when butted together.

home-made tiling gauge

pointing trowel

notched spreader

tile spacers

squeegee

grout refinishing kit

sponge

grout remover

A squeegee will be needed at the grouting stage to force grout into the gaps between tiles, while a grout finisher will provide the joints with a neat profile. If you don't have a grout finisher, you can substitute it with a short length of wooden dowel. Wipe off excess adhesive from the tiles with a sponge.

Various tools are available for removing old grout when carrying out repairs or renovation work. Take care when using them not to chip the edges of the tiles.

CUTTING AND SHAPING TOOLS

Straight cuts can be made with a simple tile scorer, straightedge and tile snapper, but an all-in-one tile cutter or tile jig will make life easier for the beginner. Most incorporate a measuring device, trimmer and snapping mechanism in one unit.

Tile nippers can be used for cutting off small pieces of tile, while a tile saw is good for cutting out complex shapes. Once a tile has been cut, you can smooth its edges with a tile file.

tile scorer

tile snapper

tile nippers

heavy-duty tile cutter

tile saw

tile jig with adjustable width and angle facility

tile file

WOOD AND VINYL FLOOR TOOLS

For laying woodblock and woodstrip floor coverings, you will need general woodworking tools, adhesive and a spreader for woodblock floors, and pins (tacks) or fixing clips for woodstrip floors, plus varnish or sealer if laying an unsealed type. For marking out, you will require a retractable steel tape measure, a pencil and a straightedge. Wooden blocks and strips can be cut to length with a tenon saw, while cut-outs can be made in them to fit around obstacles with a coping saw, pad saw or electric jigsaw (saber saw).

For laying sheet vinyl, a tape measure and sharp utility knife are needed. A long steel straightedge will also be invaluable. For bonding the lengths to the floor along edges and seams, use either double-sided adhesive tape or bands of liquid adhesive, spread with a toothed spreader to ensure that a uniform amount of adhesive is applied.

Lastly, for both wooden and vinyl floor coverings you will need a pair of compasses or a scribing block and pencil, plus a shape tracer with adjustable steel or plastic fingers, to transfer the outlines of the various floor-level obstacles along the edges of the room so that they can be trimmed to fit around them.

Unless they are to be continued into an adjoining room, both types of flooring will need finishing off at doorways, This is achieved by fitting ready-made threshold (saddle) strips.

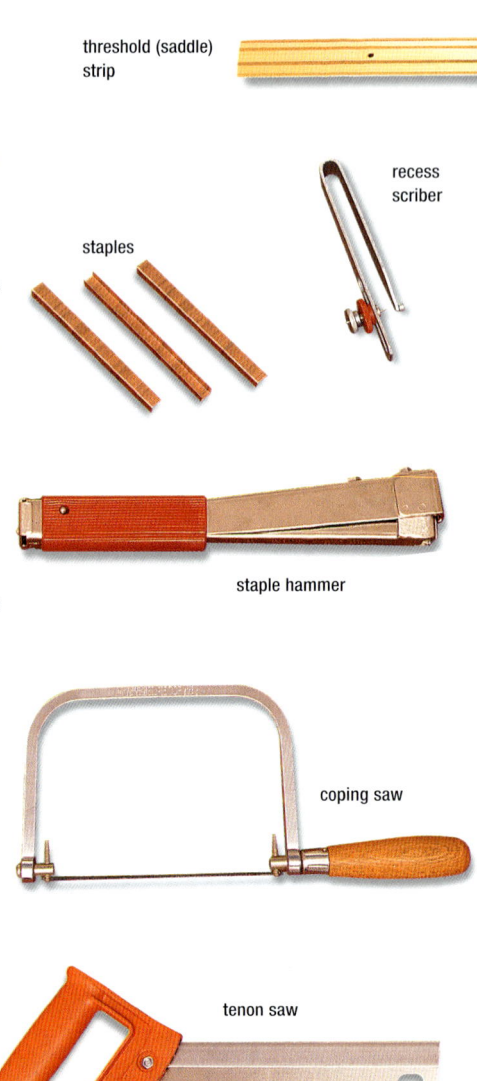

threshold (saddle) strip

recess scriber

staples

staple hammer

coping saw

tenon saw

FINISHING TOOLS • 315

adjustable straightedge

pad saw

double-sided tape

tack hammer

liquid adhesive

retractable steel tape measure

electric jigsaw (saber saw)

dividers

CARPET TOOLS

For laying carpet, the basic essentials are a tape measure and a sharp utility knife. As an alternative, special carpet shears can be used.

For a woven carpet, a carpet stretcher is invaluable. This is a device with a horizontal pad of metal spikes at one end, which is locked into the carpet, and a cushioned pad at the other end, which is nudged with the knee to stretch the carpet into place. It is probably best to hire this tool.

Also needed are some carpet gripper strips to hold the carpet in position around the perimeter of the room. These are thin strips of plywood fitted with angled nails that grip the underside of the carpet, and are nailed to the floor about 10mm (3/8in) from the skirting (baseboard). The edge of the carpet is tucked down into the gap, usually with a carpet fitter's bolster. A wide brick bolster (stonecutter's chisel) may be used, as long as it is clean.

Foam-backed carpet may be stapled to the floor or stuck down with double-sided adhesive tape. Adhesive seaming tape may also be needed to join sections of carpet together, and threshold (saddle) strips are used to trim the carpeted edge off at door openings.

Lining paper or cloth underlay is recommended for foam-backed carpets, as it prevents the foam from sticking to the floor surface. For woven carpets, use either a foam or felt underlay: they are available in various grades and should be matched to the carpet.

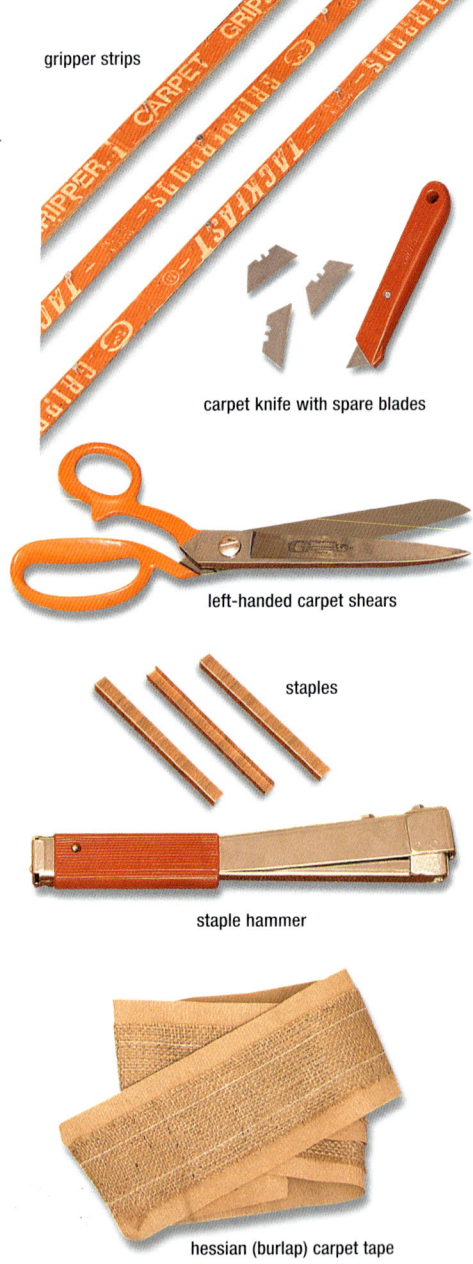

gripper strips

carpet knife with spare blades

left-handed carpet shears

staples

staple hammer

hessian (burlap) carpet tape

FINISHING TOOLS • 317

single-sided brass threshold (saddle) strip

aluminium carpet-to-vinyl strip

carpet-to-carpet strip

carpet fitter's bolster

right-handed carpet shears

double-sided tape

recess scriber

tack hammer

dividers

retractable steel tape measure

adjustable straightedge

carpet stretcher

INDEX

A
access 24–5, 311
 equipment 138, 142
acrylic paints 16, 17, 18
adhesives 314, 315, 316
 flooring 213, 236
 tiling 150, 158–9, 171, 180, 184, 186
aerosol paints 43

B
bathrooms 94, 205, 209, 212–13, 234, 252
battens (furring strips) 162, 163, 172, 182
bedrooms 205, 213
bench hooks 286, 287
bench-top vices 271
binders 19
bits 272, 273, 275, 290–1
blockboard 276
bolsters (stonecutter's chisels) 316
bolts 293

C
cabinets 273
cable detectors 268
cam clamps 294
carpenter's vices 271
carpets 204, 210, 212, 216, 223, 238–9, 240–2
 carpet tiles 211, 254–5, 257
 tools 316–17
 wallpaper 94, 99, 100, 114, 115, 131, 138–40, 146, 147
ceramic tiles 150–1, 153, 180–1, 218
chipboard (particle board) 215, 219
chisels 260, 272, 275, 278, 282–4, 285, 316
clamps (cramps) 260, 271, 273, 293, 294–5
clothing 158, 159, 188, 263, 264–5, 266–7, 269,
colour schemes 212, 247
colourwashing 54, 58, 59

combination squares 276, 277, 278
compasses 314
concrete floors 215, 216, 219, 220–1, 236, 250
coping saws 284, 314
cork tiles 150, 153, 156–7, 184–5, 186–7
 floors 204, 209, 212, 213, 216
corridors 210, 247
counter top, edging 178–9
crackle glazes 57, 71

D
dado (chair) rails 102
decorating
 equipment 260, 261, 303, 306–8, 309, 310–11
 light fittings 25, 130, 131
 preparation 12–13, 15, 23, 24–5, 26, 103, 107, 112, 118–19
diluents 17, 19
dining rooms 213
distemper (tempera) 12, 16
distressing 55, 57, 68–9
 floorboards 248–9
dividers 278, 315, 317
double-sided tape 314, 315, 316, 317
 floors 209, 238, 240, 254
dovetail nailing 297
dowelling 270, 313
dragging 62–3
drills 260, 275, 283, 284, 290–1, 299
dust sheets (drop cloths) 13, 24
Dutch Metal (simulated gold leaf) 76–7

E
edge-jointing 294, 295
edging techniques 178–9
embossed wallcoverings 102, 103, 146
emulsion (latex) paint 16, 17

F
faux effects 83, 84–5, 86–7, 88, 89, 90–1
filler (spackle) 15, 103, 112, 113, 114

filling 23, 34–5
fire extinguishers 268
first aid kits 266, 267
fixing clips 314
floorboards 204, 212, 213, 215, 217, 223, 224–5, 309
 distressing 248–9
floors 9
 choosing 205, 207, 212–13, 223, 247
 concrete 215, 216, 219, 220–1, 236, 250
 conditioning 218, 226, 228
 sanding 215, 224–5
 stripping 216
 tiles 153, 156–7, 166–7, 180–1, 184–5, 180, 184
 wood 204, 209, 250
 wood mosaic 228–30
 woodblock 204, 208, 212, 216
 wood-grain chequerboard 250–1
 woodstrip 204, 208, 212, 223, 216, 226–7
foam-backed carpets 210, 216, 238–9
friezes 151, 154

G
G-clamps 294
glazes 19, 57, 71
gloss finishes 13, 16, 17, 18, 20
gluing 293, 294, 295
gripper strips 238, 240, 243, 316
grouting 150, 158–9, 171, 177, 312–13

H
halls (lobbies) 102, 209, 212, 247, 252
hammers 260, 293, 296–7, 312, 314, 315, 316, 317
hand-painted tiles 193
hand-printed papers 95, 100
hardboard 215, 216, 227, 218, 236, 250, 252
hinges 299

J
jigsaws (saber saws) 314, 315
joints 284, 286, 290

K
kitchens 94, 205, 209, 212–13, 252

knives 260, 275, 278, 288–9, 309, 310, 314, 316
  wallpapering 122, 123, 127
knotting (shellac) 18, 23

L
ladders 264, 269
lining paper 102, 103, 107, 114–15
linoleum 209, 252–3
  lino tiles 150, 153, 157, 184–5, 211, 236–7
living rooms 213

M
mallets 284, 297
marbling 55, 90–1, 308
marking out 172–3, 275, 278–9, 288, 289, 314
masking tape 24, 25, 309
mastic (caulking) 158
matt (flat) finishes 13, 16, 17, 20
MDF (medium-density fiberboard) 276
mitre clamps and boxes 271, 286, 287, 294, 295
mitring wallpaper 136–7
mortise gauges 278, 279
mortises 283, 284, 288
mosaic tiles 150, 155, 188–9
mouldings 286
  tiling 178–9, 198

N
nail pullers 300
nails 293, 296–7, 300, 301
  flooring 217, 218, 220, 224–5
nuts 293

O
oil-based paint 12, 13, 16, 17, 18, 83

P
pad saws 314, 315
paint 12–13, 16–17, 18, 43, 83, 223, 303
  estimating quantities 15
  paint pads 306, 307, 12, 37, 42–3
  stripping 27, 28–9, 30, 108–9
  textured 30, 40, 44–5, 108–9
paintbrushes 15, 37, 38–9, 303, 306–7,
  cleaning 12, 19
painting 7, 37
  around glass 49
  ceilings 24
  doors 13, 46–7
  metal 18
  walls 24
  windows 13, 48–9
panels 108, 110–11
  tiled 151, 154, 198–9
paperhanger's brushes 95, 103, 127, 130, 132, 139, 310, 311
parquet 208, 213, 231
pasting wallpaper 94, 95, 107, 118, 119, 134–5, 310–11
patterns
  carpets 211, 257
  tiles 184, 194–5, 196–7, 198–9
  wallpaper 95, 97, 98–9, 104, 120, 122, 134, 135, 146
pets 207, 223
picture frames 294, 295
pincers 260, 300–1
pins (tacks) 218, 314
pipes 270
planes 267, 275, 280–1, 285
pliers 260, 300–1
plug cutters 290
plumblines 120, 124, 309, 310
plywood 215, 218, 250, 276
pointing trowels 312
polystyrene boards 219
polystyrene tiles 31
primer 17, 18
printed wallcoverings 104–5
professional help 261
  decorating 104, 105, 110

Q
quarry tiles 153, 156, 180, 182–3, 212, 218

R
ragging 66–7, 308
ready-pasted wallcoverings 118
rebates (rabbets) 283
relief wallpapers 102–3, 146
residual current devices (RCDs) 268
roller cutters 310
rollers 12, 37, 40–1, 261, 303, 306, 307–8
heart grainers (graining rollers) 84, 86, 309
roller fidgeting 54, 65, 308
routers 283
rubber combs 84, 86, 309
rulers 276, 278, 288, 289, 309

S
safety 6, 263, 264–5, 273, 283, 289, 301, 309
  decorating 19, 24–5, 28, 30, 108, 130, 131, 142
  equipment 266–7, 268, 269
  flooring 224, 256
  tiling 158, 159, 188
sanders 15, 23, 34, 261, 303, 304–5, 309
sanding floors 215, 224–5
sash clamps 294, 295
satin/silk (mid sheen) finishes 13, 16, 17, 20
sawhorses 270
saws 260, 264, 267, 272, 275, 283, 284, 286–7, 312, 314, 315
scissors 95, 122, 123, 124, 127, 139, 261, 310
screwdrivers 260, 293, 298–9
screws 293, 298–9
scribing blocks 314
sealant (caulking) 158
seam rollers 103, 134, 135, 146, 261, 310, 311
self-levelling screeds 215, 219, 220–1
self-smoothing compound 220–1
shape tracers 234, 314
sharpening equipment 285
skirtings (baseboards) 307, 316
sliding bevels 278, 279
soaking troughs 311
sockets 293
solvents 12, 13, 19
spacers 312
spanners 260, 293
spirit (carpenter's) levels 260, 276, 277, 309, 312
  wallpapering 114, 120, 134, 136, 147
splashbacks 151, 154, 161, 165, 171, 172–3, 196–7
sponges 37, 308, 311, 313
sponging 55, 60, 61
spreaders 312, 314
squeegees 312, 313

stairs 210, 212, 243–5
  wallpapering 137, 142–3
stamping 55, 73, 76–7, 308
staples 238, 240, 314, 316
steam strippers 108, 109, 112, 113, 169
stencilling 55, 73, 74–5
stepladders 13, 24–5, 94, 138, 311
stippling 64
straightedges 114, 276, 277, 288, 310, 312, 313, 314, 315, 317
stripping floorings 216
stripping paint 27, 28–9, 30
stripping panelling 110–11
stripping textured paint 108–9
stripping tiles 31, 108, 110, 111
stripping wallpaper 32–3, 107, 112–13, 168–9
sugar soap 23, 26
synthetic fibres 204, 210

T
T-squares 276, 277, 278
tack lifters 300
tacks 300, 301
tape measures 260, 309, 310, 312, 314, 315, 316, 317
tenon saws 286, 287, 314
terracotta tiles 156, 190
textured paint 30, 40, 44–5, 108–9
textured wallpaper 95, 102, 108–9
threshold (saddle) strips 238, 240, 254, 314–15, 316, 317
tiles
  borders 151, 174, 178, 198, 200–1
  ceramic 150–1, 153, 180–1, 218
  cork 150, 153, 156–7, 184–5, 186–7, 204, 209, 212, 213, 216
  cut 165, 176
  cutting 174–5, 188
  estimating quantities 162–3
  fixing 172–3
  floors 204, 209, 212, 218
  lino 150, 153, 157, 184–5
  mosaic 150, 155, 188–9
  printed 80–1
  quarry tiles 153, 156, 180, 182–3
  removing 31, 108, 110, 111
  soaking 182
  tile supports 172–3
  vinyl 150, 153, 157, 184–5, 216, 236–7
tiling 8–9, 172–3, 303
  centring 164–5, 166–7
  corners 176
  doors 151, 164
  light fittings 169, 186, 187
  planning 162–3
  tiling gauge 162, 163
  tools 174, 175, 312–13
  windows 151, 165, 171, 190–1
tongue-and-groove 208, 219, 226
tools 6, 261
  power tools 264, 267, 268, 269, 272–3, 299
  storage 263, 272–3
  tool boards 260, 273
try squares 271, 278, 279

U
undercoat 17, 18
underlay 210, 226, 228, 236, 238, 240, 316

V
varnish 13, 20–1, 50, 223, 224, 231, 314
veneer 288
vices 270–1
vinyl 314
vinyl flooring 204, 209, 212, 213, 232–3, 234–5
vinyl tiles 150, 153, 157, 184–5, 216, 236–7
vinyl wallpaper 102, 103, 104, 105, 107, 113, 145

W
wallpaper 54, 73, 94–5, 102–3, 107, 303, 310, 311
  borders 95, 102, 134–5, 136–7
  choosing 97, 98–9, 102, 105
  cutting 118, 119, 128, 129
  estimating quantities 97, 100–1
  soaking 103, 112, 114, 118
  stripping 32–3, 107, 112–13
  trimming 120, 122, 124, 126, 127, 141
wallpapering 8, 117, 120–1
  alcoves 117, 140
  arches 141
  ceilings 94, 99, 100, 114, 115, 131, 138–40, 146, 147
  corners 99, 103, 114, 117, 120, 122–3, 124–5, 136–7
  doors 117, 126–7, 136
  fireplaces 120, 122, 132
  guidelines 114, 120, 121, 122, 124, 136, 138, 139, 140
  problems 144–5, 146–7
  radiators 133
  tools 310–11
  wall fittings 133
  windows 117, 128–9, 136, 140
walls 24, 107, 168
  tiles 153, 154, 164–5, 168–9, 186–7, 200–1
washing walls and ceilings 107, 168
white spirit (paint thinner) 18, 19
windows 294, 307
wood washing 51, 70
woodblock flooring 314
woodchip 102, 103
woodgraining 55, 309
  beech 89
  mahogany 88
  oak 55, 86–7
  pine 84–5
woodstains 13, 21, 51, 231
woodstrip flooring 314
woodwork, decorating 23, 26
work platforms 138, 142
workbenches 270–1
worktops 153

ACKNOWLEDGEMENTS

The publisher would like to thank the following for supplying pictures: **The Amtico Company** 209t; **Axminster** 288bl; **Crossley** 206tr, 210t; **Forbo Nairn Ltd** 205t, 209bl; **Heuga** 211t; **Junckers Ltd** 202ml, br, 206b, 213t, b; **Kosset** 205b, 210b; **Mr Tomkinson** 212t; **Wicanders** 206tl, 212b.